Jane Cochrane

A Figure in the Sand

ãRP

Published in 2011 by Antony Rowe Publishing
48-50 Birch Close
Eastbourne
East Sussex
BN23 6PE
arp@cpi-group.co.uk

© JANE COCHRANE 2011

The Right of JANE COCHRANE to be identified as the Author of this work has been asserted by HER in accordance with the Copyright, Designs and Patents Act 1988.

All Rights Reserved. No part of this book may be printed, reproduced or utilized in any form or by any electronic, mechanical or other means, now known or hereafter invented, including photocopying and recording, or in any information storage retrieval system, without permission in writing from the publishers.

A catalogue record for this book is available from the British Library

ISBN 978-1-907571-02-2

Printed and Bound in Great Britain by
CPI Antony Rowe, Chippenham and Eastbourne

For my mother

1943	**THE LOSS**	
	1. The Telegram	p 1 - 8
1943 - 1988	**THE SILENCE**	
	2. The Silence	p 10 - 14
1988 - 1992	**THE SEARCH I**	
	3. The Search Begins	p 16 - 25
	4. Visit to Jack	p 26 - 33
	5. Tunisia	p 34 - 39
	6. Ceremony at Alamein	p 40 - 48
1914 - 1984	**MY FATHER'S STORY I**	
	7. My Father as a Small Boy	p 50 - 63
	8. Marlborough	p 64 - 71
	9. Woolwich	p 72 - 78
1942 - 1988	**MY STORY**	
	10. Reeves and Folkestone	p 80 - 88
	11. Hawkhurst	p 89 - 101
	12. My Mother's New Start	p 102 - 107
	13. One Big Happy Family	p 108 - 119
	14. Teenager	p 120 - 126
	15. Adult Life	p 127 - 132
1934 - 1942	**MY FATHER'S STORY II**	
	16. India	p 134 - 146
	17. Phoney War	p 147 - 155

	18. War 1940	p 156 - 162
	19. A Dichotomy	p 163 - 168
	20. Wedding	p 169 - 174
	21. Married Life	p 175 - 187
	22. Round the Cape	p 188 - 200

1992 - 1998 THE SEARCH II

23. Windlesham	p 202 - 214
24. To Libya	p 215 - 227
25. The Only Tourists in Libya	p 228 - 235
26. To Benghazi and Back	p 236 - 250

1942 - 1943 MY FATHER'S STORY III

27. The Battle of Alamein	p 252 - 256
28. Alamein to El Agheila	p 257 - 266
29. Christmas and New Year's Eve 1942	p 267 - 272
30. Jack Swaab	p 273 - 282
31. Dash Across the Desert	p 283 - 290
32. Battle of the Hills	p 291 - 300
33. Tripoli to Pisida	p 301 - 310

1998 - 2005 THE SEARCH III

34. The Cochrane Family	p 312 - 322
35. The Family in Libya	p 323 - 331
36. Graves in Tunisia	p 332 - 341
37. The Dream	p 342 - 353
38. Loose Ends	p 354 - 359
39. Back to Libya in 2005	p 360 - 367

1943 THE LOSS

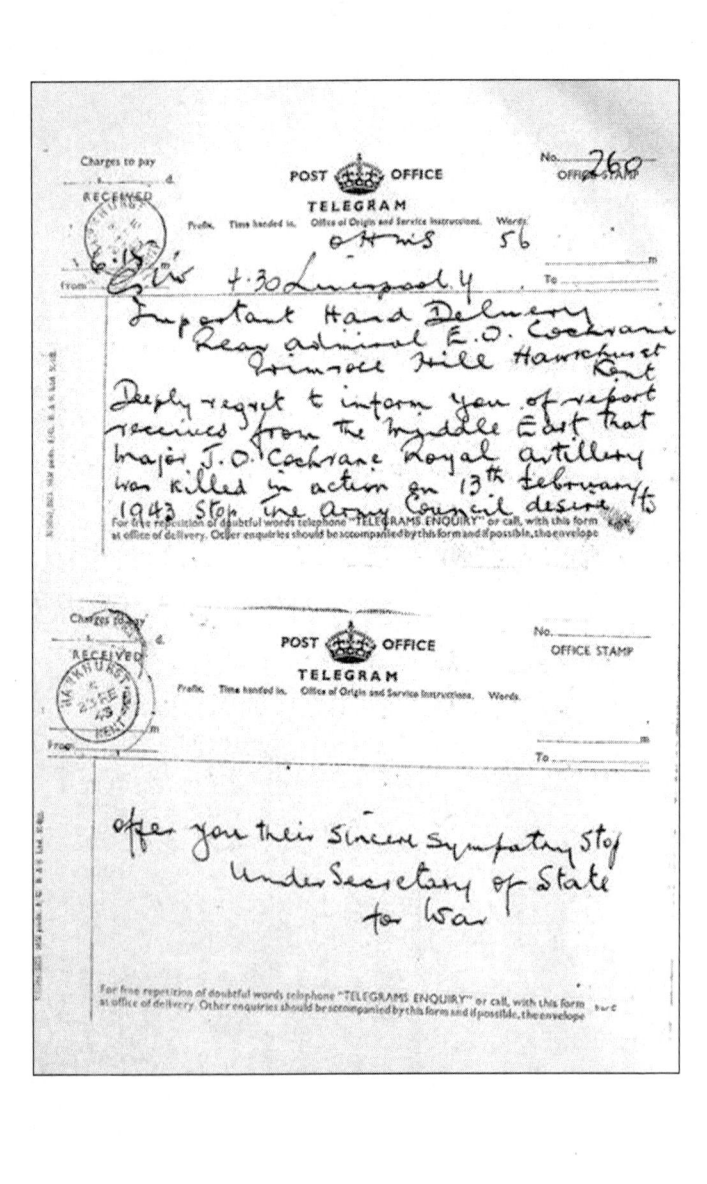

POST OFFICE TELEGRAM

No. 760

6.15 — 4.30 Liverpool 4 — 56

Important Hand Delivery
Rear Admiral E.O. Cochrane
Grimscott Hill Hawkhurst Kent

Deeply regret to inform you of report received from the Middle East that Major J.O. Cochrane Royal Artillery was killed in action on 13th February 1943 stop. The Army Council desire to

POST OFFICE TELEGRAM

offer you their sincere sympathy stop
Under Secretary of State
for War

1. The Telegram

My grandmother liked to sit at her writing desk, placed below a south facing window at the front of her house. From there she could look down the length of the driveway towards the front gate to see if anyone was coming or going.

Tuesday 23rd February 1943 had been grey, cold and uneventful. In the early evening when the postman arrived the light was beginning to fade. He dismounted from his motorbike and, holding his helmet under his left arm, began to walk slowly up the driveway towards the house. In his right hand he held a telegram.

My grandparents' usual postman was a familiar figure in the village. He often accepted their invitation to come in for a for a cup of tea in the kitchen, as their house was on the edge of the village, at the end of his round. But the postman who came up from the little post office in Hawkhurst that day was a different man, a man they didn't know. He came not in the morning but in the evening, not on a pushbike but on a motorbike. He knew the message he was carrying was the one that every family in the country was dreading.

The telegram was addressed to my grandfather; Rear Admiral E. O. Cochrane, Primrose Hill, Hawkhurst, Kent. That evening he was home on one of his rare periods of leave. My Cochrane grandfather had been recalled into the navy when WW2 broke out and led Atlantic convoys from Liverpool to America throughout the war to keep up supplies of food to the UK. It was he who opened the front door and he must have known as soon as he saw the telegram that it would not contain good news. He opened it and read;

Deeply regret to inform you of report received from the Middle East that Major J.O.Cochrane Royal Artillery was killed in action on 13th February 1943 stop the Army Council desire to offer you their sincere sympathy stop Under Secretary of State for War.

James Owen Cochrane, my father, was their only son. At home they had called him Jock since he was a child. The nick-name came from his initials, J.O.C. It is a curious coincidence that Jock is also the colloquial name for a Scottish soldier, which is what he grew up to be.

Later that evening my Cochrane grandfather made two phone calls. The first was to my Round-Turner grandparents' house in Layer-de-la-Haye, near Colchester, Essex. These were my mother's parents and, since she and I had no home while my father was away on active service, we were staying with them. I was seven weeks old. There were several people staying in the house in Layer-de-la-Haye that evening; not only my maternal grandmother, my mother and me but also another friend and a temporary nurse. My Round-Turner grandfather was away from home on war work and so it was my Gran who answered the phone. That evening she considered the news and wondered what to do with it. She didn't breathe a word to anyone. She was very fond of my father, whom she had known since he was a boy; just as she loved his parents. My mother's and my father's parents were all naval people and they had been friends from way back.

My mother had so often said to Gran, "If anything happens to Jock, and you get to know about it before I do, you will promise to tell me right away, won't you? I couldn't bear to think that anything had happened to Jock and that I didn't know". Yet my Gran didn't tell my mother that evening. She saw that my mother was having a difficult time with her seven week old baby and by the time the telegram arrived my father had already been dead ten days. She decided she would give her daughter just one more night of peace before she told her the terrible news.

After that call my Cochrane grandfather rang his daughter Suzanne, my father's younger sister. Her employers were sympathetic and she was given immediate leave from her job in Suffolk as a land girl. She set out that evening and travelled through the night to get down to and across London and on to Kent. When she arrived the following morning she was met by her mother at the same front door where the telegram had arrived the previous day. Yet although it was only two weeks since Suzanne had last been home, she barely recognized her. Her mother's hair had turned white, she told me, in the course of that night.

No-one who had been close to my father could altogether believe the news and, in the curious osmotic way that outside feelings make their way into the brain of a child before its relations think it has any conscious life at all, I absorbed their sense of shock and disbelief. Even now I find it hard to be sure that a strong young man, 28 years old, was there one day and gone the next. And be sure that he ever existed. Even as an adult I find that I need reassurance that my father once truly lived. That he once truly walked on this earth.

So I was born and my father died. My mother was devastated. Her whole future, which had seemed so full of promise, was taken from her. Her life as a married woman had hardly begun when it was over. She was a bright and pretty young woman in her early twenties but now she faced a future of poverty and homelessness, a future of life on a widow's pension. She couldn't go back to her previous life as a popular young woman with a promising career in the WRNS, the life she had left less than a year earlier, as her baby demanded constant care and attention. I was there every moment of the day to remind her of what might have been.

To cap it all I was a colicky baby. The birth hadn't been easy and now, like so many babies, I cried a lot. My nappies had to be washed by hand with rationed wartime soap grated into the washbowl. My dutiful mother tried to feed me spinach, like the book said. She picked it from the garden, cooked it, sieved it by hand and fed it into my mouth, then I spat it out all down my clothes. They were white, newly washed and ironed. This is what babies do and in some circumstances my mother might even have laughed. But after my father's death nothing was funny. She couldn't bounce me on her knee or chat to me. Her relations and friends tried to cheer her as much as they could but there was no outside help for a grieving widow available in those days. It was a tragedy and I was in the middle of it. Luckily for me my mother is a dutiful person and she forced herself onwards. She took it day by day.

Later my mother rarely spoke to me about my father and I never spoke to her. I could see that the subject caused her pain and I didn't want to do anything to make things worse for her. Luckily for me she kept close to my father's parents. They were the best parents-in-law that anyone ever could have, she said, and it was they who spoke to me about my father. I often used to go and stay with them and it was my Cochrane grandfather who told me how my father had died. By then I was five years old and I understood in the way that a five-year-old understands these things. My father was in the desert in Tunisia, in North Africa, my grandfather said, when he trod on a mine hidden under the ground and it blew him up into the air and killed him. He was on a track where many soldiers had passed before, so it was very bad luck the mine went off just then, when my father passed by. Now he was in heaven, and when my grandfather died too, he said, my father would be waiting for him up there.

My grandfather first went to sea when he was fourteen and every ship he ever sailed in had a cat. When they reached port in a foreign land the ship's cat often went ashore to look around but it always knew to come back before the ship left harbour. A ship's cat only stayed behind when it chose to, my grandfather said. All his cats would be in heaven to welcome him when he arrived, he said, including Stouty, my grandparents' tabby tom-cat, if he died first. I looked at Stouty lying on his chair in the kitchen. I often used to draw him there when he was asleep, and this is one drawing I did at the time.

I imagined my father in heaven with all my grandfather's cats. They were sitting in a line. My father sat tall and slim to the left and the cats were arranged to the right of him in height order. Near him were the big rangy hunting toms like Stouty; some had torn ears like him too; farther away were lithe female cats, black and tortoiseshell. They were all waiting for my grandfather and me to come to heaven too.

After I said my prayers at night my grandparents tucked me up in my father's big bed. They each gave me a hug and went quietly downstairs. As my eyes got used to the darkness I could see the outline of my father's cabinet hanging on the wall. Inside it his Indian animals stood in single file. The little wooden tiger led the way, his yellow and orange paint slightly chipped, his mouth open and his wire tail twisted round his back leg. He was followed by a camel and a spotted cow with stiff black horns. A smaller horse, cow and dog brought up the rear. My father had brought the animals back from India, where he was stationed with the army before the war.

There were tins of fishing flies that my father had tied in the cabinet too, little trout flies and a salmon fly with a jointed body, red stripes down the outsides of its long legs and a spotted tail. Along the lower shelf were a few books about water divining, a group of John Buchan adventure stories and four books by H.V.Morton 'In Search of'.. England, Scotland, Ireland and Wales, which had been given to my father by his school as prizes for Science.

As I lay quietly and looked at the ceiling with half closed eyes I could see patterns and blobs which shifted and merged. Some of them slipped down the wall where the fishing rods in their long canvas bags leaned up in the corner beside a leather case of golf clubs. Over the fireplace hung a Harrison water-colour of grouse flying over the Scottish moors, and in front of it stood a small, low armchair with a loose cover of pale blue cotton.

The curtains in my father's bedroom had patterns copied from Indian embroidery, printed on woven linen in primary colours with stylised leaves, flowers and fruit on inter-twining branches. The large window behind overlooked the garage where my father left his model 10 Ford when he went off for the last time to the war. Stouty had a den between the back of the garage and the wall to the kitchen garden. He brought his kill back here to eat when he came home from a night out hunting. I often visited Stouty's den. It was full of rabbit bones.

I lay in my father's big bed, specially made long so his legs didn't stick out the end, and wondered about him. Maybe he wasn't really killed, I thought, but just lost his memory and is wandering round in the desert wondering how to get back to us. Maybe he will remember one day and find his way home. He will find me lying here in his bed but there is plenty of room for him too. If he comes back he will come in quietly and close the door and snuggle in with me. In the morning everyone will be so pleased to see him back again. My grandparents will be here and so will Stouty. Aunt Suzanne (who had gone to America after the war) would come back to see him and Mummy would smile again. We were all waiting for him to come back now that the war was over.

1943-1988 THE SILENCE

2. The Silence

My father never came back. Our lives went on without him and, during the forty-five years which followed his death, I didn't speak about it to anyone at all. Nor did I speak about his life. During my childhood a few adults from his family talked to me about my father and this was something which I treasured. But the curious thing is that I think I never replied. On my own I would never bring up such a conversation, even within the family.

Yet I have always known, somewhere deep down, that my father's death when I was six weeks old has profoundly affected my life. All my life my father has been present in his absence; absent in person yet so often present in my mind. It is hard to say exactly what it was that changed forty-five years later when I began to actively search for my father. It wasn't much. A slight tipping of the balance. Perhaps some improvement in my circumstances. Perhaps some undefined point I reached in my life. But once the search began it became a compulsion too strong for me to resist.

It was only in 1988 when I was forty-five years old that I began for the first time to speak about my father. Immediately I found I had a problem. As I had never spoken about him before, I had never given him a name. His real name was James but the people who had known him called him Jock. But I couldn't call him Jock. When I was young no child would call their father by his Christian name, let alone a nick-name and even though I was by then quite grown up it still seemed cheeky, somehow, for me to refer to him that way. Yet to call him 'my father' seemed too remote for someone to whom I felt so close; for someone who was (I had begun to understand) so intimately bound up with my emotions and my sense of self. I realised that although other people had spoken to me about my father when I was a child I had never needed to do more than listen. I never initiated the conversation and I never replied. How could it be that in this world where every last atom has a name my own father had become anonymous?

When I was seven years old my mother re-married. I kept my own surname and this was important to me. It is still important to me and I keep it still. After my mother remarried the name 'Daddy' was taken by my step-father; a man who filled my father's shoes so badly that the whole concept of fathering became a travesty in my mind. So I couldn't call my real father 'Daddy' and I couldn't call him 'Jock' or 'James'. I had no way to refer to him yet I couldn't delay any longer. Not only did I myself now have a feeling of urgency but I realised that the sources of the information I wanted might soon dry up. By the time I began to talk about my father, forty-five years after his death, the people who had known him were few, and they were getting old. His family was small and I didn't have time to waste. I never found a good solution. I decided I would have to call him 'my father'. It was a bit formal but it would have to do.

Outside the family the public silence was just as profound. For fifty years following WW2 the documents concerning the war were classified. As a result very little research was done and little new material was published. Few documentaries were made. In addition to this my sympathies, from an early age, were with pacifists and Quakers.

Nor did I mention my father's death to my friends. Most people are fearful of death. They don't like to think about it. To bring up such a subject would be to cast gloom over any gathering. As I grew up I didn't want to embarrass anyone by talking about my father. I didn't want to put anyone into a spot where they didn't know what to say. I didn't want my friends who had no such old scars in their lives to think me ghoulish. I didn't want to be different to anyone else and most importantly and above all else I didn't want sympathy. So very early on I learned to keep quiet about my father. Death is a taboo subject I have lived with all my life.

I was used to speaking to myself about my father so, as I began to search for my father's grave, I wrote down the details to keep them clearer in my mind. But I began to find much more than I could ever have imagined; not only the details of my father's death but also those of his life. I began for the first time to know my father as a person and, oddly enough, that has made a huge difference to me. My journey has improved both my sense of self and my relationship with my mother. It was only after I finished this book that I have discovered that I have fellow-travellers on this journey and the extraordinary thing is, that although we are all quite different as people, our experiences have huge similarities.

Yet the subject is still one which is kept under wraps and there are reasons for this. I wondered whether I might mention my father's death in WW11 to a neighbour in my street who I know lost her own father in this way. The answer is that I didn't. Unless she initiated the conversation I wouldn't risk bringing up such an emotive subject for fear of upsetting her. Still, after all these years, I know how painful this subject can be.

So how many are we? Nobody knows. As far as I know no lists of children who lost their fathers in WWll were kept by any government agency in any country. But in America the number of dependents receiving benefits given to war widows was 183,000 from a total of 416,800 American military deaths. Taking that rough and ready ratio I calculate that, from the 382,600 deaths of UK servicemen there may have been 168,550 children left fatherless, and from the estimated 25 million military deaths worldwide, the number of children left fatherless by WW2 may be around 11 million. Even though this figure is very approximate it is, I think, a large number, and our experiences are worth considering.

1988-1992 THE SEARCH I

3. The Search Begins

I began my search for my father in 1988 when I was forty-five years old. I began surreptitiously. I had a strong feeling that I wasn't allowed to make this search, to broach this barrier. I felt guilty and I was quite certain that I would get into trouble in some way or another. Yet my compulsion to search was almost irresistible. I didn't feel I could come straight out and tell even my partner Alec that I wanted to go to Tunisia to see where my father was killed, but when he said he wanted to have a break from his work and find somewhere sunny to go for Easter I managed to find some cheap return tickets to Djerba Island. It was a convenient excuse. In some absurd way I was wondering if I could search for my father's grave without anyone noticing, even Alec with whom I normally shared all my secrets. Of course that wasn't to be.

So I assembled the facts as I knew them at the time. My father was killed in Tunisia, I had been told. He had never been reburied in an official war cemetery . Yet I thought my mother might have some idea where in Tunisia he was killed so I could go and pay my respects. A few weeks before we were due to leave I broke the silence that had so long surrounded my father. It was the first time I had ever taken such an initiative. I plucked up my courage, picked up the telephone and dialled my mother's number. I have always found her to be quite a conventional person, I can usually predict with some accuracy what she will say, but this time her reply came as a complete surprise;

"Jack Swaab is the man who would know the answer to that question," she said. "He was in your father's battery at that time."

I was shocked. No sooner had I had broken one taboo than my mother broke another. Jack Swaab. His name had been unmentionable for over thirty years. I knew that, after my father was killed and the war had ended, Jack Swaab had asked my mother to marry him and that she had refused his offer. Later she missed him and changed her mind but it was too late; he had fallen for another lady and soon he was married. Since my mother too remarried when I was seven years old, Jack's name had become even more taboo than that of my father. I had no idea that he had been in my father's battery during the war.

Two days after this unusual telephone conversation with my mother I received a brown envelope from her through the post. Inside, wrapped in a brief covering note, I discovered two crinkled old air-letters, one faded blue air-envelope with a letter and a ribbon inside, and a newspaper cutting from The Times. They dated from 1943. I had no idea that these letters existed. Where had my mother been hiding them over the past 45 years? How long was it since anyone last opened them up and looked inside?

I glanced at the newspaper cutting from March 19th 1943. It announced that my father, since killed in action, had been posthumously awarded the Military Cross. I didn't have much interest in military honours and I put it on one side. Then I looked at the two air-letters and the air-envelope. They were each rubber-stamped with a crowned ring about 1" diameter enclosing the words 'Passed by Censor' and a number. The brown three-penny postage stamps with the head of George VI were simply post-marked 'War Office' as, for security reasons; even close relatives were not allowed to know the positions of soldiers during the war. I placed the letters in date order and opened them one by one.

The first to be sent was addressed to my mother at her parents' house at Layer-de-la-Haye near Colchester in Essex where she and I were staying with my Round-Turner grandmother at the time of my birth. It was an air-letter from Jack Swaab. and it was headed;

Lieut. Jack Swaab RA., 127 Highland Field Regiment, Royal Artillery, Middle East Forces.

Jack and my father had been part of the huge allied 8th Army under General Montgomery crossing North Africa from Egypt through Libya into Tunisia. This letter was written in North Africa on 20th February 1943, a week after my father's death but still three days before the delivery of that fateful telegram in England. There had been a ten day time delay between my father's death and the arrival in England of the telegram giving the news. The time taken by communications is getting faster all the time. When I first read Jack's letter this time delay already seemed striking but nowadays we get almost instantaneous news from war zones.

The air-letter from Jack Swaab was written with a fountain pen. The handwriting was rounded, flowing and fluent:

My Dear Mrs Cochrane, I don't expect you'll remember me but we last met in Yeovil when Jock was commanding 496 Battery a year or more ago. When I found out he was in the Middle East I managed to get to his battery and I am writing now to tell you how deeply I sympathise with you over his recent death. I fully realise nothing I can say will help you at this time, but I should like you to know that if he had been my own brother I could not have been more unhappy about it. I suppose quite apart from his qualities as a man, he was the finest soldier under whom I shall ever serve, and as a person he was so completely reliable, fair, and unflurried that one could not have asked for a better or more understanding commander.

His personal bravery was always a byword. During the 8 or 9 months I served under him in England and again for the short time out here, I think I got to know him better than most people - perhaps because we were such different sorts of people - and in the many long talks I had with him at various times, it was obvious that for such a young man his mature judgement would take him far. I can only tell you that your personal grief is shared by every single man in this Battery. One of the drivers said to me the day after it happened - "He was such a fine gentleman, Sir. He'd only been with us a short time but there wasn't a man in the Battery who wouldn't have followed him anywhere." - and for an epitaph from his man this takes a lot of beating.

I hope you won't feel it is any impertinence when I say that if I get back to England I should like to call on you and perhaps be able to fill in any details you want to know. Please excuse my writing and any incoherence in this letter but I know you'll understand circumstances are difficult. I didn't want to take a chance on being unable to write to you.

I wish I could feel this letter had been some use to you and if it offers any comfort at all I shall be glad. I only hope the passage of time will help a little and close by hoping the future will bring you every possible happiness remaining, though I well realise what a mockery this must seem at the present time.

Yours very sincerely,
Jack Swaab.

I began to realise that Jack Swaab was the messenger who filled out the news contained in that telegram. All my life I have sensed that my father was special to everyone around him, so that aspect of Jack's letter didn't surprise me. The thing which struck me was that, as he wrote that letter, Jack obviously felt that he too might be killed at any moment. Yet he had survived the war and later he had proposed to my mother.

The second letter, from Lieut.A.Y.Watson Cowie

R.A., was written two weeks later on 5th March 1943. The handwriting was less clear and the words became darker and paler as the ink ran out and the pen was re-dipped into the ink well. There are a few words missing and the odd grammatical error, but I leave it as I found it myself. It said:

Dear Mrs Cochrane,

I felt I had to write you to express my deepest sympathy with you in the loss of your husband. I was his Command Post Officer since early in December and although I was only with him for three months or so soon found out his really great qualities.

For a Battery Commander to be liked and respected by his officers and be worshipped by his men needs great character, and I can assure you that Major Cochrane certainly had that quality. Every man in the battery thought he was a great chap and every officer gave secret thanks that they had such a fine leader.

It came as a sad blow to us to be talking to him one morning and to learn in the afternoon that he had gone. We were aghast and stricken with a sense of irretrievable loss. And I realise that when it was such a shock to us who were his comrades and junior officers, how much more by you would the loss be felt.

I know that I express the sympathy of all in the battery when I write, though this is not an official but a private letter.

I pray that God may sustain you and comfort you in the knowledge that you're husband - a gallant brave and fearless man, will be in that great roll of honour of men who laid down their lives for their country in a just and righteous cause.

May God uphold you in your grief.

It was good to know that the father I never knew had been so important to his colleagues, and so loved. Yet it surprised me that Cowie was so sure that he was fighting in a righteous cause. It was obvious from the way he wrote that this was important to his motivation and commitment.

It seemed that these men were not fighting because it was their profession or because they had no option. They felt they must continue the fighting, even if it meant putting their lives at risk on a daily basis, because they believed that the cause was just.

I turned to the fatter letter in the air-envelope. Carefully I pulled out the small length of striped ribbon. Either it was provided to hold my father's Military Cross or it denoted the North African Campaign. That ribbon had never met up with the medal for which it was intended. These military memorabilia had little interest for me and I laid it aside with the newspaper cutting. Then I pulled out the thin blue papers with their precise, forward-sloping handwriting. Ten weeks had passed since my father's death before this letter was written on Sunday 25th April 1943. By that time I would have been nearly four months old and I wondered, as I looked at it, how things might have been at home for me and my mother by that time. This letter was headed Major W. Melia, 127th (H) Field Regt. R.A. M.E.F. and read:

No words of mine can express to you what I and others feel about the loss of 'Jock' as I and others who knew him well called him. A first class officer and man if ever there was one - beloved by all ranks of his Battery.

I first met J.O. when I joined the 28th Field Regiment at Lahore in India. At that time I was serving with the 28th Regiment. After I returned home just before the war I did not see him again until he arrived during the Battle of Alamein to take over my battery (491) as I had to take over Second-in-Command of this regiment.

When 'Jock' fell, I was not very far away and arriving at the place later in the day I was met by Major Reg Hamden, an Anti-Tank Gunner Officer who told me that he had taken charge of the burial service and showed me the grave. I tried hard to get a photograph for you but without success. Eric Harbin, another old friend of J.O.'s, also asked me when he joined us and learned that Jock had fallen if I could get a photograph to show you, but I have been unable to do so. I did however make a sketch and I enclose it with this letter.

The action for which your husband was awarded the Military Cross took place at Corradini on the way up to Tripoli when he was a tower of strength and courage to all around him - Infantry and Gunners alike. He and his guns were the first British Troops to enter Tripoli.

War is a grim business and we all know that it is not us who have to do the fighting who suffer but the loved ones we leave behind at home.

God grant you strength and courage to bear your great loss. It is such courage which helps us who are left in it, to remember and to go on in the hope of finishing the business once and for all so that the little ones now growing up shall be spared such suffering.

On behalf of all Officers and Men of this Regiment, I join the C.O. in offering our deepest and heartfelt sympathy - we cannot forget those who have marched and fought with us and those loved ones we leave behind.

The grave is in Tripolitania, about 300 yards south of the main coast road and about 3 kilometres from the border Tripolitania - Tunisia.

Very sincerely yours,
William Melia"

The grave is in Tripolitania. I had understood that my father had no grave. And where was Tripolitania? Not in Tunisia, I knew, but in Libya. I turned to the fourth sheet and discovered a small neat drawing.

It showed a little humped earth grave headed by a small wooden cross. A tin helmet was placed on the hump over the body. Behind it was a large bush, its shadows falling to the left. To the south side of the grave, to judge by the direction of the shadows, a track is indicated. In the background, on the horizon, there seemed to be a small settlement or village. The drawing was signed W.Melia Feb. 1943 and titled "Grave of the late Major J.O.Cochrane

R.A. (Near the Tripolitanian - Tunisian Border).

I was hugely reassured to find that my father had once been buried in a proper grave and that I was holding in my own hand a sketch that had been done at that place and at that time to commemorate the burial. I had always found it distressing to think that my father had no grave. I never liked to think what might have happened to his body as he was blown up by that land mine. This, as my Cochrane grandfather had told me, was the way that he died. The fact that he had no known grave had made me, as a child, consider two equally unpleasant scenarios: either his body had been blown into so many smithereens that his colleagues had been unable, even, to collect enough of it to bury in one place or, alternatively, that they had cared so little about him that they had slung what was left of him into a pit with many others and carried on without a further thought. One should never underestimate the ability of a quiet child to imagine the worst. Nobody wants their father to end up in one of those seemingly endless rows of graves in an official war cemetery, but that is much better than to be told that your dead father has no grave at all.

Yet my initial feeling of relief at seeing the drawing was soon driven out by another emotion. The little sketch reached down into a knot of sadness deep inside me which, although I had never known it, I must have lived with all my life. I began to cry. I could hardly remember when I last cried. I was brought up to keep a stiff upper lip. Crying is something I very rarely do and, if I occasionally succumb, I feel I am being self-indulgent and soon manage to push it back. But now I was quite unable to control myself. The tears burst out of my eyes on the London Underground and fell onto the hard pavements as I made my way to work. There they fell and crinkled up the tracing paper of my architectural drawings. I went to sleep but then in the middle of the night, night after night, I was woken by my own sobbing. I wept almost continuously for four days and nights. Then finally I began to feel a little better. A weight had lifted from my heart and the relief was tangible. This little sketch had tapped into a deep pool of grief inside me that I never knew was there. As the grief began to siphon out I watched as if I was watching myself in a film. I found it hard to believe what was happening to me.

My father was twenty-eight when he died. I never knew him. He never even got home from the war to see me. So how could he touch me in this way? I wondered if I had ever felt this strength of emotion about anything in my life up till that point. Certainly I had never felt such grief. Yet these emotions seemed to have been formed before my earliest memories. What lay behind this extraordinary rush of emotion? Who was this man whom no-one had mentioned for years and what had happened to him?

4. Visit to Jack

My extraordinary outpouring of grief was replaced by an unstoppable compulsion to find out more. I began to wonder if Jack Swaab might still be alive and, if he was, whether he might possibly remember my father after all these years. Even though I was only four years old when I last saw him I remembered Jack. He might have been my step-father if things had worked out differently.

Then, when I was seven years old, my mother re-married. She put the war behind her. After that she neither saw nor mentioned Jack Swaab again and, in some way that I still can't fully define, she made it quite clear to me that I was not allowed to speak about him either. Because of my mother's previous taboo on even mentioning Jack Swaab's name, I was still afraid to ask her if she knew if he was still alive or where he might live. I wanted to go and speak to Jack yet I was afraid that if my mother found out she might stop me. I still had a tattered copy of Johnny Town Mouse by Beatrix Potter which he had given me when I was four, before he left my mother to marry someone else, and I remembered my mother's story about that book:

"It was a joke between us. Jack was so like the town mouse, so neat and well dressed, and I was like the country mouse, all plump and dishevelled. That is why I could never have married him," she had said firmly. "I could never have lived in London."

What if Jack still lives in London, I thought now, as I do myself? His name is unusual. There was just a chance that I might be able to find him without even mentioning it to my mother. I was quite grown up by this time but I felt like a naughty child as I picked up the London telephone directory to look for his name. I found it immediately along with his telephone number and address. Some things in life are extraordinarily simple. I wrote him a short note saying that I wondered if he might still remember my father and sent it off by first class mail. The very next morning he rang and asked me to dinner.

It is odd, when you are forty-five years old, to meet someone you last saw when you were four. I had grown up and left home early; qualified and worked as an architect; married, had two children and divorced; travelled widely; lived for ten years as a single parent; not only worked as an architect but also taught at art school. So much had happened. I knew hardly anything about Jack.

When my partner Alec and I arrived at Jack Swaab's house in Wimbledon I saw at once what my mother meant when she said he was like Johnny Town Mouse. Jack was still good looking, slim, upright, intelligent, neat and precise. His wife was petite and bird-like, bright and quick. Their little house was tidy and on the long low bookshelves around the walls of their sitting room were framed photographs of their two handsome sons, born rather late in their lives. I was taking all this in but Jack was watching me too.

"You are very like your father, you know," he said.

When I was a child people often told me I was like my father but it was a long time now since I had heard it. On my father's side I have no brothers, sisters, first cousins or uncles, only my aunt Suzanne. I rarely meet anyone now who knew my father when he was alive, yet Jack was one of these people.

"Your gestures, your smile, are just like your father's and you consider things in just the same way. It is unbelievable," he said.

Yet I can't have copied these things, I thought. Then he said something which amused me;

"I used to take you out of your cot when you cried in the night. I used to put you on my knee and sing 'Loch Lomond' to you," he said.

"I still love that song," I replied.

Then Jack told me about his war-time diaries. Although it was strictly forbidden he had kept diaries all through the war. In an old ammunition box in his attic he still had the seven densely hand-written notebooks, he told me. I was bursting with curiosity but I had to wait several more years before I was able to read them. Recently they have been published under the title "Field of Fire". I asked Jack if he knew whether my father was killed in Tunisia, as my grandfather had told me, or in Libya as Major Melia's letter had said, but Jack said he couldn't remember that now. Later he checked his diaries written at the time but he told me they weren't clear on the matter.

Jack seemed proud of his service in the war. This came as quite a surprise to me as I had been a long term pacifist. In my student days I had marched with the CND and protested against the Vietnam War. Most of my friends shared my views. It had never crossed my mind to be proud of my father's wartime efforts. I hated the whole idea of war. The concept was too painful for me even to consider. It seemed obvious to me that no war is worth the loss of even one good man. I had closed my mind to the subject. Although my son Thomas played with dozens of tiny plastic soldiers as a child I never took any interest in his war games. For years he spread his little soldiers up the stairs of our house and I cursed as I trod with bare feet in the darkness on their upturned bayonets. I have always hated anything to do with violence or killing and as a teenager I couldn't even watch a cowboy film. Yet Jack was unaware of this. He explained how his wartime service was his university. Then went back to talk about my father:

"He would have gone right to the top in the army, you know, if he hadn't been killed. That was obvious. He was a bit of a hero to me. He was terribly brave. He used to wear a shaggy Afghan coat and a monocle and he kept a German Luger pistol stuck into his belt. It sounds odd now," he added shyly, "but we all thought him awfully dashing at the time".

During the long silence which had followed WW2 I assumed, though he was often in my own thoughts, that my father was long forgotten by others. It was hugely reassuring for me to discover that Jack Swaab still remembered him so well.

After our meeting I found myself mulling over something else that Jack had said:

"You know you are not at all as I expected" he said. "I know I haven't seen you since you were a child but I didn't expect you to be so different to your mother."

My life has been very different to that of my mother. I have lived most of my adult life in towns, she has lived in the country. Politically I tend to the left; she sticks to the right. I have always worked for my living; she has been a full-time mother and housewife. I left home at sixteen and went my own way. So much had happened in my life which we never shared.

"We keep in touch but I'm not very close to my mother," I admitted.

Jack said nothing, but I thought he looked sad at the news.

Jack sent me home with a book. It was a 1946 first edition of 'Alamein to Zem Zem' by Keith Douglas printed on cheap post-war paper browning at the edges. I started to read it as soon as I got home and immediately I was gripped. Keith Douglas began his account;

I am not writing about these battles as a soldier, nor trying to discuss them as military operations. I am thinking of them - selfishly, but as I always shall think of them, as my first experience of fighting.

He had written about what it was like to be there in North Africa with the 8th Army fighting over the same patch of desert where my father fought too and I wanted to know exactly what it had been like for him. Like my father he too was killed before the war was over. But even now I was in two minds about it. I had to force myself to read Keith Douglas's book. I will have to steel myself now, I thought, and face up to this. Whatever happened out there in North Africa in WW2 I have to learn the truth and accept it, however painful it might be. I needed to find out about the father I never knew, and what he was doing when he was killed. For the first time I began to read about WW2 without allowing my lifelong horror of war to make me close the book. Yet there was a pen and ink drawing in that book that the author had made in North Africa in 1942, which made my blood run cold. It showed a local dog pulling a dead soldier from a shallow grave.

Was this what had happened to my father?

When I rang them, the Commonwealth War Graves Commission confirmed that my father had no known grave. His name, they told me, is commemorated on the 31st column of the Alamein Memorial, amongst all the other soldiers from the North African Campaign who were never re-buried in an official war cemetery. Yet now I knew that he once had a proper grave marked with a little wooden cross. So why wasn't my father's body ever collected up and re-buried in an official war cemetery along with the other soldiers?

Now I wanted to find out more but I didn't know

where to begin. I started by visiting the library at the Imperial War Museum.

"Huge numbers of people were killed in the war, you know," the librarian told me, "so you mustn't hope to find out anything specific, but if you know the details of your father's regiment and battery at the time he was killed you could look up the War Diaries at the Public Records Office in Kew."

At the PRO I put in my application and sat at the desk I had been allocated. Within minutes, two fat and tattered bundles of papers tied round with a length of thin khaki tape were placed in front of me. They were the wartime diaries of the 127th Highland Field Regiment for 1942 and 1943 written at the time in pencil on fragile lined paper by the commanding officer of my father's regiment Lieutenant-Colonel Perry. There he listed his officers: four Majors; William Melia, who had written the letter to my mother and three others, one of whom was my father J.O.Cochrane. Below the Majors in rank were ten Captains and twenty Lieutenants, one of whom was Jack Swaab and another Lieut., Watson Cowie, my father's Command Post Officer who also wrote to my mother; and one Quartermaster. I had been warned not to expect to find anything but, reading on through Perry's notes, I found my father mentioned, first once, then again and again. In one place, during the 'Battle of the Hills' which took place at Corodini on the approach to the capital Tripoli, his actions were recorded all through the night.

I was thrilled. Here again was evidence that my father was once a live person, that he truly once existed, that he once walked this same earth as me. For a brief six weeks we were both here together. I could even find out what he was doing, hour by hour, sometimes throughout the day and night. All through my life there had been a gap where my father should have been and now I could hardly believe I was able to hold in my own hands this evidence of his one-time existence. I was delighted by these small practical notes;

Abandoned stores litter the area.... Hold up caused by minefields... Water: 1/2 gal/man for 3 days... Reach Autelat and move forward in 4 columns as a precaution against minefields... Most of area is very bad salt marsh and many vehicles bogged... Very dark wet and cold night and country very difficult.

Then it came to the day of his death, 13th February 1943. The word PISIDA was written in the left hand column next to the words;

07.00   *One section of 491 Battery goes forward to Kilo. 163.*

09.00   *Major J.O.Cochrane is forward at Operation Post for roving section.*

14.00   *Recce parties go forward along causeway south of road.*

14.20   *News is received that Major J.O.Cochrane was killed by an 'S' mine boobied to a Teller mine at K0103. Body is buried 200 yds. south of road 200 yds. east of Kilo 2. Captain R.C.W.Arbruthnot assumes command of 491 battery.*

Only a full stop separates the details of my father's burial and the news of Captain Arbruthnot taking over his battery. Then the diary, and the war, went on as if nothing had happened; as if he never existed. Yet, in that second, my mother's life, and mine, and that of his parents, was changed forever.

On 14th February 1943 the day following my father's death, the diary noted that my father's battery crossed the frontier into Tunisia. Both Major Melia's letter and the contemporary regimental diaries were in agreement that he was killed not in Tunisia but in Libya, at a place named Pisida. It happened at K0103; a map reference but with no map attached. The position given by the diaries seemed to differ from the position given by Melia by about 800 metres. The distance into Libya from Tunisia was small, only a couple of kilometres. But in order to cross the boundary at all we needed Libyan visas, and in 1988 those were no longer obtainable in the UK.

Relations between the UK and Libya had been worsening since President Ghadafi first started to apply his revolutionary principles in Libya in the mid 1970s. During the last few years the relationship between our two countries had deteriorated more quickly. In 1984 Ghadafi's revolutionary committees took over the Libyan Embassy in London. That April a shot was fired from inside the embassy which killed a British policewoman, PC Fletcher, in the road outside. In 1985 the US accused the Libyans of involvement in Palestinian attacks in Rome and Vienna airports in which 20 people were killed. In April 1986, a bomb went off in a Berlin nightclub frequented by US soldiers, killing two and injuring two hundred. The US blamed Libya and President Reagan retaliated by bombing the Libyan cities of Tripoli and Benghazi. It was an attempt to assassinate President Gadhafi. Two of Gadhafi's sons were injured and his adopted daughter was killed, along with several other Libyan civilians. The US bombers took off from an RAF airport in Britain. As a result of this affair diplomatic relations between Britain and Libya were broken off.

In the two weeks which remained before we were due to leave for Tunisia I tried to get a Libyan visa in Paris. But I didn't succeed.

5. Tunisia

Two weeks later, on 1st April 1988, Alec and I started our holiday in Tunisia. We sat outside a street cafe in Houmt Souk on the Island of Djerba. It is known as the island of the lotus-eaters and, as if to confirm it, the sun shone down from a clear blue sky and above us the fronds of palm trees rustled softly in the breeze. A smiling stocky Tunisian speaking excellent French brought us two glasses of sweet mint tea and they sat steaming on the battered metal table between us. Alec put his feet up onto a chair and settled down with a thick American novel. I listened to the regular gurgle from behind me where our neighbour at the next table pulled bubbles of pungent tobacco through the cool water and up the long tubes of his hookah. Beyond Alec two men were slapping down the circular wooden discs of a backgammon game and across the road another group were playing a game of boules. These men seemed to have all the time in the world to relax and after the relentless pressure of our work in England we were happy enough to join them.

I began to sketch the conical minaret of the Mosque of the Turks. Its summit rose to a crisp point neatly enclosed in an upturned jam jar. Lower down the muezzin's little balcony was decorated with a string of brightly coloured electric light bulbs. Down at our level in the fish market the pillars of the arcaded streets were hung with necklaces of little fish strung through their eyes. On our way to the café we had passed the chopped-off head of a sheep lying in the road in front of a butcher's stall while at the back a group of animals queued up to go to their death. But it didn't offend me. In London we are sheltered from these things but they go on just the same. I felt it brought me closer to the realities of life and death and I liked the honest way it was all on show.

Suddenly everything seemed possible. Even though we had no visas we decided to hire a car and drive as far as the Libyan frontier. I allowed myself to hope there might be a little office at the border where we could buy day-passes into Libya. That afternoon we drove out of Djerba Island over the causeway which joins it to mainland Tunisia past orchards of silver-leaved olive trees extending in regimental rows into the distance. Neat white cube-shaped buildings stood in clearings, their hemispherical domes glowing in the evening sunlight.

After an uncomfortable night in the little town of Zarzis we emerged the following morning to find that the weather had turned. A brisk wind sent small grey clouds scudding across the sky and blew the sand up behind my contact lenses. Our guide book assumed that no tourist would go along this coast road towards the Libyan border, and we saw no others. The wind was getting stronger as we drove out of Zarzis in our tinny little hire-car and the sky turned to a strange dense yellow. This coast was called the Cote Sauvage, the savage coast, the guide book said. The flat, marshy, rutted land between our road and the distant sea began to look ominously like a battlefield. This land was still mined, our guide book advised, so anyone leaving the road should stick to well-used tracks. We drove gingerly, passing the occasional mule cart where Arab families in bright coloured clothes huddled together to protect themselves from the sand-laden wind. We didn't envy them. From time to time huge lorries overtook us, flinging sand onto our windscreen and right over the people in the open carts. Piles of rubbish were dumped to the left of the road and later two great dark shapes loomed up amongst them. They looked like tanks. Surely, we thought, there can't still be old tanks here since the Eighth Army came this way, forty-five years ago now. We parked our car beside the road and set off towards the hulks taking care to keep to the large track which led in their direction, although the sand was fast blowing over it. The two huge old WWII tanks lay stranded like beetles on their backs. Tangled lengths of broken track spiralled upwards from their massive rusted wheels.

The road passed on through sand dunes and marshes. A large group of white sea birds and a single stately heron hunched themselves against the sand-filled wind and we strained our eyes to see a hawk which hovered above us. The wind was getting stronger. By the time we reached the decrepit little town of Ben Gardane we knew we were driving into a sandstorm. There the single street was still gapped where some houses had been blown up, or maybe they had simply fallen down. Alec decided to stock up while he had the chance. He disappeared alone through the bead curtains of a roadside shop, emerging later with a bottle of water, a loaf of bread, two oranges and a bag of nuts. A road sign said Tripoli 202km.

As we drove on humps of sand began to snake their way across the road and, lurching across one of them, the back bumper fell off our car. I got out and fetched it and, pushing it onto the back seat, we carried on. Now the road was reduced by the sand to a single track and the dunes were drifting across it fairly thickly. Huge dark shadows rose out of the yellow gloom as passing lorries approached and ran out into the sand to avoid us. We could just see as far as the electricity posts beside the road. I had read that the German soldiers in retreat strung wires across the road between these poles to take off the head of any unwary

British soldier in a truck. I was wondering if anyone was killed this way when we reached the first of three police posts. They were surprised by the large dark blue British passports we had at this time, but they let us through after we explained in French the reason for our visit. Then we reached the Tunisian frontier building.

When my father's division crossed this frontier at Ras Ajdir on 14th February 1943, the day after his death, the British newsreel cameras were there to record the event. They wanted to show their pride in the troops and to encourage the people back home. To form the background of the picture an enterprising soldier had painted the Highland Division sign on the customs shed along with a note "First Across HD".

The HD sign gave the division the nickname the 'Highway Decorators'. They were also, because of their kilts and fierce fighting, known as the 'Ladies from Hell'.

That day the 5/7th Gordon Highlanders were first over the frontier. They were headed by their second-in-command because (I discovered later) their commanding officer Lt-Col Saunders had been severely wounded by the same explosion which killed my father. The soldiers had polished up their boots and badges. The pipers puffed out their chests as they passed the camera at the frontier playing 'Cock of the North'. It was all going well until the head cameraman rushed out into the middle of the road shouting 'Stay! Stop! There's no film in the camera!' So the whole parade stopped, marched back again and once more swung across the border for a re-take.

By the time we arrived the HD sign was long gone. Now the wooden walls of the Tunisian frontier shed were painted black and robed Arab women squatted in groups around the outside, huddling against the sand-filled wind. Inside the air was thick with tobacco smoke and packed with men all shouting together. We were the only Europeans and I was the only woman. Through the murky atmosphere we could just make out the border police who carried the passports up onto a staged area at one end of the room and into an enclosed office beyond. From time to time a policeman emerged from there with an armful of stamped passports which he piled on a counter at the front of the stage. He picked them up one by one and, glancing inside, shouted out an Arabic name. Then, as the passport holder waved his arms and began to fight his way towards the stage, the policeman skimmed the passport through the air towards him and continued to the next.

At last we spotted our large dark blue passports at the bottom of a new pile and Alec didn't wait to see how the officer would deal with them. He pushed his way quietly through to the front of the crowd. Reaching up he slipped them out from beneath the pile of small green Tunisian passports and put them quickly into his pocket. We escaped through a side door and, bracing ourselves against the wind, we walked the two hundred yards to the Libyan frontier shed. We could just make out the giant portrait of Colonel Gadafi in sunglasses painted on the large flank wall of the building.

Inside the Libyan passport shed the officers were friendly; but they only spoke Arabic. We tried English, French, Greek and even the small amount of Italian we could muster, but to no avail.

"Pisida, Pisida, we only want to go two kilometres to Pisida," we said.

The man behind the counter smiled but he didn't seem to recognise the word 'Pisida'. I showed him a photocopy of the little sketch of my father's grave but that only made him more confused. Using sign language we filled in the little green entry cards they gave us. The official raised his rubber stamp above our passports and I held my breath. Then he hesitated and spoke to his neighbour, who quietly shook his head.

I stood in the windswept road and gazed out through the swirling sand into Libya. My father had been killed and buried only a couple of kilometres down that road. But would I ever be able to go there?

Later that same year, in November 1988, a bomb exploded in a PanAm airliner bound for the USA over the Scottish town of Lockerbie. Two hundred and seventy people were killed. Two Libyans were blamed. In 1992 sanctions were imposed on Libya and these included a ban on all civil flights into the country. From then on no European or American tourists were issued with Libyan visas for any reason. But I had made up my mind. One day I would get into Libya to look for my father's grave.

6. Ceremony at Alamein

Following our unsuccessful attempt to cross from Tunisia into Libya in April 1988 the political situation between Libya and the UK got steadily worse. As the years passed by it seemed less and less likely that I would ever be able to get to Pisida to look for my father's grave. But something had altered inside me; now I actively wanted to know more about my father and, although I had only so far plucked up courage to mention it to my mother, I was also trying to find out more about WWII and this was something right out of character for me. My new interest was soon rewarded. At last it appeared that the silence I had lived with all my conscious life was lifting.

When I first went to the Public Records Office to read the War Diaries before our trip to Tunisia I found they were classified documents. I had to sign a paper to say that I wanted the information they contained for personal reasons and that I would not publish anything I found there. This classification lasted for 50 years. But in September 1989, only eighteen months after our trip to Tunisia, the fifty year embargo began to expire. This had an immediate effect. Documentary films about the war were assembled and shown on television. The silence was broken and people began to talk again about the war. A new generation who had never known a world war began to be interested in this extraordinary piece of European history.

In the spring of 1990 my search was made easier by an unexpected and unconnected event. My stepfather who my mother had married when I was seven years old died suddenly of a heart attack. After his death my mother felt she could talk to me about my father in a way she hadn't wanted to while my stepfather was alive.

The television documentaries continued to be produced as the classification of wartime documents expired year by year. November 1992 was the 50th Anniversary of the Battle of Alamein. This was the battle which finally turned the tide of the war against the Germans. They had been trying for many years to get through to the oil fields of the Middle East. Between 1940 and 1942 battles waged to and fro across the desert. Finally the Germans broke through and advanced into Egypt but there they were stopped by the allied forces at Alamein, a tiny place with a railway halt 50 miles to the west of Alexandria. Alamein held a strategic position on a narrow passage between the Mediterranean Sea to the north and the Quattara Depression, a huge boggy gulley impassable to tanks, to the south. There, in 1942, the two huge armies faced each other month after month. The Germans under Rommel planted a gigantic minefield five miles deep and forty miles long. On 23rd October 1942 the Allied 8th Army under General Montgomery began to break through this blockade in a terrible 13 day battle. By the day of victory on 5th November Montgomery had lost 4,600 men dead or missing and 8,950 wounded. Rommel had lost 25,000 dead or missing and 30,000 captured. The victory at Alamein came at a time when morale in the UK was at its lowest. The course of the war changed at last for the Allies. To celebrate the victory Churchill ordered that the church bells be rung all over the UK. They had been silent since the beginning of the war, only to be rung if the Germans invaded.

To commemorate the 50th Anniversary of the Battle of Alamein a memorial ceremony was planned at the War Cemetery there. My mother was asked if she would participate in the opening of the ceremony by receiving the first Remembrance Day poppy from John Major the British Prime Minister. Now my stepfather was no longer alive she felt able to accept the invitation, and she suggested that Alec and I might like to join her there. And so it was that, as the ceremony began, I found myself looking for a place from which I could take a photograph of the scene. The officials had cleared a space for my mother and two other war widows on a small mound at the centre of a huge crowd. She was wearing formal lightweight clothes and a crisp straw hat. Opposite, on another mound, were the world press. Cameramen pointed their huge intrusive lenses at my mother and the little group around her. I explained that I wanted to take a photo of her and the cameramen pushed along cheerfully. I squeezed in between them.

  I looked across at my mother. It was hard to know what she was feeling. She hadn't expressed any apprehension about the ceremony but it wasn't her way to share her feelings with me. She and I had become accustomed to keeping our feelings to ourselves. It was something that made us feel rather separate from each other. I expect she was glad to have this huge crowd all showing gratitude for the sacrifice that she and my father had made.

  She looked pleased as John Major handed her the first poppy, then he handed poppies to two other widows and made a short speech. Repeating the words of the official programme he said that my father was a victim of the battle of El Alamein; but I knew that my father had survived that battle. The Prime Minister said that my father was buried here at Alamein; but I knew that wasn't true either. I knew that he was killed at the other end of Libya, out near the Tunisian border, and that his bones were still lying there under the desert sand. I began to feel somewhat alone with my perception. The loneliness had a familiarity and I realised it was a feeling I often used to have as a child. Now, as the press photographers zoomed their lenses in on my mother and the Prime Minister, my feelings of isolation deepened. I began to look at the facts as I saw them. In spite of the map reference in the war diaries, and the wooden cross planted by his grave, it seemed that nobody went out there to bring my father's body in to the graveyard. The cameras all around me clicked and flashed.

This scene would be reported in newspapers all over the world, I thought, yet the truth was somewhere else and I was going to be left to live with it. It was the same old story over again. I was beginning to feel a bit rebellious and I had started making some calculations. There are 7,367 graves at the war cemetery at Alamein, I thought, and a further 11,874 names, with my father's amongst them, listed on the memorial. Were none of these soldiers named on the memorial ever buried in a real grave? How many human bones were still out there under the desert sand where fit young men once ran and fought, I wondered. All these grand people are here for the show, I thought, and then they will go home and get on with their lives. They are enjoying the ceremony with all the dressing up and posh hats. It is just a game to them.

Yet the service was brief and respectful. People had come from all over the world. The Duke of Kent read from Laurence Binyon's poem 'For the Fallen';

> They went with songs to the battle, they were young,
> Straight of limb, true of eye, steady and aglow.
> They were staunch to the end against odds uncounted,
> They fell with their faces to the foe.
>
> They shall not grow old, as we that are left grow old:
> Age shall not weary them, nor the years condemn.
> At the going down of the sun and in the morning
> We will remember them.

If only my mother and I could forget, I thought, how wonderful that would be.

Poppy wreaths were laid by veterans associations from all over the world. A lone bugler sounded the long notes of the last post. As the ceremony ended the haunting sound of bagpipes spread itself over the huge silent crowd and made its way out into the desert. The lament died and a warm gust blew spiralling whorls of sand up into the silent air.

That afternoon life went on in its conventional way and my mother, Alec and I joined the crowds of people from all over the world walking up and down amongst the rows of white headstones of the Alamein War Cemetery. The grave stones stretched in neat rows on and on away into the distance and we walked up and down, up and down, up and down in the bright North African sunlight reading the names and inscriptions. Many of the soldiers were only seventeen or eighteen years old when they died. I thought how devastated I would be if I were to lose my own son Thomas, twenty-two at that time. I thought of all the love and effort which had gone into raising those young men, some of them hardly out of school, to have them cut down at the very threshold of their lives. Nearly thirty thousand died in that one battle. As I began to imagine the suffering and waste of so many young lives lost the tears welled up into my eyes and began to run in rivulets down my cheeks. But this upset my mother. She couldn't allow me to cry. She hitched me up roughly by the arm and bustled me forward saying sternly "Come on, come on". And then she commented under her breath "If only your father were here he would be able to deal with you!"

There was something familiar about her words. I hadn't heard them since I was a child but now I remembered it was something she often used to say. She must have found me a difficult, spirited and rebellious child and I know that she often wished that my father had been there to help her bring me up. Yet I didn't like the way she still felt she still had to 'deal' with me. I had left home at sixteen and I had always been quite independent. For years and years my mother hadn't had to 'deal' either with me or with my children. This time I was certain of the validity of my feelings. I was sure that to weep was the only sane reaction to such carnage, and I wished my mother was able to weep too. If only she could do that it would help her, I thought.

That evening I was still upset about the episode and I spoke to Alec about it. I told him how my mother seemed to have been threatened by my feelings even though I was sure they were appropriate. She seemed to want to block my feelings out, I said. But Alec is a kind man and he was able to see both points of view. He agreed that it was right for me to weep but he thought that my mother's grief was so deep that she couldn't let it out, even now, fifty years after my father's death.

"She is still trying desperately to keep control of her own feelings" he said. "Maybe she feels that if you cry it might set her off crying, and that if she started to cry she might never be able to stop".

The following day we went to look at my father's name inscribed high up on the 31st column of the Alamein Memorial. I managed to borrow a ladder and I climbed up and stuck a poppy cross next to his name. We took photographs of it. What else could we do? Then we went on together to the small site museum. We looked at an 'S' mine and a Teller mine. It was an 'S' mine which had been 'boobied' to a Teller, an anti-tank mine, which blew my father up. We looked at a 25 pounder gun. My father had been in charge of eight such guns. He had been proud of that. But this one had a flat tyre and my mother, who is a practical person, was saddened to see it left in this condition.

"Your father would soon have seen to that," she said.

Back at the hotel my mother linked up with two delightful 8th Army veterans who had been together at Alamein. Each day they helped her with their realism, their humour and their camaraderie. All these years she had swallowed her feelings and her memories, keeping them buttoned up inside her. She had kept them entirely to herself. It was only now, fifty years later, that she began to visualise where her husband had been in 1942 while she was pregnant back in England. Her visit to Egypt was helping her put her feelings of sadness and loss into some kind of context. She began tentatively to connect again with the person she had been before she re-married when I was seven years old; with the part of her life we had shared. A slow process of healing had begun and immediately it brought us closer.

My mother began, at last, to talk about my father. She told us how she first had the idea she would marry him when she was only nine. Her own father, at the time, was Commodore in Charge of the naval barracks at Devonport, on the south coast of Devon. At the same time my Cochrane grandfather was in command of the gunnery school there. The two families had always been friends. On Sunday the Round-Turners and the Cochranes sat opposite each other in the front row of the pews at the Royal Naval chapel. My father was thirteen, nearly five years older than my mother.

One Sunday after church my mother went to lunch with the Cochranes and for pudding they ate stewed plums. My mother always counted the stones to see who she would marry.

"Tinker, tailor, soldier, sailor, rich man, poor man, beggar man....." It was a bad result, but my mother didn't care.

"It doesn't matter," she said, "as anyway I'm going to marry Jock."

"Oh no you're jolly well not!" he replied, she explained. Any self-respecting thirteen-year-old would reply like that, I thought.

As I stood in the War Cemetery at Alamein after the service in 1992 I looked westwards across the desert and wondered about my father's last journey with the British 8th Army in 1942. I would like, I thought, to follow the route so I could try to understand what it was like for my father and the other soldiers. But it wasn't possible. The desert road westwards from Alamein led along the Mediterranean coast through Marsa Matruh and Sidi Barrani and over the Halfaya Pass (inevitably called the Hell Fire Pass by the Allied soldiers) into Libya.

This was the frontier which no European tourist could cross.

1914-1934
MY FATHER'S STORY I

7. My Father as a Small Boy

After my trip to Alamein I began to speak about my father not only to my mother and to Jack Swaab but to my father's sister Suzanne and to his first cousin Ruth, who is also my Godmother. They all responded immediately and with no reluctance or embarrassment. In this I was lucky.

My father's immediate family decreased dramatically in size in the three generations above mine. I have no brothers, sisters or first cousins on my father's side, and only one aunt, my father's younger sister, who married late and had no children. I was the only grandchild on the Cochrane side. It was a privileged position. They loved me unreservedly and tried in every way they could to make up for the father I never had, and in this too I was very, very lucky.

By the time we came back from our trip to Alamein my aunt Suzanne lived with her husband in London.

When I rang her up and asked her if she had any letters from my father or photographs of him she said she had a photograph album I might like to see. When I arrived at her flat I found a large dark green leather-bound album immaculately laid out on a cloth on her dining table. I had never seen it before and I was astonished by what I found inside. As soon as I started to turn the pages I began to wonder if my grandparents knew that I would find it one day. The album was a record in pictures of my father's life. My grandparents made the album in 1954, Suzanne told me, when I was twelve and my grandmother lay dying of cancer. My grandfather spent most of his time with her. Knowing they had so little time left, my grandparents used the last few months of their marriage to look back over their lives together and to share their memories. My grandfather collected up photographs, telegrams, letters, postcards, menus and paintings for the album and discussed with my grandmother which ones should be included. Then he stuck each chosen piece in carefully with stamp hinges and titled it in neat handwriting. From the bedroom window he could look down the driveway towards the gate where the telegram courier arrived on that fateful day.

The yellowing pages of my grandparents' album were densely packed with black and white photographs, many now faded to sepia, interspersed with my grandmother's sensitive water-colour paintings, my grandfather's postcards from far places and important telegrams from both world wars. As I looked through its pages I found that the photographs, so neatly ordered and titled year by year, formed a diary in pictures of my father's life. The first pages of the album tell the story of my father's birth at the Devonport Naval Base on 21st July 1914 just one week before the outbreak of World War I. My grandfather was already away at sea. It continues with his idyllic-seeming childhood in the inter-war years and ends with his death in World War II just twenty-eight years later. As I turned the pages I began to understand that my grandparents had made the album for me.

On the first page I found photographs of my father's christening on 20th September 1914 when he was two months old. Already I could distinguish that long Cochrane face with the large eyes and definite features. His fair hair is carefully brushed into a quiff and he is held in the arms of his proud nurse. She is wearing a special hat for the occasion and a stiffly ironed white cravat edged with handmade lace. She is holding the baby with her hand in an odd position so she can display his beautiful long christening gown to the camera.

My father was christened James Owen Cochrane so his initials, J.O.C. , were the same as mine. Both the Owen and the Cochrane names are family names from his father's side and both show a strong naval heritage. My father came from a long line of fighting men. He would have liked to follow his father, his grandfather and his great-grandfather into the navy but he failed to get in due to short sight inherited from his mother's side. But the army let him in. It crossed my mind as I thought about those names that with them he was handed his destiny.

The early photographs show my father as a little boy sitting on his rocking horse, helping in the garden or playing outside with his friends. In spite of WWI his early life was peaceful and privileged. I looked at the photo of the chubby two year old toddling between the flower beds with his full-sized bucket. He is dressed all in white. The pleated hem to his neatly cut jacket came down to cover the top of his short white trousers. His podgy turned-in feet are encased in clean white socks and his little black shoes are fastened with a strap and button.

In 1917, when my father was two and a half, the first signs of war creep into the family album. A photograph shows a German Prisoners' compound at the Frith Hill Army Camp, near my grandfather's family home at Windlesham in Surrey. The prisoners stand about listlessly inside a tall, barbed wire fenced enclosure.

In a postcard from 1917 a long squat tank, the very latest weapon of war first used the previous November at the Battle of the Somme, has been driven on to the square near the central pond. The base of a nearby statue is enclosed with placards urging 'Buy Your War Bonds at the War Bond Tank'. A huge queue is just distinguishable from the rest of the tightly packed crowd leading towards a small hut where the bonds to raise money for the war effort are being sold. The buildings surrounding the square are barely visible through the thick coal-fire smog. My grandfather spent two years of WWI working at the Admiralty in London. That is right nearby Trafalgar Square and he must have known the scene well.

My Cochrane grandfather was a dapper figure as a young man, tall, relaxed and confident. In January 1918 he was appointed to command the battle cruiser HMS Lord Nelson. In the photograph of the forty officers and the ship's chaplain on deck it is easy to find my grandfather with his long face and neck and sloping shoulders. Painted boards hung behind the group with the words "ENGLAND EXPECTS THAT EVERY MAN......." Just what was expected is hidden behind a white ensign hanging from the bridge but doubtless England expected its men should "..DO THEIR DUTY". It is a quotation from Nelson himself and my father was brought up with this principle.

My grandfather was Acting Captain of the HMS Lord Nelson in Malta in October 1918 when he received a telegram announcing the birth of a daughter. This was my Aunt Suzanne. Now the family was complete. This was to be a modern family with only two precious children.

The photograph of my father at the time of his sister's birth is one I have known all my life. It is one of three photographs which, in spite of her remarriage, my mother has always kept in her bedroom. In 1918 the four year old boy stands alone with his little spade on the huge empty sandy beach. Wearing a baggy sun suit and a straw hat on his head he gazes pensively out to sea. My mother always told me it was typical of him and I often used to look at that photograph when I was a child. There was something about it that I immediately recognized in myself. Perhaps it was the apparent isolation of the small child which made me identify with that photograph.

The telegram announcing the end of WWI is carefully stuck into the album with a note to say that it was received in the Dardanelles at 07.22 on 11th November 1918. It came from the French Commander in Chief, Marshal Foch and was relayed from the Eiffel Tower;

Hostilities will cease upon the whole front from the 11th November 11 o'clock French o'clock. The Allied troops will not cross until further orders the line reached on that date and that hour.

It was the eleventh hour of the eleventh day of the eleventh month which has become Armistice Day, still the time of the two minute silence to remember the dead of the two world wars. The new baby daughter was christened Suzanne Gloria. Her second name was chosen to celebrate the end of WWI. This was a family where war played a central role.

In April 1919 my grandfather was ordered to take HMS Lord Nelson to the Dardanelles to collect the Grand Dukes Nicolas and Peter Romanoff who were fleeing Russia following the assassination of Tsar Nicholas and his family at Ekaterinberg the previous July. My aunt Suzanne told me again how her father took one grand duke to Marseilles and the other to Genoa. The photograph the Grand Duke Nicholas gave my grandfather shows a bearded figure wearing a heavy, wasted overcoat and a tall Astrakhan hat. A jewelled dagger hangs from his belt.

As soon as my grandfather completed this mission he was asked to collect Maria Feodorovna, the Dowager Empress of Russia, sister of Queen Alexandra of England

MY FATHER AS A SMALL BOY

H.M.S. LORD NELSON.

and mother of the murdered Tsar Nicholas, and to bring her and her entourage back to Portsmouth. In the family album a portrait of the party on the deck of the Lord Nelson is circled with signatures.

As far as I can read them they say: Maria Feodorovna, the Count, two Countesses and N and V Mengden, P and D Obeliani and Prince Dolgorouky. Two people, probably the children of the Empress's murdered daughter Olga, have signed simply 'Rotislav' and 'Vassili'.

My grandfather has a child on his knee who looks to me too small to be either of the princes.

The Empress spent much of the journey sitting on deck and as the ship passed the Isle of Wight on its way to Portsmouth she summoned my grandfather and said, "We have passed this way before. What is going on?"

"I have orders to dock in Portsmouth Harbour at 3.00 p.m.," he explained, "and as our Royal Family are very punctual I mustn't be either early or late. We have had a strong tail wind and it has brought us to this point a bit ahead of schedule. To put us back on target I gave orders to take a loop around the Isle of Wight."

"Oh I do hope my sister will be there to meet me!" said the Empress.

My grandfather hoped so too but he couldn't be sure. He said, "Queen Alexandra is no longer young. It is a long way from London to Portsmouth and you mustn't be too disappointed if she is unable to manage the journey."

As soon as the harbour came into view the Empress exclaimed, "Oh! There is my sister! I told you she'd come! I told you she'd come!"

By 1920 it was possible again to go across the Channel to France and my grandparents took the children on holiday to Paris Plage. My grandmother's watercolour of the beach is stuck into the album next to the holiday snaps. But although, compared to many families, they were lucky in WW1 it had marked their lives. They went to find the grave of my grandmother's brother William who was killed in January 1915. He was the eldest son of the family, the nearest to her in age and her favourite. He was buried at the Guards Cemetery at Cuinchy just outside Béthune.

The photograph of the Cathedral of St. Martin at Ypres taken before the war is carefully stuck into the album next to the same view afterwards. In the second photograph the whole high cathedral nave is a pile of rubble spewing out through the gaping hole at the base of the jagged stump of the western tower.

404194. — Ypres. Cathédrale St-Martin. St-Martin's Cathedral

Between the wars the photographs in my grandparents' album shows Jock and Suzanne growing taller each year.

Their lives were secure but, like all naval families, they moved house time and again as my grandfather was posted from place to place. In their early childhood it was their grandparents who provided a continuous base for the children, just as my grandparents later did for me. Suzanne told me how each Sunday, if he was in London, my grandfather would drive his wife and children to lunch with my grandmother's family outside Ascot and then on for tea with his own parents five or six miles to the south at Windlesham. The children stayed with both sets of grandparents when their own mother and father were abroad and there they lived in the old style.

My father was sent away to boarding school when he was nine years old. I was astonished when my mother sent me another bundle of letters which he had sent to his parents at that time. Like the condolence letters I had seen already and all those she would give me later I had no idea they existed. The first letters were sent in February 1924, when my father first went to prep-school at Rottingdean outside Brighton on the south coast of England.

When I unfolded my father's first letters home his handwriting was so unruly and the spelling so unlikely that they read like a spoof. Amongst the writing whole sentences were often scratched out and the scratchings went in all directions. On one early letter the top right hand corner of the small page of stiff cream-coloured writing paper is covered in spots and blodges where he tested his nib. The letter he then wrote reads:

Laste night mister fredritch in and sead shal we don the noulyoum wich had been over laping and we when we came in to the domantry you all ways trip over it and spoal the noalyam and he tryed to pull it to the side and he foget he had nailed it down and he had to go dowen and get a hamer and touls and that took a good five minits and the time was geting on for 10oclock and then the there was all the nails to take out and pull it rite and then to nail it down aghen and it was 10 by now and the beds had to be moved and the wash stands had to be moved and then it was 12 beafor I got to sleep.

Like any small boy he was thrilled to stay up till midnight but it was odd for me, as a fairly literate adult, to find that my father had such difficulty with his spelling. Now, as I looked through his letters I found that although the words came tumbling out without any inhibition even when he was grown up they had hardly any commas or full stops. Yet it seemed, when I enquired, that my father's education had been quite conventional. My mother said, "Oh he could never spell. It didn't worry him one bit and it didn't bother anyone else either as far as I know. They just loved him as he was."

It appeared that although he tried hard at school he really struggled on the academic side:

I have got up a bit in maths as you say it is my spelling that puts me back or I mite be higher up at eney rate I have beatin Dill this week and am not botem this week.

I can only assume that my father was dyslexic and that, at that time, was not a recognised condition. My father's letters are filled with descriptions of how his garden was growing:

My nestirshams is about two inshes high and my caliopsis has started at last.

He told his parents what he needed for his stamp and cigarette card collections and about the photographs he had taken, but they never mention any academic subject. Although he struggled with hay fever he took all sports very seriously organising the times when he could practise for the hurdles, which he called 'hirdels' and the high jump. He found the swimming pool 'simply ripping'.

His parents enjoyed and encouraged my father's childish curiosity, his enthusiasm and his adventurous spirit. It was never crushed out of him. He was always keen to explore and he loved fishing. His prep school was near the coast and sometimes the children got a chance to wander along the sea shore discovering pools and caves;

I never thout that I should find a fish in the pools all though they were onlay small slingers I was looking for thoes when some one discoverd the cave ...

One day he found a man offering rides in a plane:

There is a man with an aroplane on the downs he takes people 2 miles for 5/- and right into Brighton for 10/- and loop the loop for 15/- and loop the loop and spiral nose dive for 30/- I should love to go up if he is still there by the sports. P.S. There is a boy going up at half term called Bevan.

I shall never know if his parents agreed to that.

8. Marlborough

My mother was one year younger that Suzanne, but a very different character. My mother had two elder brothers and she always tried to keep up with them. She was up for anything and hated to be left out. Suzanne was very different.

"She was a dear little girl," my mother said now. "She had a nanny, Miss Swann, who stayed with the family for years who thought Suzanne was perfect; and she really was. She was always neat and clean and she was never naughty. Miss Swann used to tie up her beautiful red hair in rags each night and in the mornings she combed it into ringlets. I always liked to play with Jock. I am ashamed to say that one time when I was a little girl, Jock and I climbed up an apple tree together and when Suzanne came by we pelted her with rotten apples. I expect we got a terrible ticking-off," she added, but she didn't seem to remember it.

In 1928 my Round-Turner grandfather was Commodore in charge of the Naval Dockyard at Devonport and my Cochrane grandfather ran the Gunnery school there. One photograph shows a royal inspection at the barracks. Naval officers line the street, capped, booted, standing to attention, their rifles held upright. They were headed by my two grandfathers in full uniform, each in turn shaking hands with Princess Mary. Another photograph shows Jock as a gangly thirteen-year-old against a distant background of ship's funnels. This was the lad who my nine-year-old mother decided she would marry.

He had just started at Marlborough College. The fees were paid by his maternal grandfather, who ran a rather profitable coal export and import firm Mann George. In my grandparent's photograph album his prep school cap was exchanged for the Marlborough College boater. It was a school which specialised, at the time, in educating boys to join the armed forces. My father soon joined the Officers' Training Corps and his letters reflect how they prepared him up for the life he was to lead. He describes how a group of schoolboys were taken out on an OTC field trip one freezing day and the weather got worse and worse;

a wind had got up and was driveing the snow right accross us. Of course I was the outside man and by the time we stopped my neck was so numb that I could hardly move it then came tea which was frightful as it was getting colder and colder and we were standing still to make it worse... we had to wate outside the station because the train had been ordered for an hour ...I think this was about the wirst time of all as they seem to have put the station on the most exposed place they could find.

In the train on the way back to school he was caught larking about and later beaten for that. But he took it all in good part and commented;

A nice day all together!

"He was tough," Jack Swaab had said. He was brought up to be tough. And he was encouraged to be adventurous. From his very first days at Marlborough he persuaded his parents to let him come home to London by bicycle and well before the end of each term he tried to find other boys to accompany him and began to make his plans.

Later he and a school-friend bought a boat So then they made their way home along the waterways. He made meticulous plans for the journey borrowing the rug and the tarpaulin from his parents' car for sleeping out:

It would render me semi-impervious to moisture whereas sleeping in a wet blanket might not result in over much rest.

He estimated the journey might take about a week:

if we are not delayed by the weather or by a stay in a local court or a lunatic asylum, all of which possibilities seem to be likely, especialy the first for keeping an unregistered boat on the thames, on the other hand if the weather is kind to us it should be glorious.

His mother's family also had a lease on a hunting lodge up on the moors in Ayrshire and each summer the whole George family and all the servants moved up to Scotland for the shooting season. My father loved his annual trips to Scotland. When I was a child my grandmother used to tell me how preparations for the move took weeks. Hampers were filled with all they needed including the sheets and tablecloths. A whole carriage was reserved on the train from Euston. I still have half a dozen starched white double-damask tablecloths and piles of napkins in a cupboard which made that journey many times. Their corners are carefully embroidered with the entwined initials, S.K.G. for my father's grandfather, Sidney King George. They are remnants from another world.

The summer trips to Scotland continued throughout the inter-war years. My father had three uncles on his mother's side, Uncles Mac, Jack and Ron, who had no children of their own. Uncle Mac especially doted on my father and gave him plenty of his time. He taught him to tie his own fishing flies, trap rabbits, shoot grouse and later to drink fine wine in the evenings as they did. At Marlborough, where my father went to secondary school, he used the training his uncles had given him to catch fish and rabbits under the cover of darkness. He supplemented his diet with his catch and sold any he had to spare to his schoolmates. From school he wrote back to his parents:

if it had not been for them I expect we should be actualy trying to live on college rations now as it is we are completely bancrupt as usual but liveing on the resources of the country in comparative ease.

At Marlborough my father shared a study with a long-suffering friend and he described to his parents how he decorated the room and things got into a bit of a mess;

I do not think you would exactly enjoy the studdy now spots of paint everywher the tea things still unwashed up and plates of fish bones strolling about and last but not least the pot of tame worms on the table

The teenage letters give precise descriptions of the

fish traps he set in the Kennet and Avon canal; how he tied his fishing flies; how he snared rabbits along with his latest recipes for fish or rabbit stew; and the rabbit hutches he made for keeping the rabbits he brought in live; and he told the story of one rabbit which managed to escape;

I caught an old and wize rabbit who at once sat down and gnawed one of the boards that constituted the bars. I caught it on Fryday morning and brought it back alive and its fate hung in the ballance as there would be no time to cook it on a Fryday and we were not anxious to have a dead rabbit hanging about a small studdy until there was time to consume it, consequently it remained in the studdy all Fryday then owing to House matches it was allowed to survive all saturday, on saturday night a court was held and the death sentence was passed for committing a nuisance and contempt of court, however on Sunday morning when I arrived down the rabbit was nowhere to be seen and had evidently jumped out of the window though how it managed to survive a jump from the second storey I cannot think, the other theory was that it had been abducted by one of the house servants, but I do not think that could have been so as as I saw that he was there at about ten oclock on saturday night and he was not there early sunday morning as I was up early to look at my snares and rat traps...

Although Marlborough is a school with a forces tradition the masters were very lenient in some ways. His housemaster must have known about the cooking arrangements in my father's study. But it seems he never interfered. He knew about the poaching too, but he turned a blind eye. My father, for his part, made an effort to conceal his activities from the school authorities, though not from his parents:

I hope to be able to drop a rabbit but I will probably not be able to do so as the authorities are begining to sit up and take notice which means that I have to take great care.

My mother told me how when my father left Marlborough his housemaster said, "I shall miss his silent figure creeping back over the fields in the early rays of dawn."

Year after year the summer visits to Scotland are recorded in the photograph album. The photographs show groups of eight or ten hatted gentlemen wearing tweed jackets and plus fours and carrying guns. Each group is accompanied by one or two gun dogs. Young Jock, the only boy, is there too. He too is wearing a tweed cap and plus fours, getting taller each year as his uncles impart to him their love of Scotland, and teach him their way of life. It was my father's responsibility to supply his grandmother, Granny George, with trout for breakfast and with grouse and rabbits for the family dinner. By the time he was seventeen my father is barely distinguishable from the adults at Craiglure. He is taller than his uncles and a little taller even than his father, carrying a gun, wearing a brimmed hat and smoking a pipe with the rest of the party.

My mother sent me bundles of letters little by little and in no particular order. I had no idea if she had given me all that there were or if she had more hidden away. I never knew if she might suddenly decide she had given me enough and decide to burn the rest. I didn't know whether, if she knew I was studying them in such detail and even writing up some passages from them on my computer, she might decide to stop. One time she sent me a bundle of my father's school reports and a report from a career advisory service he had visited. My father's school reports were very different to mine. Even though my father had such trouble with writing his teachers were never critical of the effort he put in. I was good on the academic side but my teachers often said I didn't concentrate or could try harder. Sometimes they said I was mischievous or naughty.

It seems, on the other hand, that my father always tried hard. With the school reports my mother sent another from the National Institute of Industrial Psychology, made in 1932 when he was 16 years old. It was typically modern and enlightened of my grandfather to send his son to be assessed in this way to help him decide on a suitable career. The Institute made some thorough tests.

The first was an intelligence test devised to discover innate ability rather than acquired general knowledge. In this my father scored 134 marks out of a possible 193. The average for boys of his age and education was 125. The next was a problem-solving test designed to assess not only general intelligence but also his practical abilities. They reported that his movements were characterised by above average speed and dexterity. In the next test, for mechanical ability, it was not speed but the method and accuracy of working which were important. The maximum score was 100 and the average 75. His score was 91. The final test was for powers of literary expression:

"In this brief test," they reported, "he produced some almost incredible work. His spelling is the most original we have seen for some considerable time. His punctuation is atrocious, in the course of writing over two hundred words he used only two commas and two full-stops. Thoughts tumble out of him in an extraordinarily higgledy-piggledy manner. In many of them there is neither rhyme nor reason. His saving grace is his sense of humour."

My father was physically in touch with himself, but had difficulty writing. How ironic that it should be his letters which survive for his own daughter to get to know him.

"He is of a sensitive nature," the Institute report noted, "and tends to be shy and solitary. He is of only a moderately sociable disposition but he can be very pleasant in his relationships with others. He is inclined to be critical of those with whom he comes into contact, and he possesses a greater degree of self-confidence than is usually found in boys of his age. His casual and easy-going manner seems to us to be one of his main characteristics, but there is in him too a definite streak of obstinacy."

Those who knew my father agree that this assessment was extraordinarily astute and accurate. The curious thing is that people say I am like that too.

Gaffer had suggested that my father might follow Uncle Mac and go to university to become a fuel technologist. Uncle Mac worked for Mann George, the family coal export firm. The Institute advised that this idea be dropped. They recorded that my father responded with disdain to the suggestion of a career in business. So they recommended that he should go into the navy or the army, for which, they said, he seemed well suited both intellectually and temperamentally. They noted that his main problem with entering the navy would be his poor eye-sight. Finally they summarised their advice:

"On the whole, then, we think that the Navy and Army should be given first choice. Either appears to us to be very suitable."

My father applied to the navy which he considered the 'senior service' but, as predicted, he failed to get in on the grounds of his eyesight. He was accepted into the army.

9. Woolwich

At the time of the Wall Street Crash in 1929 my father was fifteen and still at Marlborough. World economic depression followed. The UK fell deeper and deeper into economic turmoil and in July 1931, after a meeting of the Committee on National Expenditure, Ramsay MacDonald's government decided they needed to drastically reduce public spending. A reduction in spending on the armed forces was at the forefront of this package.

In September 1931 my grandfather was Captain of the battlecruiser HMS Repulse. The Repulse was one of ten warships of the Atlantic Fleet which had recently arrived at Invergordon in the Cromarty Firth in Scotland, when the Admiralty announced a 10% cut in all naval pay. Ratings below Petty Officer who had joined before 1925 faced a massive 25% pay cut. On 12th September 1931 a mass meeting was held in the local football park where the sailors voted unanimously to take strike action. Strike action, or mutiny, is very rare in the armed forces. In spite of the decision in the football park HMS Warspite and Malaya left harbour to perform planned exercises two days later on 14th September. The crews left in harbour were incensed. They intended to prevent their ships sailing out on similar practice manoeuvres the following day, the day when my grandfather's ship, HMS Repulse, was due to sail out to perform similar exercises. On the evening of the 14th my grandfather gathered together the entire crew of HMS Repulse, over a thousand men. He explained that the 10% pay cut applied to everybody, including himself, and that Rear-Admiral Tomkinson (temporarily in charge of the fleet) had made a representation to the Admiralty to try to resolve the anomaly of the ratings pay. He explained that he stood behind Tomlinson in this matter. He went on to describe the economic situation which lay behind the cuts and that the country was on the verge of bankruptcy. On 15th September 1931 HMS Repulse and four other battleships were ordered out as planned. At 6.30 am. that morning HMS Repulse sailed out precisely on time; but the sailors on the four other battleships refused orders. On HMS Hood and HMS Nelson crews carried out ordinary harbour routine, but refused to put to sea. On HMS Valiant and HMS Rodney crews carried out essential duties, such as the provision of safety patrols, without any recourse to their officers. On HMS Rodney the sailors dragged a piano on deck and sang songs, ridiculing the officers who issued orders through loudspeakers. The sailors on board HMS Centurian, Norfolk and Exeter also refused to obey orders from their officers. The Invergordon Mutiny was the widest act of industrial action by the armed forces since the Nore mutiny of 1797 and it was a key event in forcing Britain off the Gold Standard the following month. My grandfather could be seen as being a strike-breaker but on the other hand, it was a remarkable demonstration of the personal respect that his men held for my grandfather that his ship put out to sea on time on that day. His men trusted my grandfather to keep his word and to do his best to support their claims.

The following summer HMS Repulse was in the West Indies. Several pages of the album have photographs of Trinidad, Granada, St. Vincent and Barbados. The seventy-seven officers on deck are immaculate in white tropical hats, suits, socks and shoes. Gaffer also carried out an extra mission of the type he rather enjoyed. He was asked by the London Zoological Society to bring back a rare Guildings parrot from St. Vincent and the Natural History Museum asked him to bring back a collection of reptiles, insects and jelly-fish. The parrot was a large orange bird with bright blue markings on its neck. Parrots live a long time and in later years my grandfather and I sometimes went to visit him at his new home in London Zoo.

Yet on 30th December 1932 my grandfather received a brief letter from the Admiralty. The letter, addressed to Captain E.O.Cochrane A.D.C. R.N., states blandly:

I am commanded by My Lords Commissioners of the Admiralty to inform you that you have been promoted to the rank of Rear Admiral in His Majesty's Fleet, with seniority of 3rd January 1933. I am also formally to acquaint you that, in accordance with the Regulations for the Retirement of Officers of the Royal Navy, They have approved of your being placed on the Retired List from 4th January 1933.

It seems odd to me that Gaffer should have been given only five days notice to quit after thirty-eight years of exemplary service in the navy and I know that he was very upset by this. The dismissal came immediately after Christmas. From commanding over a thousand men one day my grandfather was unemployed the next. He was hardworking and ambitious, fit and only fifty-one. Although this was a time of sweeping cuts in the armed forces due to the economic situation in the country Gaffer felt that his outstanding work at the Invergordon Mutiny had not been recognized. Without further research I can't be sure but it seems possible that he was punished for his support for Rear-Admiral Tomlinson at this time without precise consideration of the role he played. However he accepted the decision and my Cochrane grandparents started to look for a house of their own for his retirement, and they bought the house in Hawkhurst where I so often visited as a child. Like my Round-Turner grandfather Gaffer immediately set about making a beautiful garden.

My father left Marlborough in the summer of 1932. He was accepted into the army and since Gaffer was a gunner, my father was sent to the Artillery Training School at Woolwich. Soon after his arrival early in 1933 he sized up what was expected of him and reported home;

I seem to have been kept on the hop very effectively so far, the stock practical jest seems to be to put you down for about three things at once then enjoy the fun as you shuttlecock to and fro across the whole academy trying to find out which you have to do. The other favourite is to make you change as many times as possible in any given day for instance one can get up and go to breakfast in uniform, change to P.E. kit afterwards, then back into uniform for Infantry Drill, then into canvas for workshops or a demonstration in the gun park and finally into uniform for lunch...then you have to sprint in heavy army boots half across the shop then do a complete change and arrive at the other end in time to parade outside the classroom...

He had a little room of his own:

The chimney is smoking furiously owing to a high wind, the whole gaseous contents of the chimney suddenly precipitates itself into the room every few seconds.

And the bed was awful. By this time my father was 6'3" tall. The bed was too short for his legs, had a hole in the middle, a lump at the end, a huge straw-stuffed bolster too high for his head and a small flat pillow too low. He tried using the pillow as a ramp up to the bolster. In the end he found a solution;

Re the bed question I have discovered why there was a bump at the foot of the bed; the mattress is very thin and when a large wad of clothes is tucked in at the ends, and the corner and side tuckings all overlap, the result is a distinct elevation of the end. Cure is to untuck the foot of the bed and dispose the clothes round the body. I have also got cunning with the bolster and by twisting it and generally arranging it with great care the pillow can be made to fit on a ledge and the result is quite comfortable. Anyway I am always sufficiently tired every morning to be able to sleep in the middle of the parade ground in a snow storm.

He knew that Ga would be worrying about him;

I am sorry I did not write before as you must in your usual way have been suffering agonies wondering whether I had by this time a bed at all to sleep in.

And he asked her if she could send him a few little things he needed. They give a glimpse of a very different world to the one we live in now:

Could you also hunt out a brass button stick and button brush the brush has a brass star on the back and is slightly knocked about, the bristles are a sort of green colour from much button cleaning, as although my servant cleans the buttons every morning their are occasions when they require an extra rub before going on parade say in the afternoon after a rainy forenoon.

On the page of the album following the letter announcing my grandfather's retirement is the first photograph of their new house in Hawkhurst. The view, from across the lake, is one which was blocked when I knew it by the large rhododendron where I used to play. The dam which held the lake broke during the war. There was no-one to mend it and the water drained away. But in this photograph the lake in the foreground is full and the elegant early-Georgian house stands back on the raised ground behind. My father and his new army friend Buster began immediately to dig out the lily pond to turn it into the swimming pool where twelve years later Gaffer would teach me to swim.

Next to that photograph is one of the Admiral Superintendent's House at Chatham. My witty and amiable Round-Turner grandfather survived the naval cuts of the early thirties. He was put in charge of the dockyard at Chatham and my mother, fourteen by now, her two older brothers and her younger sister moved there.

At Chatham Grandfather and Gran Round-Turner had a large staff so it was easy for them to organise picnics and boating parties for the children and their friends. My father sailed from Woolwich in a boat called Mysinda he owned jointly with his new army friend Buster. My godmother Ruth, two years older than Jock, went to stay there too. He had grown up since she last saw him and now she was impressed. They were carefree times for those young people. My father found plenty of time for parties, hockey and golf as well as for sailing:

We have had some good runs in Mysinda lately we got up to Waterloo Bridge last Sunday. We got through the Tower Bridge in grand style as a big boat was just coming down and we slipped through while the bridge was open, under London Bridge we had to take the topsail down in a great hurry under the bridge into Cannon Street the top of the mast just scraped along the bottom of the bridge and finally the next bridge being an iron girder one the top of the mast was dodging rivets all the way through. After that I called a halt as my nerves wouldn't stand another. We tied up to a barge and waited for the tide to go down a bit before we attempted to go down again. Going back we had our revenge on the senior service as we picked up a whaler full of the navy just after leaving Tower Bridge and beat them down to the R.N.C. by the length of Greenwich reach in spite of the fact that we had to go up into the wind during squalls or we should have capsized.

My father's passing out ceremony on 11th July 1934 marked his transition into an adult soldier. A letter from the War Office that December confirmed his posting to the 15th Medium Brigade and in February he set out for Peshawar, now on Pakistan but then on the North-West Frontier of India, in a massive troop ship HMT Lancashire (of the Bibby Line established 1821). His parents, my Cochrane grandparents, came down to Southampton to see him off on the long voyage by sea to India.

My father left England at twenty years old; his life up until that time had fully prepared him for the man he would become. He was a handsome, fit, secure and confident young man with a wonderful sense of humour. He was slim and six foot four tall. He would come back when war broke out five years later, with experience as well.

1942-1988 MY STORY

10. Reeves and Folkestone

When I was a child the people around me often told me I was like my father. These stories about my father became embedded in my sense of self, they were part of my dream world; yet I never met my father. I had no idea, at the time, what he was really like. I had no joint experiences with my father as a real person. I could never form my own view of him. This account of his childhood that I have now written, and what follows about his short later life, is built up almost entirely from material I discovered only in my late forties and fifties. In as far as I took my cue in life from my father, and I did do that, it was taken from a mythical figure, a man with no reality, the man of my dreams.

When the death-announcing telegram came through it was addressed to my grandfather at his house in Hawkhurst. My parents had only been married a couple of years and my father had not thought to register my mother as 'next-of-kin' on his army forms. It was lucky for me that my mother was close to my Cochrane grandparents as well as to her own parents and they took an essential part in my upbringing.

In February 1943 when the telegram arrived my mother and I were staying at the large old house in Layer-de-la-Haye which my maternal grandparents had bought five years earlier when my Round-Turner grandfather retired from the navy. By 1943 he was away in Folkestone where he was Commodore in Charge of Folkestone Port. In this capacity he was in charge of the defence of a long stretch of the south coast where the invasion had been expected to arrive. My grandmother was still at the big house with two older women who had been evacuated out of London, my mother and me. When I was about a year old my Round-Turner grandmother sold the house at Layer-de-la-Haye and moved to Folkestone to be with her husband. She kept on a small cottage called Reeves next door which had come with the house and my mother and I moved in there.

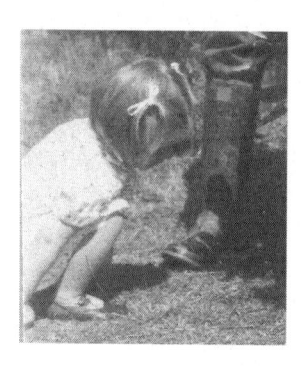

My mother and I loved the little old cottage. My first memories are of Reeves with its low-beamed rooms and of my sandpit in our sunny garden. My mother kept chickens and I had a bantam of my own until it was killed by the larger birds in a rush for food. We had a fierce white nanny-goat called Minnie to supplement the milk ration and Minnie had a kid called Violet. Each morning my mother milked Minnie and then we took her and her kid out and pegged them on the common land in front of the cottage. My mother was, and still is, practical, ingenious and hardworking. We ate well in spite of the war-time rationing. It must have looked idyllic from the outside and only people who knew her well realized how sad and depressed my mother was for much of the time.

Many people came to stay with us for a short time during those early years. My mother's sister, her baby son and springer spaniel dog came and lived there too for a while when her husband was away during the war and Jack Swaab visited from time to time when he had leave in England. My Godmother Ruth, my father's first cousin, stayed for one whole summer after the war was over. These people were all kind to me. My mother has always told me that she was too depressed to jog me on her knee or make googling sounds as people do with babies yet, although I was a quiet and somewhat isolated child, I think I was not unhappy.

Very early memories are hard to pin down but sometimes something happens which makes me wonder about those first connections which are made in babies' brains. One such occasion was when, around midday at the beginning of April 2002, I was walking along the pavement of a London street when, a second later, I found myself crouching in a shop doorway, my heart hammering. I thought maybe a car had crashed on the road beside me and that I had jumped instinctively to avoid it but when I looked out I was surprised to see that the traffic was still travelling along the road in its usual way. Then I wondered, since my heart was beating so hard, if I had had a heart attack; but I felt my arms and legs and they seemed to be alright. So I stood up in the doorway feeling shaky and rather embarrassed. I began to wonder if anyone had seen me and to hope that my mad descent into crouching position had gone undetected. Then, as my mind cleared, I heard the unmistakable drone of wartime bomber planes. I looked up and saw three of them flying in formation across the sky above my head. I was still shaking when I arrived at my friend's house and explained what had happened.

"It is the Queen Mother's funeral today," she explained. "It must be a fly-past."

How strange that the noise of wartime bombers should have affected me like that. I can't have been more than two and a half years old when the war ended so that reaction must relate to a very early connection. So I asked my mother if she remembered the bombers coming over Reeves.

"Oh yes," she replied immediately, "it was the noise of them which was so frightening. They used to come over in waves, German, English and American bombers. The German bombers were on their way to bomb London. I suppose they came from Holland, Belgium or Northern France. When I heard them coming I used to go into your room and stand by your cot. I felt that if we were going to go we should both go together. I didn't take you out of your cot," she added hastily, "I just stood at the end of it. You could hear the German planes coming for ages before they actually came overhead. It was very frightening."

She told me how one of the very first doodle-bombs came over the cottage making an awful noise ("yang-yang-yang-yang-yang," she said). She hadn't heard about this new type of bomb so she thought it was one of our own aircraft which was damaged and trying to get home. Her heart was in her mouth when she heard the engine cut out; then she knew it was coming down and thought with horror of the poor pilot inside. It landed with a terrible crash. Only later that she learned about doodle-bugs and discovered that this is what it was.

"I have always hated loud noises and bangs," she said again, and I know that to be so. Then she explained that Layer-de-la-Haye was very close to several allied wartime aerodromes, such as Birch, and Filton and the American airfield at Boxted.

"All the planes from those aerodromes flew over," she said, "and some of the troop-carrying planes towed strings of gliders out behind them, each one full of troops." Some German planes dropped strips of silvered paper to confuse the anti-aircraft lights set up to spot them and she picked some up from our garden. Bombs had often dropped on Harwich and Chatham when she was there before I was born, and when she went to London by train to Liverpool Street Station she saw the East End of London flattened and smoking. In London she saw the rockets coming in, she said and reflected on how upset she had been at the news that Coventry Cathedral had been bombed. Again she mentioned how, when the noise cut out, she knew the bomb was going to come down close by.

"It was the noise," she repeated, "which was so frightening".

My mother's fear of this noise must have embedded itself in my early consciousness. Everyone lived in fear in those days and I have discovered that my mother used to sleep with a German Luger pistol under her pillow at night in case the Germans landed and broke in to her cottage. Jack Swaab had picked it up on the battlefield in North Africa and given it to her. It seems strange to me but maybe it was commonplace, in wartime, for civilians in England to have guns.

When the war was over life didn't get any easier for my mother. The most difficult time of all for her, she says, was not at the time when my father was killed. Then the war was still on and, although it was terrible beyond words, there was a feeling that everybody was in the same boat together and that the same thing could happen to anyone at any time. The worst time for her was after the war ended. Then everyone else was celebrating the victory. Then she felt that everybody else's husband would come home, but not hers. While the whole country was rejoicing she felt even more isolated with her grief.

When the men came home they didn't want to talk about the war any more and especially they did not want to think about their comrades who had not returned. The women handed over their jobs to the returning heroes and concentrated full-time on home-making. Their husbands threw themselves into civilian work. The birth-rate rocketed; it was called 'the bulge'.

My mother was still in her twenties. The merry life she had led before the war was over. Coming from a service family she found that many of the young men she had known as a child were dead. Now the wives of people whose husbands had returned were suspicious of a pretty young widow like my mother in case she might have designs on their husbands. The men were worried that the young single mothers might be clinging, needy, and no fun.

My mother is not an analytical person and she seldom reads books. She is someone who gains nourishment from fitting in with the conventional pattern, a woman of her time. After the war ended my mother's friends were keen to re-assert the endlessly enticing family stereotype where the father goes out to work and the mother stays at home to look after the children. How much my mother would have loved to have done that too if only her husband had come home. The thought of how things might have been was so painful she dared not let it into her mind. The future was something she couldn't consider. To force herself forward each day she worked out what she would do hour-by-hour in advance and that way she willed herself to keep going.

Yet my mother is a disciplined and dutiful person. She didn't take her sorrows out on me and I was quite happy. I was already an independent child and somewhat dreamy. I was growing up in my own little world. I didn't have friends of my own age yet the adults around me were kind. I was the first grandchild on both my mother's and my father's side. All my grandparents were wonderful people and they gave their time generously. This is a gift which many children miss these days. For me, with a missing father, this was a life-saver.

When I was four-and-a-half my mother and I went to stay with my Round-Turner grandparents in Folkestone. Grandfather was a keen gardener. Together he and I looked at plant catalogues and chose plants to suit their position and soil. When the plants arrived we first dug the hole. We were careful not to hurt the worms whose holes are so good for the soil. I poured in the water, he spread the roots, we filled the hole together, then I jumped round the edge of the plant to make sure there were no air gaps round the roots. Things always grow for me now, just as they did then. It is annoying for people who try so much harder than me, read all the books and water their plants religiously, and then they die. Sometimes I sat with Gran in the kitchen and watched Grandfather out in the garden. It was my job to hammer on the window to get him in for lunch and although he was very deaf (it was the gunfire in WWI which did it, he said) he always heard me knocking.

Grandfather Round-Turner taught me to read, write and draw. He was a natural teacher. After the war we were short of paper so he split open used envelopes with his paper knife and I wrote and drew on the insides. Nothing was wasted. The odd thing is that Grandfather's lessons have seeped into my lifestyle and I still love to read, write, draw and tend the garden. While we were there my mother cut her finger right through the tendon so we stayed much longer than we intended and I started school in Folkestone. Then Gran and Grandfather sold Reeves and we never went back.

Now the war was ended we could move around more easily. Reeves was sold, the goats and chickens were gone, and we began to live a rather peripatetic life. Often my mother and I travelled around staying with friends and relations. I was happy enough but I can see that it wasn't a good time for her. Wherever we were staying I had to be quiet and good; we both had to be helpful around the house and above all else, we must never, never outstay our welcome.

Each time we were about to move on my mother washed our clothes carefully by hand and when they were dry she ironed them and smoothed them out flat on her bed. Then she rolled up white tissue paper and placed a sausage of it on to the centre of each shirt or dress and folded it over the roll to prevent it creasing and laid another flat piece of tissue below the roll so cloth never rubbed against cloth. It would have been wasteful to throw away tissue paper so she used it over and over until it yellowed with age and the creases became fine and dense. Finally all our clothes were carefully placed in my father's huge leather 'Revelation' suitcase. On the top of it his initials, J.O.C. for James Owen Cochrane, were the same as mine. The case was always filled way above the height of its sides and usually I had to stand, or even jump on it to make it shut. I am afraid to say I never liked the immaculate way my mother did her packing. For me it always meant we were moving on again.

11. Hawkhurst

Quite soon I began to stay on my own with my Cochrane grandparents at Hawkhurst. I called my Cochrane grandfather Gaffer and my grandmother Ga, after less than complete success with an early attempt at more complicated names. I will begin to refer to them by those names in this book as that is always how I think of them still. Gaffer and Ga tried to make up for the love my father couldn't give me and, although they were strict and never spoiled me, they made me feel terribly special. I was their only grandchild. They always had time to talk to me and to answer my questions and it was here at Hawkhurst that my Cochrane grandfather told me how my father was killed by a land-mine in the North African desert.

I remember so clearly still how I wandered alone through the big quiet rooms of their house and around their beautiful garden absorbing the atmosphere of peace and freedom. The big drawing room with Ga's desk below the south facing window and a sofa below the west-facing window was where she sat to darn my knitted lamb until he was all darns and there was no knitting left on him.

Outside an open lawn sloped down to a stream and, beyond it, a large nettle patch where, before the war, there had been a boating lake. Now the water had drained away. Nettles had grown up in the pit left by the drained lake and in the crater beyond where a doodlebug had landed. The doodlebugs were unmanned flying bombs. Their timing mechanisms were set to cut out so they would land on London. It was the policy to try to shoot them down in the sparsely populated countryside of Kent and Essex to prevent them reaching their destination. When this low-flying doodlebug came over their house in Hawkhurst both Gaffer and Ga heard the noise, they told me, and they both thought it must be an aeroplane about to crash into their house or garden. Gaffer ran to the front door and Ga to the back. When the bomb crashed to the ground the blast blew Ga flat onto her back and it blew out all the windows on that side of the house. Gaffer explained to me how the blast from the bomb went in through the back door, along the passageway and out through the front door where he was standing. It was lucky that he and Ga had gone to opposite doors, he explained, so that the blast ran straight through. I still have an image in my mind that if that blast had been unable to escape the whole house would have inflated like a balloon.

The crater of the doodle bomb lay beyond the nettle-patch where the boating lake drained away during the war after the little dam which had contained it was taken away. By the time I knew it a huge rhododendron had grown right over the little boat house which once housed a flat-bottomed boat made by one of my mother's brothers. Before the war groups of young people laughed and joked as they rowed out onto the lake but now the lake had gone and the great bush had closed in around the boat house leaving no trace of it from the outside. After the war only I pushed my way through the lush dark green leaf layer of the bush to the dappled-dark interior. There I found the boat house was squashed into a rhomboid by the inner branches of the plant but I could still see the remains of the boat inside it. I set up house alone in there with two holed saucepans and a mug with no handle and played for hours at the edge of the stream. I had no toys but I was never bored. I made my own imaginary games. I pulled the columbine from the rhododendron bushes which was helpful as Gaffer and Ga didn't like it there. Besides I could wind it into a crown and around my arms and legs. Then I was a flower-fairy.

Beyond the lawn an oak tree stood on the top of a small hill. In my memory the tree was massive, but looking at pictures now I realise the tree wasn't so big, it was just that I was small. I often played under the spread of its branches, amongst its roots which you can see at the top left hand corner of this picture.

I borrowed Ga's pins to make acorn men, women, children and dogs and sometimes I took them down the hill a little way to the place where a spring bubbled out of the ground.

Gaffer had put stones between the rushes which surrounded the spring. There I played out the lives of my acorn families and allowed them to hide from each other in the tall rushes. I pulled out the thin green strands which grew on the surface of the icy spring water so Ga would have space to dip in her jug to fetch fresh spring-water for our lunch, but the little water boatmen rowed themselves out into the spaces I made, leaving 'V' shaped tracks.

The water flowed down from the spring between bog irises and gushed into one end of the swimming pool my father had built before the war with his army friend Buster Compton. Buster was my Godfather I was told but I never met him. I believe that after the war he was upset by the thought of the friends he had lost and perhaps I might have reminded him of that. The swimming pool was small but deep, over six foot deep along its entire length so my father, who was taller even than Gaffer, was quite out of his depth at any point in it. Gaffer told me how, quite soon after it was built, the swimming pool had iced over. The weather was so cold and the ice so thick, my father was afraid the concrete sides of the pool might crack. Finally he broke a hole in the ice and dived down through it to release the plugged outlet from the base of the pool and let out the water through a pipe into the stream below. The family were all waiting by the pool with towels to dry him as soon as he got out. My dead father was always the hero in these stories.

Gaffer felt it was important for me to learn to swim at the earliest possible moment so, when I was four, he bought a book explaining the modern approach to swimming. I practised the strokes lying on my tummy on the tapestry-covered stool in front of the sitting room fireplace. Then together we sang his favourite hymn, the one all naval people love, whose final verse goes;

O Holy Spirit, who didst brood
Upon the waters dark and rude,
And bid their angry tumult cease,
And give, for wild confusion, peace:

O hear us when we cry to thee
For those in peril on the sea.

Gaffer told me how he had seen so many poor sailors drowning at sea. Some could have swum to safety if only they had known how to do it. As the convoys crossed the Atlantic they were attacked by German U-boats. They had to stick together and keep going , and they were under orders not to stop to pick up sailors from the sea. The image of his colleagues crying and waving from the sea must have been a terrible thing for Gaffer to carry in his mind, and quite fresh at that time (I realize now) only a couple of years after the end of the war. One time his own ship went down, he told me, but he survived. Because he could swim, I thought.

Outside by the pool, Gaffer hitched me up to his special swimming device. He strapped a canvas belt around my waist and attached it by a length of fine rope to a pole, as if I were a fish on a line. Then he walked up the side of the swimming pool supporting me in the water as I swam. I never knew when he slackened the rope and I swam on my own until he said, "You just swam the whole length." So then I could swim whenever I liked pushing out on my own into the deep dark water of the pool my father had built. I tried to swim as quietly as a water boatman. I followed their little forked tracks. The fresh running spring-water was always cold but I didn't mind. It smelt miraculous. Only the cows watched me as I swam. They leaned their heads over the field gate beyond the pool and watched intently.

When the weather was too cold or wet to swim there was a little room inside the house called Puggy where I could go and read. There I could open the glass doors of the dark brown book case and take out my father's stamp albums, his book of Epic Heroes, the Edward Lear nonsense rhymes or, my favourites, the Pip and Squeak Annuals from the 1920s. Scorcher was the boy who had all the adventures in the Pip and Squeak Annuals. These were the stories my father read when he was a boy. One story told how, one school holiday, his uncle in India took him out on a tiger hunt. The uncle shot a tiger in the leg. The illustration shows the enraged beast leaping out from above the two human forms, open-mouthed, teeth bared, his outstretched claws reaching for the uncle. At the very last second our hero Scorcher lifts his tiny shotgun and kills the tiger with a single shot to the heart.

Ga got up late in the mornings, often staying in bed long after she had eaten the breakfast that Gaffer and I brought up for her. Although I had been up and dressed for hours I took off some of my clothes and snuggled back into bed with Ga. It is something I could never do with my mother, or even with my Round-Turner Gran, although I am not sure how they made that clear to me. Gaffer slept in the dressing room next door and I was allowed to go in to his bed too in the mornings when I woke up, but not in the middle of the night. If I did this, Ga explained, he found it hard to go back to sleep again with me there and it made him tired the following day.

In Ga's big double bed in the mornings she told me stories of her own childhood, growing up in a rich and privileged family at the end of the nineteenth century at a house called 'The Brackens' near Ascot. She told me how her uncle had been rolling the croquet lawn when her elder brother, who was later killed in the battle of the Somme, fell under the roller. Her uncle bent down and simply picked up the hugely heavy roller and lifted it off the child, who was completely unhurt. When, afterwards, he tried to lift it again, he couldn't shift it even a half an inch off the ground it was so heavy. Ga was still trying to puzzle out where he found that extra strength. I wondered if my father had puzzled over it too, and known about the extra strength a person can find if a real emergency arises.

Ga told me about the many suitors she had had when she was the most eligible young lady in Ascot and how, when my grandfather asked her to marry him she replied, "Oh! I never thought of marrying you!" as he was a couple of years her junior. She realized immediately what a wonderful man he was and very soon accepted his offer. And she told me about my father. I especially liked the story about how, when he was 21, my father killed his tiger out in the jungle in India, and this is how it went:

Some villagers were bothered by a tiger who came out of the jungle and took their goats and buffaloes so they asked my father if he would come and kill it for them. My father walked deep into the jungle taking with him some goats and a few chickens. One morning in the first light of dawn one of the villagers woke him to say that a tiger had killed his buffalo and dragged it away into the jungle. My father dressed quickly and followed the villager to the field where his buffalo had been. There was blood on the ground and the grass was flattened where the tiger had dragged the dead animal back into the jungle. For an hour my father followed the drag marks until he came to a clearing and there he saw the dead buffalo lying ahead of him. The tiger hid when it heard him coming, but my father could hear growls from behind a nearby bush.

So my father made a tree house to hide in. Two Indian villagers came to help and together they found some wood and made ropes from the long dangling creepers which hung from the trees. First they made a raft with the wood and then they used the creepers to hang it from the branches of a large tree. They pulled some other branches across in front of it to hide it from the tiger. On the other side of the clearing the tiger was still growling. The villagers didn't like the sound of it so they finished the tree house quickly and hurried off home.

My father climbed up into the hide with his gun to wait for the tiger to come out. The hide was rather small and he had to curl up his long legs very tightly to fit into it. Coming from a naval family he knew about knots and now he found that his Indian helpers had not made reef knots but grannies in the creeper ropes. As they slipped the floor of the hide was moving down and down towards the ground, and if it got too low the tiger would be able to reach him.

All that morning and into the afternoon my father measured the position of the floor against the tree. At first the hide was only slipping six inches every hour but at three in the afternoon a wind blew up, the branches on the front of the hide sprang back so the tiger could see him and it shook the branches of the tree and the floor slipped faster. Now it was moving down a foot every hour and still the tiger lay behind its bush and growled.

Late that afternoon a big tigress came out and walked

quietly towards the kill. As she stood over it she looked up at my father with a long cool stare which lasted a full half minute before lowering her head to eat. He aimed the gun at her shoulder but hit her right fore-leg and, like in the story of Scorcher, she leapt towards him. He swung the gun and fired at her a second time, straight from the hip as his uncles had taught him. The tigress fell and lay still.

My father had some stones in his pocket and he threw them down onto the dead tigress from his tree. There was no movement so he climbed down from his lookout and walked out into the clearing, but as he looked down at her he heard a noise that made the hairs on the back of his neck stand on end. Another deep growl was coming from behind the bush. It was her mate and he was angry.

My father walked backwards slowly and quietly keeping his gun aimed at the bush until he was right outside the clearing, then he turned round and hurried back to the village. There he told the villagers the news and this time four coolies came back with him to help him carry the body of the tigress. It was evening now, the light was fading and the sky turned pink. By the time they got back to the clearing it was nearly dark. My father kept his gun trained on the bush as the coolies lifted the body of the dead tigress onto a stretcher made of branches and leaves, and the four of them began to carry her back to the camp. They left the dead buffalo for the other tiger and luckily he didn't come out to eat it until after they had gone.

Back at the camp they lit a hurricane lamp outside a large wooden hut and they worked together all night to separate the skin of the tigress from her flesh and bones which they threw to the vultures. When the body was opened up my father found that his second bullet had gone straight through the tigress's heart so she had died instantly. The villagers were pleased. My father salted the skin and sent it off to be cured, mounted on canvas, and fringed with black scalloped braid.

When I was a child the skin of the tigress hung down into the oval stair well at Gaffer and Ga's house in Hawkhurst.

Her head rested on a little shelf so it looked out above the banisters at about the same level as mine and as I passed her on my way up to bed in my father's bedroom I kissed her goodnight on her Bakelite nose, I felt her sharp eye teeth and coarse tongue with my finger and I stroked her ears with the pale spots. Her long tail stretched up behind her and hung over the banisters onto the stair landing above. I never touched the whiskers in case they came out. The whiskers of a tiger only bring good luck if they are kept in place.

As a child I accepted the tiger and its story without questioning my father's morality in killing such a magnificent beast. Things which were acceptable in my father's day are unacceptable now that Bengal tigers are an endangered species. Ga told me that my father killed the tiger to keep the Indian villagers safe and I accepted that. Now the skin hangs in my own stairwell and, though I love her myself, I apologise to visitors who see her for the first time, and I wonder if they are shocked that I have her skin hanging there.

After the story Ga got dressed and I loved her daily ritual. She was discreet yet she never sent me away or made me feel excluded while she dressed. I never remember any nakedness, yet I was fascinated by the piece of pink flannel, about eight inches square with a piquet edge, which she placed on the centre of her tummy below her corset to prevent its hooks and eyes from chafing. In 1908 when she and Gaffer were married, she said, she had a wasp-waist measuring only 19" and he could reach right around it with his hands, the thumbs touching in the front and the middle fingers behind. On top of her petticoat she wore a pretty blouse with a small flower print, usually in navy blue, with a collar of handmade lace she fixed with a fox brooch with ruby eyes. Ga was an artistic person and her navy blue pleated skirt always matched the blouse perfectly. Next she lit the flame of the small paraffin lamp she used to heat her scissor-shaped hair tongs. I loved the sour burning smell they made as she squeezed three neat little parallel crinkles into the top of her thinning grey hair. Then she sat at her dressing table with its angled mirrors by the west facing window. Her ornate silver-backed brushes were decorated with the initials of her maiden name, M.L.G. for Mary Lucy George entwined with those of my grandfather E.O.C. for Edward Owen Cochrane. After brushing her hair with one of the brushes Ga dipped her swansdown puff into a silver-lidded cut glass jar and dabbed pink powder onto her nose.

"Why don't you leave it shiny?" I asked.

"Oh, just fashion!" she replied.

From this description you might think that Ga was just a spoiled society lady from an age long past, and good riddance; but there was more to Ga than that. As well as being very loving she could also be quite strong and practical when the situation demanded it. Another of her stories I particularly enjoyed was the one about the shipwreck.

In August 1923 Ga set off for France with Jock aged 10 and Suzanne aged 4 with her adoring nanny Miss Swann. They set out from Southampton on the Southern Railway Company's steamer the Princess Ena on an overnight crossing to St. Malo. The ship sailed at 9.00 p.m. and passed Portsmouth, the Isle of Wight and the Channel Islands on a flat calm sea. But while they slept soundly in their two cabins a dense fog came down. At 4.00 a.m. they were woken up by a great bang and a crunch at the bow end. Then the engines swung into reverse with a roar and the boat reversed a little way until a crash from the stern signalled that they were stuck on the rocks both fore and aft. A sailor walked down all the passageways inside the ship ringing a hand-bell and shouting, "All on deck! All on deck!" They all scrambled into their clothes and came up on deck to find the sailors lowering lifeboats over the side into the foggy night.

Ga looked overboard into the darkness. She was not at all keen to get into a lifeboat. She felt the ship might re-float as the tide came up and that they would do better to stay on board. But the sailors insisted. "Women and children first!" they shouted. With six other passengers and two young men from the crew my grandmother and the two children were lowered into a lifeboat. They were told to stay in sight of the ship, which was sending out S.O.S. signals. It was only as a swift current carried the lifeboat out into the fog that Ga realised that the two young sailors who had been put into the lifeboat with them couldn't row to save themselves – or to save any of the rest of them either! Luckily she had many years of rowing experience on the Scottish lochs and Jock was good with the oars as well, so Ga and ten-year-old Jock took over the rowing. But the Princess Ena was already out of sight, and the lifeboat holed and shipping water. Eventually they spotted a buoy. Ga insisted they tied up to it and organised shifts for bailing out the water, and in due course another lifeboat full of people came and tied up next to them. When the tide rose the Princess Ena floated off the rocks and managed to limp in to St. Malo as Ga had predicted, but the two lifeboats tied up to the buoy were reported missing. Little Suzanne asked what they would be having for breakfast, but breakfast time went by and lunchtime too. Luckily there was a small supply of water on board and the sea was calm. The bailing rota continued.

Back in England Gaffer, who was working at the Admiralty, came out into Trafalgar Square and saw the headlines on the evening paper "Princess Ena on the Rocks! Two lifeboats missing!" All afternoon he tried desperately to get in touch with the harbour-master at St. Malo to find the names of the passengers who were missing, but luckily he didn't succeed or his worst fears would have been confirmed. Finally, at around 5 p.m., the two lifeboats were picked up by a cargo boat, which had been out searching for them, and brought safely in to harbour. For Jock and Suzanne the shipwreck had been a thrilling adventure.

12. My Mother's New Start

In the autumn of 1947, when I started school, my mother and I were moving around quite a bit. That time, following the end of the war, was particularly difficult for my mother. My first school was in Folkestone where we had come to stay with my Round-Turner grandparents. But after a year Grandfather, who smoked over forty Players Navy Cut cigarettes a day, fell ill with lung cancer.

My mother and I moved on and stayed with my mother's brother's wife and daughter, while he was away in China with the navy. I loved my second school in Chichester. There we were taught reading, writing, French, the high-jump and how to make matchboxes into tiny chests-of-drawers with a silk tassel to open each drawer. The wonderful and perceptive teacher found me hardworking and clever but rather absent-minded, so she worked hard to help me integrate with the other children there. When my uncle came home my mother and I moved into a residential hotel nearby so I could carry on at the same school. I once brought back some yellow and black stripy caterpillars to our hotel room from a school walk on the South Downs but there, naturally, they escaped and crawled along the corridors into other people's rooms! The only other children at the Bedford Hotel were the cook's children and I was sad that I was never allowed to play with them out in the back yard, but all the same I was used to being on my own so it didn't bother me much.

My mother didn't go out to work and I suspect she didn't feel it would be proper to do that. So she was lonely and money was tight. She felt very unsettled at that time.

One thing was a constant. Wherever we were staying in November we never missed going to church on Remembrance Sunday. When I was six I had just learned to ride a bicycle so we cycled together to the service at Chichester Cathedral. My mother rode ahead along the road and I followed. The occasional car was parked on the edge of the road and we had to bicycle round them. My mother set off boldly into the centre of the road from quite a distance back but I left it until it could no longer be avoided. At the very last minute I held my breath and swerved out around each car, then I had to cycle on fast to catch up with my mother.

During the service I noticed the tears were flowing down her face. I had never seen my mother cry before; she is not someone who shows her emotions if she can possibly help it. After the service we bicycled home fiercely to blow away our tears. For me her tears seemed natural. I knew how sad she was that my father wasn't with us. I understood it and I didn't mind her crying. But I think she felt it wasn't right for a child to see that her mother was vulnerable. I had no preconceptions but she had a strong idea about how mothers should be and crying didn't fit into it. I think it was after that Remembrance Day service that something crystallised in her mind. She decided she must put the past behind her and get on with her life.

My mother and I were living at the Bedford Hotel in Chichester when I first met my stepfather-to-be. He arrived in the dark brown front hall, where the hotel manager kept her pot plants with the red and white striped leaves. She kept those plants in the dining room too. I liked them but my mother didn't. My mother and I came down from our room and the man who had come to see her took us out into the road where he had parked his car. It was a dark green Riley with leather seats, heavy doors and a dashboard of polished walnut. On the front of the bonnet above the radiator was a silver model of a man skiing. My mother sat beside him in the front of the car and I sat in the back. The smell of the leather and the smooth engine of the car made me feel sick.

He drove us to another brown hotel where we sat and ate cream scones with our tea. I didn't think much about the visit at the time. I went along with my mother on all her visits as there was no-one to leave me with at the hotel. My stepfather-to-be talked with my mother and I watched. I don't know if he noticed me. He was someone who thought that children should be seen but not heard and I was used to fitting in with that. In an ideal world I suppose he would have preferred neither to see nor to hear any children as he was not a child-lover. But unfortunately for him he had four children and his wife had died of cancer. A mutual friend had suggested that my mother might make a good wife for him and this was an initial interview for that job, I suppose. Of course I had no idea what was going on. My mother said nothing to me afterwards either about the meeting or our tea together, but there was nothing odd in that. I thought no more about it and my life went on as usual.

After that I went to stay with my Cochrane grandparents, Gaffer and Ga, for a few months and went to a new school near their house in Hawkhurst. The local children felt I was an outsider. They told the teachers when I wandered off into the woods on my own, as I often did. This was my third school and I had just turned seven. One day my mother came to visit me at Gaffer and Ga's house at Hawkhurst. She slept in the spare bedroom down the corridor but I was sleeping in my father's bedroom as usual. One evening she came into my room and sat down on the low, pale blue cotton covered chair between the fireplace and my father's big bed. She said she had something important to tell me so I went and sat on her knee.

"You are going to have a new daddy," she said.

I hadn't been thinking about what my mother might be up to while I was staying at Hawkhurst and dealing with my new school there. I had no idea what having a 'new daddy' might mean. I was quite happy with my life as it was but my mother was searching for something more conventional. She wanted to 'normalise' the situation, to have some position and status in society and she assumed that the new arrangements would be good for me too. This assumption cut the ground from under any objections I might have had and turned out to be quite a stumbling block.

"This is for your sake as well as for mine," she said.

I don't remember the wedding but I know I was there as it was recorded in a photograph and I am in it. I am smartly dressed for the occasion in my Cochrane kilt fixed with a curly silver pin and a Scottish sporran and beret.

After the wedding my mother and I moved into

my new step-father's house back in Colchester. It was a large red brick late-Victorian house in the next road to the nursing home where I was born and there, for the first time, I met my new 'brothers and sisters'. Two were older than me and two, the twins, were younger. Now, it appeared, I was third in a family with five children.

They all had dark hair. My mother's hair was black like theirs. But mine was fair like my father's. They all had brown or hazel eyes. But mine were blue, like my father's. My mother changed her surname. It used to be Cochrane like mine, now she changed it to be the same as theirs. I kept my real father's name. I liked it then and I like it still. But it made me feel different and a little left out. Now all the children called my mother 'Mummy'. I called my new stepfather 'Daddy', and I included him in my bedtime prayers.

God bless Mummy and Daddy, Gaffer and Ga, Grandfather and Gran, and all my aunts and uncles, and make Jane a good girl. Amen.

I tried very hard to be a good girl. I tried, like my mother, to fit in and look forward. The new life didn't feel all that good to me but that was something I wasn't allowed to say. After my mother re-married our previous lives became an out of bounds subject. My mother and stepfather made a new family, a fresh start. History began again. Yet for me the previous history hadn't been going all that long. I was only seven.

I think my mother always kept some photographs of my father in the new big bedroom she shared with my step-father, but we children were not allowed into that room so it was hard to be sure. There were never any photographs of the mother the other children once had. She had died of cancer, and now her name was never mentioned again. Her memory was obliterated. It was at this time that Jack

Swaab's name too became unmentionable. I took my memories underground and kept them to myself. I was known as Dreamy Jane.

My mother was busy. She threw all her energy into her new life as a mother of five. 'It's cheaper by the dozen' went the words of a popular song at the time. My mother has a beautiful singing voice and she sang with feeling as she stood in the steamy bathroom stuffing our clothes into her new open-topped, dual-action washing machine. Then she heaved them out with a long wooden stick and folded the buttons carefully inwards to save them as she wound the clothes through the mangle on the top of the machine. But corduroy should never be mangled, we understood. Corduroy trousers had to be thrown from the first floor bathroom window and David and I stood below as the steaming drenching objects landed on top of us. Then we carried them off to peg them onto the wash-line. My mother organised everything. She fed us, she bathed us, she patched our wounds, she drove us around in her new little car. She was so busy her feet hardly touched the ground.

We didn't see much of my new stepfather. Right from the start he kept himself separate. When he came home from work he sat in a large conservatory looking out onto the garden and put on his record player. My mother brought him in his tea on a tray with tea in a tea-pot and milk in a jug. We children were told that my step-father had had a hard day at work and we were not allowed in. My mother tried to protect him from us and us from him. She tried especially to keep me away from him in case I annoyed him in any way. Only my stepfather was allowed to show anger and he was never criticised. We children soon learned to keep our feelings to ourselves.

13. One Big Happy Family

So how did we children feel about the new family? What did my mother anticipate we would feel and how different was it in reality? These are modern questions which my mother and step-father certainly never asked. I think they both assumed, in as far as they thought about it at all, that in forming a new family we would all fall into our newly designated roles and all our past problems would be solved, and no doubt this was the conventional thinking of the time. They assumed that their own lives, so rudely pushed awry by the deaths of their spouses, would now return to the normal pattern with a mother, a father and a cluster of happy children. My mother couldn't afford the luxury of considering her own actual feelings in the aftermath of WWll, let alone ours.

Yet the new family group came as a shock not just to me but to all of us children and we each of us had to adjust and adapt as best we could. We all tried very hard to fit in with the new system. We tried hard to forget the past. We never spoke about our feelings. Organisation was the thing and my mother organised everything a good mother should organise. Even though food was scarce she fed us well. She kept our clothes clean and mended. She even organised ballet and riding lessons for me and took us on trips to the sea-side. But I was still dreamy and forgetful and sometimes I began to be a little bit naughty as well.

A new step-uncle had a beach hut at Frinton, an ultra-respectable seaside resort on the east coast not far from Colchester. In this photograph we children are sitting along a rather unsafe diving board positioned so that people could dive from it into the sea when the tide was high.

Vicki, the oldest child, is not present in this photograph. She is six years older than me, thirteen at the time of her father's re-marriage, and she seemed like a grown-up to me. In the photograph I am sitting at the end of the diving board looking out to sea. As usual I am not really concentrating on the photograph being taken, but David, sitting next to me, has noticed and he is making a face. The twins, Mike and Tessa, were only three and a half at the time of the re-marriage and their mother had died a mere six months earlier. They are sitting together at the left. Like so many others their mother fell pregnant as soon as her husband came home from the war. When the pregnancy set off cancer she went to stay with her parents on the south coast in Hampshire, and they helped look after her and the two new babies. Vicki and David, the oldest two children, were left in Colchester with their father and David was sent off to boarding school.

At the time of the re-marriage Mike and Tessa had lived all their lives with their maternal grandparents. Now they were brought back to their 'Daddy' and new 'Mummy'.

At night Mike had terrible nightmares. He terribly missed his grandparents and his real mother. My mother got him out of bed and took him from room to room around the new house in Colchester to show him that everything was normal. This system might have worked in her own family where everything was actually more normal, but this family was a new construct. I don't think Mike was reassured by his nightly visits to Vicki, David and me as he hadn't known any of us before. Tessa had trouble with eating and going to the loo. She sat on a special commode half the morning and my mother spent hours flying little morsels of food into her mouth as aeroplanes.

David was nine and the nearest to me in age. He had been sent off to boarding school aged six when his mother had moved away from home and now she was dead. I was small for my age and skinny but David, although eighteen months my senior, was smaller and skinnier than me. His arms and legs were covered in weeping eczema so my mother bound them with zinc poultices under huge bandages. It was the remedy of the day. She said that David was a hard child to love, but she did her best.

David and I were grouped together like a second pair of twins. In the garden of the house in Colchester we lay flat on our faces on the lawn and tried to make sense of our new situation. To our left were two long rectangular flower beds whose bare-branched rose bushes produced big summer blooms in unlikely colours, pale mauves and bright oranges. Around them the earth lay bare to the edge of the beds where pansies were park-planted at one foot centres, so different from the overflowing jumble of subtle-coloured sweet-smelling flowers which I loved in both my grandparents' gardens. Beyond the tortured roses was my step-father's shed where he kept battery hens in tiny wire cages and the garage for his very smart car. On that lawn

David quizzed me about the latest things he had learned at school;

"What makes the waves in the sea?" he asked.
"The wind," I guessed.
"No, the moon; silly."

Having asserted his superiority, he gave his verdict on the new family. It struck to the very core of the anxiety I was feeling:

"Your mother isn't your mother any more," he said. "She's our mother now."

He is right, I thought. I had already lost my father. That had really happened and now, just as easily, I seemed to have lost my mother as well. Looking back as an adult I can see how much this needy little boy wanted to claim my mother for his own and how I, so near to him in age, was the chief rival and obstacle to this claim. But as a child I was devastated. I tried to tell my mother about my worries. I thought it was time for us to move on, but when I suggested it she got really cross.

Once in those early days when my new Daddy came up into my tiny bedroom to say goodnight I pulled down his head to give him a hug and a kiss on the cheek as I always did with Gaffer. He froze and recoiled jerking his head back from my grasp. I never tried it again. He was not a man with whom a child could be intimate. Especially not someone else's child. Maybe even the child of a rival man in my mother's affections.

My mother was too busy to think about my problems. All of us children had problems and she was worked off her feet. She hired several nannies to help deal with us all. Gloria was kind and played the piano and we liked her, but my mother wasn't so keen. Freida was strict and had us all ready and standing in a row when my mother wanted to take us out. My mother liked Freida but we weren't so keen.

At night in my dreams I fell and fell. Down and down I went past windows and more windows until I landed - whoooomph - sometimes I was on the floor but more often still in bed, slippery with sweat with my heart pounding. On other nights huge animals chased me, getting closer and closer until I could feel their fiery breath burning the back of my neck as I ran and ran. But I was tied in one spot. Sometimes my legs were tangled in barbed wire. Sometimes they simply failed to take me forward. They just went round and round in circles.

I tried to tell my mother how scared I was of losing her but that seemed to make things worse. My mother had made her decision and she didn't want feedback from me.

"The new family is for your benefit as well for mine," she repeated, "and the sooner you knuckle down and accept it the better."

'Knuckling down' and 'bracing up' were my stepfather's key concepts but I never found them helpful. Kindness and understanding were unfortunately in short supply. This was a bad time for me and this, I know now, is a problem I had in common with many war orphans. The need of the mothers to get on with their lives lay in direct conflict with that of their children, who needed, for their own sense of roots and identity, to hang on to their own past and to the knowledge of their lost parent. In my case this was exacerbated by the fact that my step-father was not child-friendly and by the simultaneous arrival of so many step-siblings: all of them traumatised, all of them needy.

My mother made huge efforts to be fair so she used to say she couldn't remember which children were her own and which were 'steps'. This must have been good for the others but I didn't find it reassuring. 'Daddy' had no such lapses of memory. He was a businessman and money was important to him. It was up to him to give us children our pocket money each Saturday. He gave the others 6d each but he told me I didn't need any as when I grew up I would inherit some money which had belonged to my own father. I was proud and I wasn't going to show him that this upset me. I didn't want his ruddy money anyway, I decided. Ruddy was a new word I had learned from him.

After my mother married his father, David began to come with me when I went to visit my Cochrane grandparents in Hawkhurst. Gaffer and Ga were kind to David. I think they were pleased that I had some company and, like me, they became fond of him.

I expect Gaffer treated us both in much the same way as he had treated my father as a child. Gaffer's ideas about bringing up children were old-fashioned and tough, but David and I were happy with that. He was strict, but also loving, practical, honest and straight-forward. He always had time to discuss the principles behind his suggestions and we knew he had our best interests at heart.

Before the marriage I used to go alone into the morning room, where Gaffer had his plain dark mahogany desk. It was a man's room. It used to be called the smoking room before Gaffer gave up smoking, I was told. The carpet, furniture, and even the walls were brown and it was silent but for the rhythmic tick of a big old clock on the mantelpiece. When the sun came out bright swords of light penetrated deep into its darkness. I watched the little white flecks of dust floating in the sunbeams and made them into patterns in my mind.

After the marriage, when David and I went together to Hawkhurst, we found an old pianola standing in a dark corner of that room and, next to it, a bookshelf filled with dusty boxes of punched paper pianola rolls. All we had to do was open the sliding door on the front of the upright pianola, slip in a roll and pedal away while the notes moved up and down as if struck by invisible fingers. Together we pumped out the music of Dresden at the end of the 19th Century where Ga had been sent for a year as a young woman to have lessons from the best pianists of the time. David, who was wonderfully musical, soon learned to put his fingers over the notes as they played. The music soared and swooped as his fingers hovered above the keyboard. After a short time he could play the pieces by himself without the rolls in the style of the old masters. Our favourites were the classic old romantic pieces, Chopin's nocturnes, polonaises and mazurkas and Beethoven's Moonlight Sonata. Then we played the old dance music, waltzes, quick-steps and gavottes, finishing up with a lively gallop or polka. On 13th February 1945, on the second anniversary of my father's death, Dresden had been destroyed by allied bombers. Over 30,000 civilians died in the firestorm which followed. Six years later as the city lay in ruins, David and I still pedalled out the music from the old days when Dresden was the musical centre of the world.

Sometimes David and I took bamboo canes and helped Gaffer destroy the nettles which had grown up in the pit where the boating lake once lay. We slashed until our hands were blistered. Later Gaffer bought a flame-thrower to kill the nettles and we pushed through the head-high undergrowth behind him as he blasted them. It was a typically Cochrane idea and we loved it. We dug a huge den under a tree in the woods and burrowed down into it. We swam in the pool with Willy the plastic whale specially brought for us from America. David did a splashy dog-paddle; he wasn't nearly as fast or neat a swimmer as me, but I did my best not to show him up.

On rainy days we stayed inside and carried on with my father's stamp collection. It was a reminder of the days of the empire. The main collection was built up in the '20s and '30s with complete sets of George V stamps from 'Uganda, Tanganika and Nyasaland', Rhodesia, Northern Rhodesia and from India. Then there were oddments from when Gaffer was stationed in the West Indies, stamps from

Barbados, St.Helena, St Kitts and Nevis. The names on the tiny fragments of paper caught our imagination and made us wonder about far places. David kept up this collection even as an adult. Maybe it was these little stamps which inspired us both to travel when we grew up.

We both read my father's old books: the Book of Epic Heroes, the Pip and Squeak Annuals from the 1920s and Edward Lear's Nonsense Songs and Stories and Nonsense Botany and Nonsense Alphabets. Together we chanted;

> *Who, or why, or which, or what*
> *is the Akond of Swat?*
> *Someone or nobody knows I wot*
> *Who, or which, or why, or what*
> *Is the Akond of Swat?*

Oddly enough Gaffer knew who he was. The Akond, he said, was the great-grandfather of the Wali of Swat who lived up beyond Peshawar where my father was stationed on the north-west frontier of India in the years leading up to WWII. The Akond started life as a shepherd boy but he rose to lead his mountain people against the mighty British Army. When he beat us back his people called him the Messenger from God and began to worship him for his power. The English had the good sense to leave him alone to rule his mountain principality, Gaffer said.

Unsurprisingly David was a fairly disturbed child. When he first came to Hawkhurst he used to pull the wings off the bluebottles which buzzed around the inside of the west facing window in the sitting room. Gaffer saw what he was doing but said nothing about the wingless, and sometimes legless, bluebottles. But when David brought in the corpse of a snake Gaffer decided he should take this up with the boy, and he did it in his own particular way.

"Why did you kill it?" he asked. "That is a grass snake, you know, it doesn't do you any harm."

Obviously Gaffer was not against killing per se. He had fought in two world wars. Sometimes he leaned out of his bedroom window in the morning and shot a rabbit on the lawn for our lunch. Then he skinned and gutted it and made us a fine rabbit stew. As a gunner he accepted death as the inevitable corollary of life. But he felt that if you kill you should understand what you are doing and why. He taught us to take responsibility for what we did , and to see it through to the end.

So when David killed the mole he was sure that Gaffer would approve because of the damage they did to his lawn. We were playing by the spring when the mole popped out right beside us and David caught it in his hand. When it bit him he threw it, picked it up and threw it again until he got it near the house where he finally killed it with a stone.

Gaffer made sure that we saw the job through. He took us, and the dead mole, to the place where the water from the swimming pool flowed out into the stream and there he split its little body down the front and gave us a biology lesson. As he removed each internal organ he held it up and made us look at it carefully as he explained its function. "These are the intestines," he said holding up a long string of little sausages, "just like we have inside us to digest our food." Only when he was sure we had had a good look at each part he threw it out into the stream.

The insides of a mole are particularly stinky. Because they eat worms, we decided. Then Gaffer scraped the moleskin clean and helped us to peg it out flat on a board. Every day for ten days we rubbed salt into the skin until it was cured, although it was rather stiff. I made two tiny purses and sewed around their edges in blanket stitch. Inside each purse I put two of the mole's horny little black feet. After that David thought very carefully before he killed anything again.

When my mother and I moved to Colchester I had started at my fourth school, a girls' day school. It was not far from our house so I went there by bicycle. But once a teacher saw me riding on a mile beyond the school lost in my own thoughts. Unfortunately she told my mother and I was teased for weeks at home about that. I quite liked the school in Colchester but after only 18 months I was moved on again to a convent boarding school in Berkshire. I was nine and it was my fifth school in four years. But I was getting tough. I was scornful of the girls there who were homesick. School was no worse than home, I reckoned.

This was the situation when my mother got pregnant with a sixth child. My stepfather was not pleased. He had hoped that his family would be complete after his first two children were born and somehow now he had accumulated five. After the baby was born my mother had six children to care for and we all needed her. She was as strict with herself as she was with us children. I don't know if she was happy. She had made her own bed, she reasoned, and now she must lie on it. But emotionally she had left me behind somewhere in a past life of hers. I still treasured my memories of the days before her marriage to my stepfather and held them tightly in my mind. I pieced together my own opinions and I kept my thoughts to myself.

Yet I was also desperate to fit in with the new family. I tried really hard to be as like my new brothers and sisters as I could, but somehow it never seemed to work. And my feelings towards my mother became somewhat ambivalent. She had recently bought new green clothes which matched her surprisingly bright green eyes and bright red lipstick by Helena Rubinstein. I decided that red and green were hard, harsh colours. I didn't like them any more and I left red and green out of my paintings at school. My eyes were blue like my father's, and that is the colour I liked best.

I began to question the conventional sentimental beliefs of the 1950s and draw my own conclusions:

'Home is where the heart is' went the saying, but it didn't seem like that to me.

'Love and marriage go together like a horse and carriage' was the chorus of a popular song. I didn't believe that either.

'Money makes you happy.' Well I certainly didn't believe that. My mother and I had so much more money now than we ever had before but somehow nothing seemed right to me.

A perceptive solicitor friend of my parents was one of the few people who seemed to listen to what I said.

"You're a little cynic," he commented as he tousled my hair through his fingers, "but I love your big blue eyes."

14. Teenager

The life decisions had been made and now my mother and stepfather carried them out. They accepted traditional roles. My stepfather earned the money and my mother looked after us children. I soon got on well enough with my step brothers and sisters, but however hard I tried to fit in I always felt very different to the other children. During school terms we were away from home and in the holidays I was often sent away as well. My mother fixed for me to visit all kinds of relations from both sides of the family as well as with Gaffer and Ga, and this made it difficult for me to find my feet.

David and I loved the time we spent with Gaffer and Ga; but all too soon it came to an end. When I was eleven Ga took me on one side. She told me that she had gained weight, then lost it, and the doctor had told her she had cancer. Grandfather Round-Tuner had died of cancer in the year that my mother remarried and I knew that, in those days and with that diagnosis, that was the only possible outcome. The following holidays my mother asked me if I would like to go on my own to visit Gaffer and Ga even though she was ill and I said, "Oh, yes please, please do let me."

But my mother never fixed it up and I stayed in Colchester all that summer. When I got back to my boarding school I counted each day as it passed and with each one I was glad to think that Ga was still alive and grateful for the extra time. One morning a letter came from my mother and I looked at it on the green baize letter board, then I watched the other girls take theirs but I didn't pick mine out. Some seventh sense had told me the news it would contain. I was playing for time, wishing it wasn't there. Finally, when it was the only letter left, I took it down and went alone with it up to my bedroom to cry.

I was never taken to Ga's funeral and my mother never spoke to me about her death. A silence lay between us about the things which really mattered. I expect it wasn't conventional in those days for children to go to funerals but nobody even spoke to me about Ga's dying and I felt terribly sad and alone. She had been the most important person in the world to me. Missing her funeral made me feel the adults thought she wasn't important to me or that I didn't matter to her. If I had been there I could have seen how much she was loved by everyone, not just me. It would have helped me come to terms with her death. Many, many years later it was my Round-Turner Gran who told me about Ga's last days and how, the day before she died, she had asked Gran, who was staying at the house, to go and pick the raspberries for her from the garden.

After Ga's death Gaffer was lonely in the big house in Hawkhurst. He sold the house, put the furniture in store and went travelling around the world with his daughter Suzanne working with an idealistic movement called Moral Re-armament (or the MRA). He became a kind of missionary, I suppose. My Cochrane grandparents, along with seventeen-year-old Suzanne, joined the group in 1935 soon after my father left for India. They were aware of the build-up of tension in Europe and the re-militarization of post WWI Germany. Gaffer had fought through the first world war and he hoped the MRA might prevent the second.

The MRA was formed as the 'Oxford Group' in the early 1930s by Frank Buchman, an American Lutheran minister of Swiss descent. The name was changed to MRA in 1938, when preparations for WWll were already under way. Buchman was convinced that moral compromise destroyed human character and relationships and that moral clarity was a prerequisite for building a just society. He believed that war could be avoided only by changing the hearts and minds of people and sought to use personal change to build a 'hate-free, fear-free, greed-free world'. The movement had some good ideas although it also had anti-Communist and anti-gay obsessions for which, in the 1960s, it became discredited. It still exists, though much diminished, and in 2001 its name changed again to 'Initiatives of Change'.

Gaffer's absence with the MRA was a painful loss for me. I missed both him and Ga terribly. He was away throughout my adolescence. Wherever Gaffer went he wrote to me and I stuck his postcards from all around the world into a plain-paper book which had once belonged to my father. It had 'Artillery Rough Notes' stamped on the cover. Another world had vanished. It too went away as if it had never existed.

My mother chose my convent boarding school in Berkshire because it turned out 'nice girls'. Educating girls was not a priority in conventional society in the 1950s and in any case my stepfather felt that educating women was a waste of time. The nuns at my convent school were kind but their interest was religion; the message of the Bible was the one they aimed to pass on. Many of the girls came from 'society' families. On leaving school they 'came out', were presented to the queen and spent one whole summer going to balls so as to meet up with and marry an aristocratic or at least rich husband.

I rebelled against all these things and yet, at the same time, I was used to adapting to each new situation and I thought of many ways of coping with the school environment. To make money one of my schemes was to collect up old fountain pens as they were discarded broken throughout the year and before the exams I combined the parts to make working pens and sold them. I didn't know my father had sold rabbit and fish at school when faced with the same predicament. To manage the endless services in chapel (on Good Friday we had to fast all day and spend a total of five hours in chapel wearing an extraordinary starched linen 'chapel cap') I got myself a job as a 'sacristan'. My job meant that I didn't have to endure the services but could stand outside the door of the chapel ready to rush in and pull out the floppy bodies of my fellow schoolgirls when they fainted, as they did every Sunday. Then I sat them on a bench and pushed their heads down between their legs to get the blood back into their brains. If ever I had to spend a whole service inside chapel I always fainted too. Lack of food, standing upright, and a good sprinkling of incense never failed to bring it on.

I was desperate to escape into the world outside so a friend and I thought up a suitably religious excuse to persuade the nuns to let us out into the little town which was otherwise totally out of bounds. We hit on the idea of bell-ringing in the local church and the nuns swallowed it. For many years we practised campanology twice a week with a few local folk.

On his occasional visits to England Gaffer always came to take me out from school and then he would report back on how he found me. By chance a scrap of one of these letters, written to my mother, has survived. It says:

Yes, self contained. Her Pa all over, 'I can take anything they care to hand out and be damned to them!'.

I was battling on through my teenage years and Gaffer had picked up exactly how I was feeling. Dear Gaffer lived to be ninety and to the end he was always sensitive to the person I was inside my skin, always realistic, always loving. He did his best to stand in for the father I never knew but I think he never knew the full value of what he did for me.

I was quite precocious but David found all academic work a struggle. I always had to cut back in order to fit in both at home and at school. My mother believed in 'taking us down a peg or two' and making sure we didn't get 'too big for our boots'. But there was no need for that as we were neither uppity, boisterous nor assertive. It has taken me a lifetime to abandon the need to melt into the background as soon as the attention turns to me.

But many of my mother's ideas on childrearing worked well. Sometimes she was gutsy and interactive. As a teenager David used to spend hours in the bath. Once when the twins and I had finished supper he still hadn't appeared and my mother told him if he didn't come down in five minutes the twins and I would eat his supper. Five minutes passed and we ate his supper. When David finally appeared he complained that nobody could have a bath in five minutes. My mother said, "Oh yes they can," and vanished. We all watched the clock and three and a half minutes later she re-appeared in her dressing gown smelling of soap;

"I wasn't in the WRNS for nothing!" she declared.

It was a good demonstration. David went to bed without his supper and we all thought it was fair and took care to be on time for meals in future.

In my teens I sped ahead of David and this caused some difficulties. I grew pretty but David was still very small for his age. I became excruciatingly shy and self-conscious. I learned stock responses to any question and kept my real thoughts to myself. We spoke in a jolly format-type of speech, which I learned easily.

After I left boarding school I wanted to live at home and study art. I just wanted some ordinary everyday life and a bit of company. I got myself a place at the Colchester School of Art and began to go there every day on my bicycle. I loved the easy friendly atmosphere of the place and the way we all shared a studio. I learned quickly and soon excelled, but my parents disapproved. After a few weeks I was taken away and sent to Paris.

"If only I had been able to learn a language when I was your age," my mother said. "You are so lucky".

There was no point in arguing with my mother so I adapted and coped in my customary way. Someone in the house stole what little money I had but the French family didn't sympathise or investigate. I was lonely and when I was approached by the local MRA group who wanted me to join I was tempted, but I couldn't entirely or unquestioningly accept their principles. I considered the four absolutes carefully; absolute honesty, absolute purity, absolute unselfishness and absolute love. I found absolute honesty especially appealing and it has landed me in quite a bit of trouble over the years! One evening I thought I would join, but as soon as I woke up the following morning I knew I couldn't trap my mind into that rigid framework. I thought there was something in it, especially when it came to interpersonal relations on a small scale, but I have never found it easy to belong to groups and I found I couldn't make the required leap of faith. But at the time I was sorry as I had always wanted to be an insider.

At home too I really wanted to fit in but somehow I always ended up different. The girls in my step-family were supposed to be nurses or secretaries. Two of my sisters became secretaries, the other a nurse, while one of my brothers married a secretary, the other a nurse. But I didn't feel good with the prospect. I had to act fast. I wasn't allowed to go to art school so I plumped for architecture. I thought it would use my artistic talents and also enable me to do something socially useful. Luckily, in those days, I was able to get a full grant from Essex County Council and my stepfather was not required to make any contribution.

My mother stayed with my stepfather until his death in 1990. In all those years, like the good wife she was, she played second-fiddle to his tune. She adapted to her new role and brought out the side of her character which fitted in with him. When it came to the crunch it was he who had the final word. Difficult family decisions about any of us children were referred back to the man of the house: to a man who had no sympathy for me.

My mother used to say, "I couldn't possibly have married two men more different." And then she remarked how like my father I was, and how different from her. She didn't communicate and nor did I. I went my own way.

15. Adult Life

It is difficult for me, being so close to it, to separate the consequences of my father's death from things in my life which might in any case have happened. Of course if my father had lived my life would have been easier, happier and more conventional. I would, no doubt, have had real brothers and sisters and a loving father. How wonderful that would have been! To be honest this is the first time I have ever allowed myself the indiscipline, the lack of control, to think this unimaginably wonderful thought! But I know I must shut it out. We all have to live with the destiny we are given.

The loss of a parent at an early age is always a disadvantage. Such a child will always be vulnerable. Yet many children are affected in this way for reasons other than war. The outcome for the child or children depends very largely on the quality of the care and love the remaining family are able to give the child.

There is a book on war orphans written by Susan Johnson Hadler and Ann Bennett Mix in America, who both lost their fathers in WW2. Ann Mix began to search to find out about her father and she was later joined in her quest by Susan Hadler, a trained psychologist. Together they collected stories of many war orphans which they published in 1998 in a book titled 'Lost in the Victory'. These stories are striking in their similarities both to each other and to my own. Reading these stories, which I found only after I had made my own record, has made me feel much better, and much less alone. By publishing this book the authors hoped to bring home to others the incredible sacrifice that was made, not only by those who fought in WW2 but by the families of those who died. They aimed to help others to understand the cost of war in terms of human suffering, a cost which does not end with the armistice or with the burial of the dead. I found I was not alone in my search for a father lost in WW2. In story after story the people interviewed by Hadler and Mix started in middle age to search desperately for evidence of their fathers' lives, for stories which had been buried for decades. Like me some have written books about their search. Others have written about the part their fathers played in the war. Over and again, like me, they have found it necessary to dig up these old tragedies in order to come to terms with them, and to make sense of their own lives.

My mother was deeply traumatised by my father's death, which occurred so soon after my birth. On the other hand my mother is a strong woman and many war widows managed less well. Of the examples found by Hadler and Mix many mothers became alcoholics, some had nervous breakdowns and others committed suicide. Many mothers had less family support than mine. I was lucky to be the first grandchild on both sides of the family and to have magnificent grandparents. I believe that my father's death made all my grandparents feel even more loving and protective than they might otherwise have been. It was unfortunate that cancer took two of my grandparents at a comparatively early age.

The conventional assumptions of the time, in case after case recorded by Hadler and Mix, were those of my own mother and stepfather. The re-marriage of the mother (and in some cases the adoption by a step-parent) is supposed magically to put right the loss the child has sustained. In practice this happens only rarely. Research by Martin Daly and Margo Wilson, for instance, shows that a child is a hundred times more likely to be abused or killed by a stepfather than by a generic father. This research, which is in its infancy, shows the tip of an iceberg. The conventional assumption that the mother's remarriage will improve the situation of the bereaved child is particularly difficult for the child when this does not, in practice, prove to be the case. In my case my own perception at this time was totally at odds with that of my mother. For me her remarriage and its consequences were by far the most difficult and confusing part of my childhood. My unhappiness and my sense of isolation were greatly increased by the fact that even my perceptive grandparents now assumed I was better off in my new family than I had been before. My mother put my occasional protests down to simple contrariness and, in spite of my best efforts to fit in, I was soon regarded as the black sheep of the family.

As an adult I suffered a certain identity loss resulting from the fact that I never felt at home in my stepfamily. "Where do you come from?" is a normal question that, even now, I find impossible to answer. My friends would be amazed if they knew how that question can still (though mercifully people seldom ask me now) tap in to my deepest anxieties. (Where on earth, indeed, do I come from? And who am I anyway?) If my father had lived I would never have had these problems. I think my father knew exactly where he came from, who he was, and why, as did his father and grandfather before him. My mother is the same. But for me it is different. What could I say in answer to that question? Obviously I didn't want to embark on a conversation either about my dead father or about my step-family in Essex or my convent boarding-school in Berkshire.

I had always wanted to go to art school but this was not allowed in my step-family where the girls were expected to become nurses or secretaries. The architecture course was hard for me as it was a long course and my schooling had been rudimentary. But it widened my horizons and encouraged my creativity, it taught me skills which enabled me to earn my keep and to bring up my little family though, for a single parent, the job of an architect is far from ideal. For years I worked for a housing association where I was able to provide houses for others who, like me, had experienced homelessness. Later I completed another postgraduate course and worked in conservation. I have also taught at art schools, been a potter and a painter. Luckily I have plenty of energy and I like to use my talents.

I spent the ten years of my thirties as a single parent and my strategy in that role was different to that of my mother. Unlike her I always worked for a living. She considered I was depriving my children by doing this and, even though I didn't think I had much option, I worried about that too. Yet when it came to the crunch (and several times it did) I put my children first, way in front of any notion of career. And I wouldn't give any man priority over my children. I sometimes feel a little wistful, I admit, about the career opportunities I have missed, but in the end I believe my priorities were right. I considered I was a hopeless mother but amazingly neither Thomas nor Amy complain. "It was fine, Mum, stop worrying," they say.

To my surprise and delight my children have grown up straight and beautiful. Between them they have produced five marvellous grandchildren. They all live nearby and I feel truly blessed. At last I have achieved the wonderful close and loving family I never had as a child.

For David things didn't work out so well. After David and I left home when I was sixteen, and he a little older, we hardly met each other except at the annual Christmas family gathering. I got on with my own life, only rarely visiting David. But one weekend when I was in my fifties I went down to the pretty little house he shared with his loving wife outside Cambridge. Now his two sons had grown up and left home we chatted about old times. I told him about the research I was doing and how much I was finding out about my father, and I asked him how much he remembered about his own mother who had died when he was eight years old. I was shocked by his reply.

"You know I don't remember anything. I don't remember her at all," he replied.

How is it possible that a little boy of eight years old could completely forget his own mother? I had heard she was a lovely person, I said, and suggested that he did some research to find out more. Nobody talked to David about his real mother after his father and my mother married when he was nine and I was seven, and it seems that David pushed the past right out of his mind. It may have been difficult for our remaining parents to wipe the slate clean but at least it was only a part of their adult lives which had to be forgotten. For each of us children it was our entire life up till that point. I silently guarded the memories of my life before my mother's re-marriage and pieced them together in my mind. But David's early memories from before the marriage of my mother to his father were more painful than mine. Nobody will ever know if it might have helped him had he tried to make sense of it all.

Soon after he left home David began to drink quite heavily and by his fifties it was more than his body could stand. His funeral was a sober affair as we all loved David but, true to family tradition, nobody cried. Then, uncharacteristically and as at the Alamein ceremony, I found the tears welling up, spilling over, and running down my face.

"I am so sorry, so sorry," I found myself saying, "so sorry I couldn't save you too."

1934-1942
MY FATHER'S STORY II

16. India

The Cochranes had been fighting men for generations and I realised as I read his letters that my father was a chip off the old block. With my father the child led seamlessly to the man. When my Cochrane grandparents said goodbye to their son at Southampton Dock in February 1935 he was fully prepared for the life he would lead. He was confident, resourceful, responsible and practical. He had a wonderful sense of humour. As soon as his parents left the soldiers began to arrive and he discovered by default that he had been left to organise their embarkation:

About 1/2 hour before the first batch was due to arrive I started looking for Major Prain, who as you remember was in charge of the draft. I first went to the Orderly Room and discovered that he had not been on board at all yet. Then I went ashore and looked round there not knowing in the slightest what I had to do. Finally the first batch arrived and thank heaven they had some of their own officers with them and between us we got them on board. During the respite before the arrival of the next batch I again had a look for Major Prain without any success. The second batch arrived and they got on board. After they were safely stowed I had a last despairing search for the major and this time found him, he must have turned up while the second batch was arriving. However he seemed to know even less than I did which was remarkably little. The third and final batch arrived and got on board under their own steam while we were thinking about things and to cap everything he mentioned something about parading the whole bag of tricks and seeing what we had got hold of that afternoon and then disappeared off the face of the earth. I didn't find him again for two days.

His Majesties Troopship Lancashire set out for India in mid-February 1935. It sailed past Cape St Vincent, Gibraltar, the snowy mountains of the Sierra Nevada and up the length of the Mediterranean to Port Said. There my father had his first experience of Egypt:

We hung over the rail and watched the various robbers in their boats. The police seem to run a complete racket here. There were two fat specimens in a boat hanging on the outskirts of the crowd. From time to time they seize one of the rogues and confiscate half his stock and retire to their place on the fringe. The robber seized wails loudly expressing extreme grief, but after a decent interval he rows up to the police boat and begins a parley and after a while a little palm oil is passed and all the confiscated stuff returns to its original owner.

The huge ship passed down the Suez Canal towards Port Sudan and troops from the ship and Egyptians from the banks yelled to each other in their own languages. Then the ship set out over the open sea to Karachi. As soon as he arrived my father engaged a bearer. He described him as a villainous looking man wearing a sort of black dressing gown over a khaki shirt worn outside his trousers and a black turban wound round a brass centre piece. The bearer helped my father take a draft of soldiers from Karachi up to Peshawar on the North West Frontier of India.

The British had been trying to control the mountains along the North West Frontier since the 1850s when they first feared the Russians might march down into

British India through the Hindu Kush. Alexander the Great took this route in 327 B.C. and he left a settlement of Greeks whose descendants still live there. Later it formed part of the Silk Road as it passed from China along the strip of Afganistan which still separates Pakistan from Russia. These mountain areas seem as remote as could be yet their passes form links between ancient civilisations. That area is still as wild as ever and, with our extraordinary inability to learn from history, we are back there again. In my father's day they called it the cockpit of Asia.

Here my father fought in local wars against the tribesmen of the Lashkar, Malakand, Kalangai, Dargai and Kot. They were the last colonial wars of the British Empire. His photographs, sent home and lovingly stuck into his parents' album, show sniper's posts, dust devils, shaggy Berbian camels and street scenes in Peshawar. There tribesmen and animals jostle for space between the coppersmith's stalls; a turbaned salesmen carries sweetmeats in baskets each suspended by six long strings from each end of a shoulder pole and a legless shoemaker plies his trade with a bees-nest of shoes attached to the tree trunk behind him.

My father's first experience of war was all good fun for a tough young Englishman:

On Friday I took the pay out to our section which is attending the local war. They were looking disgustingly fit and well fed spending their time between basking in the sun and bathing in a nicely sheltered valley in the hills high enough to be pleasantly cool. At Kot (pronounced coat) where our guns are friend tribesman with his rifle spent an all night session sniping and wounded one mule in the neck. Armed with 6 inch Howitzers we went one better and actually killed two cows, and that is the whole casualty list as far as the artillery is concerned, though the P.B.I. may have done more damage but they have the advantage of being much closer. Our cows were 9,000 yards away and we cannot go any further till the sappers build a road for us.

The British were making roads into the north. They wanted to be able to march the army up quickly if the need arose, to secure the frontier. The tribesmen resisted. In the album, next to a photograph of Gaffer planting irises round the edge of the new swimming pool in Hawkhurst, is a report from the local Indian newspaper of my father's first action.

The object of the operations on April 12 was to drive the hostile lashkars still east of the Swat river over to the west bank, and thus out of the protected area. By 9 a.m. the Guides Infantry had secured a position north and north-east of Loi Agra whence to support the advance of the column towards Ghund. Covered by the 4th Mountain Battery and the Guides machine guns, the 3rd Battalion and the 2nd Punjab Regiment then made good the ridge from north of Inzargai village to the west of Ghund Kandao. A section each of the 66th Field Battery and the 15th Medium Battery* (*here my father had written 'me'), which had previously occupied positions near Kalangai in the Swat valley above its junction with Panjkora, proved of great assistance in breaking hostile concentrations and driving them towards the Swat.

My father described the process more clearly (when you add in a few punctuation marks as I have done)

So far the scheme has been that the tribesmen gather themselves together and shoot up a party of coolies road making. Road making ceases. All the available army marches out and sits in the hills all around these fellows with guns trained on them and planes flying overhead looking as if they are loaded with bombs. The tribesmen promise to be good boys and the army marches home and returns its ammunition to store. The road making party perks up its head and puts out a tentative feeler and promptly gets shot up again. Then the show starts at the beginning again.

Gaffer questioned him about some details, but he replied:

I do not know anything about Rendell who got the jingler out of our local war as I as not with the main body but miles in front lobbing eggs onto the enemy's back areas, especially the crossings over the Swat river to prevent reinforcements coming up.

He would be out in front, I realise now. He was out in the lands of the Wali of Swat and that is how Gaffer knew about the Wali's ancestor the Akond of Edward Lear's 'nonsense rhyme' which David and I had so enjoyed. My father looked around carefully and commented in his own cryptic way:

Friendly tribesmen look exactly the same as the enemy and we are convinced that they are the chaps who snipe the camp at night.

But he respected a brave soldier whichever side he was on:

I take my tin hat off to the Mohmands, a lot of the fellows doing the attacking had no rifles of any sort but attacked with the sword or knives and prized the Guides out of their holes like winkles on a pin.

In the letters and photographs I found the tiger story again and the story of my father's horse. "He was the colour of carrots with a temper to match," I had been told as a child. My father began to search for a horse as soon as he arrived in India in April 1935. At first he couldn't find one he wanted for the price he could afford to pay:

Remounts having nothing worth taking and outside horses being either aged or toothless or very much patched in the legs or else costing 1000 chips or more which is nearly double what I can pay.

After three weeks he found a horse already named 'Safety'.

The name was a joke as the horse was far from safe. Jock wrote home to tell his parents:

I mounted in under 5 minutes today - a local record. I get a syce to hold his head and he stands on his hind legs and you just have to stand around till he decides to come down. There is one spot on the side of the beast which is far enough from the front end to be out of range of his teeth and far enough from the back end to be out of range of his heels to have a shot at mounting.

Once mounted you sit tight and wait till he has worked off his first little show of enthusiasm. The first day I had him out he was hardly ever on four feet at once. He was scared stiff of a small pole jump but once he understood he had to go over he showed that he could jump. Now after 8 days he jumps a three foot pole with zest, clearing it by miles. He learns quicker than any horse I have ever known. He has been Indian owned and somebody has teased him in the stable. The prize joke is that somebody has named him 'Safety'.

My father got up at 5.00 am. each morning to exercise his horse before the sun got too hot and after two weeks Safety could clear a 5' fence with ease. One week later he got out of hand when he was riding bareback and jumped out of the school over a six foot wall:

He took the top off the wall and we all landed in a heap the other side, but not bad considering that I was trying to pull him up at the time and generally being as much hindrance as possible.

After 3 months Safety was so well-behaved that Jock almost forgot that others might not find him so easy. An airforce officer was having trouble with a horse which was scared of water, so my father gave him Safety and brought the other back to the schooling ring:

I started schooling the cause of all the trouble in the riding school when the next thing I saw was my animal coming home under its own steam at a steady canter. I left him to it knowing that he would go to the stables. The next to turn up was a rather brow-beaten ride complete with a foot-slogger. I learnt that after taking his rider for a little chase round the countryside my beast returned to the ride, his jockey being still in the saddle clinging on like grim death but not making any attempt to control him, and quietly tipped him off. He then with very nice judgement bit him and broke loose, he then dealt with every attempt to catch him on the principle that attack is the best method of defence.

Having suitably subdued the ride he left them and trundled home having bitten each member of the ride separately and severally and kicked three of them, when I got back to the lines he had the impertinence to walk up to me and ask for a lump of sugar which made me laugh so much that he got it.

Both Ga and my mother told me about Safety when I was a child. I wonder if I was trying to follow my father when, as a teenager, I used to ride a naughty, clever retired racehorse called George. He belonged to a neighbour who owned apple farms. George used to bolt under the apple trees so that once my shirt was torn from my back by their branches. He was scared of cars too and, when once I was commissioned to take him in to Colchester to the blacksmith, he walked up the length of the High Street on his hind legs on the wrong side of the road. I can still see in my mind the look of horror on the face of one driver protected only by his windscreen from George's flailing front legs.

In November 1936 Gaffer and Ga set sail for India on the P.& O. India, China and Australia mail and passenger ship, the S.S.Narkunda to visit my father in Peshawar. They took with them Suzanne and Ga's niece Ruth who later became my Godmother. Ruth was my father's first cousin. I used to go to stay with her as a child and we always got on well. She is an independent person, intelligent, straight-talking and feisty. You can always get a straight opinion out of Ruth. At the time of the trip to India Ruth had been working as a salesperson for high-class sausages. Her family weren't happy about that so Ga offered to take her to India where she thought Ruth might find a suitable husband amongst my father's army colleagues.

After the six week journey out by ship they drove up from Bombay in an open car, Ruth told me, with their trunk on the luggage rack behind. Ga wore a fox skin scarf round her neck and the people in the street thought it was a live animal. In the 20 months since Jock left home his parents and Suzanne had joined the Oxford Group, which later became the MRA, and Gaffer, Ga and Suzanne arrived in Peshawar with all the enthusiasm of new converts. As soon as Gaffer arrived in Peshawar he began organizing meetings to spread the word. Jock was taken aback by this change in his parents and sister. The situation was acutely embarrassing for the young soldier. He observed that the men in his regiment who joined the Oxford Group were those who were had difficulty fitting in socially and he and Ruth made common cause. It drove a bit of a wedge between my father and his parents which was only resolved a few years later by his marriage to my mother. She had loved his parents since she was a child and she was not going to let this be affected by their new absolutist principles.

One photograph taken at this time shows the party drinking tea together outside the rifle factory on the Khyber Pass. A formal English tea has been laid out in this outlandish spot. The family are sitting around a small wooden table covered with a heavy crocheted cloth. The two Indian men standing behind them in the photograph are headless as if, to the photographer, they didn't exist. Two large teapots with traditional English flowered design and china cups and saucers stand on top of it. Ruth and Suzanne are wearing thick camelhair coats and felt hats. The men have taken off their hats and placed them on a day-bed standing nearby. They are wearing tweed jackets and ties, and their leather shoes are nicely polished. They are all behaving exactly as they would in England at that time. On the left, also half out of the picture, my father reaches for his cup of tea. On the right of the table, leaning back confidently in his chair, is the man that Ruth would marry. My father didn't think much of her choice. "I'll give that marriage a year at the most," he said.

Ruth's prospective husband was an Intelligence Officer in my father's regiment. He was a great ladies man. He already had a girlfriend in Peshawar, as my father knew. After the marriage Ruth lived with him out in the Himalayas beyond Peshawar where he spoke several local languages. Ruth was the only European woman out in those wild parts. My father would drop in to see them when he passed that way. He used to sit on their terrace in the evening light to smoke his pipe and enjoy the glass of whisky they provided.

"And how did you find him?" I asked Ruth, so many years later.

"Well he was a quiet man," she replied, "but it wasn't that he had nothing to say. He thought hard about the world. But he was always happy to sit quietly and look at the view. He was a peaceful person to be with."

My father may have been keeping his thoughts to himself, and he was right about the marriage. After two years of married life Ruth and her husband were brought back to England and separated by WW2. She worked for MI 5 in Wormwood Scrubbs (in the building which is now a prison) in London and her husband was a founding member of the S.O.E. in Scotland. Their marriage didn't survive the separation and Ruth never had children.

In the Indian section of the album I found another photograph I have known all my life. It has always been in my mother's large photograph frame on the chest-of-drawers in her bedroom. In spite of my jealous stepfather she always kept it there. It is a small snapshot.

A tall man stands on his own in a wide outdoor space, maybe a parade ground. He is wearing riding uniform: high tightly-fitting boots, jodhpurs and a leather-belted jacket. In his hand he is holding a wide-brimmed riding hat and a crop. He has stopped to think, maybe he has forgotten something, and his hand is raised to his bent head.

"That gesture was so typical of him," my mother said.

When he first bought Safety, my father's idea was to train him up and sell him for a profit. The following summer he was given a good offer for the horse. He agreed to sell him but, almost immediately, he began to have second thoughts, and he thought of an excuse to cancel the deal. He kept Safety until 1939 when war in Europe was imminent. When he was recalled from India my father was afraid to leave the horse with someone who might ill-treat him again. The story goes that, rather than risk his future ill treatment, he shot the animal himself. I don't know anyone who would think like that these days and it seems rather shocking to me, yet I am told that in Egypt at the end of WWI the cavalry shot their horses before they returned to England, rather than leave them with the Egyptians.

If my father had not been killed he might still be alive today. All these years as the world has changed we would have been able to discuss our impressions and exchange our views. When he was alive he could never have imagined the world that we live in now. Even when I was a child the remnants from my father's world seemed old fashioned and now, although we can none of us get him out of our minds, the details of his life are stuck in a time warp, the warp of those who die before their time.

My father's relationship with animals was close but unsentimental. As a child he trapped fish and rabbits and shot grouse on the Scottish moors. Later in India he spent most of his army leave hunting game. To him it was a game. He shot snipe and duck on the lands of the Wali of Swat. He went pig-sticking on horseback in Uttar Pradesh. He went up into the mountain kingdom of the Mehtar of Chitral and thought about larger beasts:

I have heard of a panther so shall probably buy a couple of goats and see if I can collect him then have a look round to see if any bear have come down for the mulberries, but again the real time for those lads is later on when the pomegranates are ripe.

And he shot the tigress. We try to enforce different rules now when it comes to killing tigers. With human soldiers, it seems, the view of many politicians has not changed. Yet for the families of young soldiers there should be a compelling and unarguable reason before they are sent out to war: to kill or to be killed.

17. Phoney War

In the summer of 1939, as the situation in Europe worsened day by day, Jock was brought back from India. For all its efforts at appeasement the British government was gathering in its depleted forces in preparation for war.

On 24th August 1939, six days after his 58th birthday, Gaffer received a telegram: 'YOU ARE APPOINTED AS COMMODORE R.N.R. AND WILL BE REQUIRED TO LEAVE ENGLAND VERY SHORTLY BE READY WITH UNIFORM AND AWAIT PASSAGE INSTRUCTIONS ADMIRALTY.'

Gaffer's uniform fitted perfectly. He hadn't put on an ounce of weight since his sudden retirement from the navy five years earlier. Although he had a good appetite (his favourite meal was steak and kidney pudding followed by 'Spotted Dick', a suet pudding with raisins) he believed he should always finish a meal leaving enough space to eat another, if for politeness sake it was ever necessary. He only ever actually had to do it once, he said. Now he dusted down his uniform and reported for duty. The job he was given, leading food convoys to and fro from America, was one of the most dangerous, responsible and challenging of all. The Atlantic was a cruel rough sea at the best of times and in the early years of the war U-boat attacks on convoys were frequent and often deadly. Gaffer escorted the first food convoy out to America and the last one back, by which time he was sixty-four years old. During that time he escorted more convoys and lost fewer ships and men than any other Convoy Commodore.

Jock's telegram, dated 31st August 1939, is stuck next to Gaffer's in the family album. It reads 'YOU WILL REPORT IMMEDIATELY TO OFFICER COMMANDING 22ND MEDIUM AND HEAVY TRAINING REGIMENT ROYAL ARTILLERY AT SHOEBURYNESS'. My father's new job at the army station at Shoeburyness, on the Essex marshes to the east of Southend, was training new recruits in a rushed programme to build up the army.

Three days later, on 3rd September 1939, Britain and France declared war against Germany. But Hitler had not yet turned his attention to England and for most civilians life went on much as usual during the first six months of the war, so much so that at this stage it was called the 'phoney war'.

My Round-Turner grandfather had been retired from the navy with a rank of Vice-Admiral. He and Gran had bought a large house at Layer-de-la-Haye in Essex, the house where my mother was staying at the time of my birth. Grandfather had immediately set to and made a beautiful garden behind his house, building the retaining walls and steps himself. As soon as war broke out these activities were interrupted when nineteen Barnadoes children from Barking were billeted on them there. The children stayed with their two minders in a large room previously used for parties. Now Grandfather used his garden for games he organised to entertain the Barnadoes children. Some of them were fairly wild. One little girl he nick-named 'the Murderess'. But the Barnadoes children stayed only for six months until they were re-housed somewhere in the country out of the way of the bombs which, as everyone feared, would fall on the suburbs of London.

By Easter 1940 the Barnadoes children had already moved on and as Gaffer had some Easter leave he arranged to go with Ga and Suzanne to stay with my mother's family at Layer-de-la-Haye. They wanted to try to see Jock who was only forty miles from there at Shoeburyness, if they possibly could. Jock was working through his weekends and he wasn't sure he would be able to make it. In the end he managed to negotiate some leave and he drove over on Easter Saturday to join his family. It was to set off something more than he expected.

The children of the two families had long been friends so my mother's brother Dick fixed tickets for himself, Jock, Suzanne and my mother to go to the Saturday night dance that evening at the George Hotel in Colchester. My mother hadn't seen her childhood flame since she was fifteen. Now she was popular among all the young men and had several boyfriends. Bobby, her favourite, was over with the army fighting with the expeditionary force in France. She was apprehensive about meeting up with Jock again and not only because of Bobby. She had heard a rumour that Jock, once her childhood flame, now had a reputation as a 'woman hater'.

As my godmother Ruth had known my father when he was out in India I wondered if she might know how his reputation as a woman hater had come about. At first she said she didn't know. Then, as she went on speaking, I realised she had a pretty shrewd idea. My father never had a girlfriend when she knew him at Peshawar, she said, but he used to go to Kashmir on leave from time to time. He liked to sail up there. In those days there were plenty of parties and social life for the British in Kashmir and Ruth thought he had fallen for a young widow who hadn't treated him well. I looked at the photographs titled 'Jock's leave in Kashmir, May and June 1939'. They show my father fishing on the Desu and the Upper Nowbug rivers, his little white tent pitched below the trees. A slim and relaxed young man is leaning back, barefoot and smiling, as he sails a small boat. There is no sign of a girlfriend, but there must have been someone else who took the photograph and maybe it was her.

Jock drove back to Shoeburyness late on Easter Saturday after the party at the George Hotel in Colchester. He was on duty on Easter Sunday. At breakfast the following morning my mother remarked to her parents that he didn't seem like a woman hater. Nobody expected to see Jock again that weekend, but on Easter Monday he reappeared to join the young of the two families on a trip to see the Suffolk punches at the annual Easter Monday horse show at Woodbridge. My mother had to leave early as she was due back at Harwich where she was working as a coder for the WRNS.

The WRNS was disbanded after WW1 and my mother, aged twenty, was one of the first new young wren ratings to join after it was re-formed in April 1939. She went up to Harwich with two Wren officers from WW1 who were experts in coding and de-coding. My mother was sent to learn their trade. The three women took over an empty house. Streets and streets of houses lay empty in strategic ports such as Harwich, she told me. There was a huge movement of people around the country in the early months of the war when an enemy bombardment was expected any moment. A large marmalade tom cat had been left in this house and the three women took over his care too. It was some time before a new WRNS uniform was issued and my mother bought herself a Girl Guides hat which she wore with a hat band saying HMS Badger over her own navy blue suit. The two older officers still had their uniforms from WW1.

My mother's two elder brothers were already naval officers and her younger sister joined the WRNS as soon as she left school. Grandfather Round-Turner, who had been retired from the navy as a Vice Admiral, immediately signed on as an air-raid warden. They all wanted to do what they could.

On the afternoon of Easter Monday 1940 my mother had to leave the Woodbridge Show early as she was due back in Harwich on duty. Jock drove her to Shotley Pier so she could catch the 8-person ferry over the mouth of the Stour to Harwich Town. As they said good-bye she realised she had left her handbag in his car. He rushed to get it but the ferry left before he could get back to it. Back at the Woodbridge Show he found another Wren who was going back to Harwich who could take my mother's handbag back to her. The very next day, on Tuesday 31st March 1940, he wrote her a letter. It was to be the first of many. His writing was unusually neat, the spelling was perfect and he even put in commas and full stops:

My dear Pegs,

I gave your bag to a girlfriend of Dick's to be taken back to Harwich. Actually I arrived back on the end of the pier just as your boat pushed off, and consequently abandoned the chase. My fault, I should have searched the car before I left. I only hope you have got it safely by this time. Can you get away to town the Wednesday after tomorrow i.e. 4th or 5th April. I might be able to get away after lunch that day. Should have to leave London at about midnight.

He must have paused at this point as the ink had time to collect in his pen and the writing was darker as he started again. He had been trying to hold back his feelings but they got the better of him:

Pegs you little horror you have got under my skin in a most alarming manner. The whole of yesterday's party seemed flat after you had left. Since then I have been on edge wanting quite impossibly to be with you. Write and tell me if you can make town come Wednesday. I simply must see you again.

Yrs, Jock.

He wondered if he might buy a small boat so he could sail from Shoeburyness round to Harwich in the old style, arriving as he once used to with his friend Buster on the dockyard steps at Chatham. The route by sea is quite direct, as I can see on the map, but even in the days of the 'phoney war' I imagine this was a fanciful idea. My mother told me that wooden fake submarines were assembled along that coast to act as decoys to the German surveillance planes which flew over.

After their meeting in London that Wednesday

Jock caught the half past midnight train from Fenchurch Street Station back to Shoeburyness and the following day when he wrote to her again, he ended his second letter:

I love you Pegs and am just waiting till I can see you again.

When on 9th April he wrote to ask her for a list of times when she might be off duty so he could catch her on the telephone, he admitted:

Fortunately or unfortunately for me you occupy a considerable amount of my thoughts these days and I get worried by such horrors as the thought that you may not be able to get away or that some opportunity has been missed. A most reprehensible state of affairs I admit, but one which I am assured is apt to happen.

It was all very sudden. At first my mother didn't take him seriously. But his love shone like a thin ray of light through deepening cloud. As he wrote the German troops were marching into Denmark and Norway. The thunder of guns was moving towards him. Denmark capitulated right away. The consequences of the German advance were to push their way into my parents' lives and change them forever.

In my mother's office opposite Parkestone Quay in Harwich five or six Wrens worked in pairs, day and night on three or four day shifts. One held the heavy coding book, weighted with lead so if it had to be thrown overboard in an emergency it would sink down to the bottom of the sea and not fall into enemy hands, while the other wrote out the coded messages on a signal pad for the Chief Petty Officer who passed them on to the trawlers and minesweepers in the area. The messages were mostly only to do with stores and supplies, but they were sent in code all the same.

When the message came through to offer Grandfather Round-Turner the job of Naval Officer in Charge of Folkestone Port the Flag Officer asked my mother to put the signal through to her father. But coming from her he assumed it was a joke. When he realised it was real he was thrilled to take on the job.

My mother's three-day shifts ran continuously, with the pattern beginning again on every third day. On the first day they were on duty from 1pm to 8pm, the following day from 8am to 1pm, that evening after an eight hour break they were on duty again at 8pm and worked overnight till 8am. Sometimes during a slack night watch the Chief Petty Officer would say, "You could go and get your head down for a bit Miss," and my mother could go next door into the empty room once used as a ticket office for the ferries from Harwich to the Hook of Holland. There she curled up under a knitted patchwork blanket on the brown linoleum counter and passing sailors made cheeky comments through the hole where the tickets were once sold. At the end of the night watch they had 36 hours off before the cycle began again. That was the only time she could get to see Jock.

At Harwich my mother was surrounded by handsome young men and she had dozens of friends. There were, as she put it, 'Loose chaps all over the place'. She was terribly fond of Jock, but he had been in India for the last five years and she had been growing up while he was away. Now many of her friends were fighting in Europe, a few had already been killed and others were lost. She had not been surprised when Jock fell for her but she was a bit taken aback when he began to get so serious so soon; when almost immediately he began asking her to marry him. The world was getting more uncertain by the day and the last thing she had been thinking of was committing herself to one man for life. Jock was coming on a bit strong; he was moving rather frighteningly fast. He seemed to be so sure of his feelings and of what he wanted. Every second or

third day he sent her another letter:
It is just to say that I love you and that I have a sort of itching longing all over me to be with you. My Pegs you have absolutely turned me upside down. Have a feeling of only being half alive when you are not there.

"I didn't realise at first," she said, sixty years later when she told me the story for the very first time, "what a terribly special man he was. How much I would give," she added, and a faraway look came over her face, "still to be married to that man now."

18. War 1940

On 10th May 1940 the German air force began bombing barracks and air fields all over France, Belgium and Holland. Within hours half the Belgian and nearly all the Dutch air forces were destroyed on the ground. The R.A.F. bombers, sent out to attack the hugely superior German forces, were practically wiped out. In France German fighter planes strafed the allied forces on the ground. In Britain Winston Churchill, First Lord of the Admiralty, formed a new coalition government and a five man War Cabinet. The German army were heading for Britain and they were moving fast. Jock's leave was suspended until further notice. He spent most of his time dashing around on a motor-bike trying to organise a local civil defence scheme around Shoeburyness; starting work at dawn he was lucky to finish by midnight. There was panic in the air but he wasn't going to let it ruffle him.

"This part of the world has got a bad fit of parachute jitters," he told my mother.

On 14th May the Dutch army capitulated and four days later the Germans took Amiens. Jock had made some progress in setting up the local civil defence scheme and he was wondering how he could get to see my mother. He couldn't think of a credible pretext for going up to Harwich on work and his leave was still suspended. His only hope was to persuade her to use her precious 36 hours after the night shift to come to Southend to see him:

So it looks as if the only hope is for you to come down here though it is a horrid journey for you my sweet.

On the 28th May the Belgian army capitulated.

The British forces in France were pushed right back to the coast and the evacuation from Dunkirk began.

Ships of every type arrived at ports all along the south and east coasts of England. At Harwich my mother saw the port filled with destroyers, corvettes and submarines. Poles, Dutch and Free French swarmed onto Parkestone Pier. The Wrens were asked out to parties on board ship and when these were interrupted by the air raid sirens they had to go ashore quickly in rowing boats in total darkness in case the ships put out to sea. The Germans were bombing the MTB base just on the other side of the water at Felixstowe. The situation was dire, but my mother never thought for a moment that her side might not succeed. Now it was even more difficult for my parents to meet and sometimes it was impossible:

My darling, I was so disappointed about Sunday. It was the only solution, to call it off, though my sweet I did not get in till about 7.30 in the evening, dead tired and soaked to the skin. In fact when you wired on Saturday to say that you couldn't come I was just waiting to get a minute spare to phone you to say that it was no good as a storm was brewing. Of course having got the wire I did no more. Keep on getting brighter periods when most things out of the ordinary seem to have been done then another bombshell occurs and we are back at the beginning again on 24 hour shifts.

By 4th June the evacuation of Dunkirk was complete but the 51st Highland Division, one of the army's best fighting units, and the one in with which my father would later fight and die, was still in France. The division had been taken under French command in an effort to demonstrate to the world that Britain was standing firmly by her ally.

That day Churchill made his famous speech which was to unite the whole country behind him:

I have, myself, full confidence that if all do their duty,

if nothing is neglected, and if the best arrangements are made, as they are being made, we shall prove ourselves once again able to defend our island home, to ride out the storm of war, and to outlive the menace of tyranny, if necessary for years, if necessary alone....
Even though large tracts of Europe and many old and famous States have fallen or may fall into the grip of the Gestapo and all the odious apparatus of Nazi rule, we shall not flag or fail. We shall go on to the end, we shall fight in France, we shall fight on the seas and oceans, we shall fight with growing confidence and growing strength in the air, we shall defend our island, whatever the cost may be, we shall fight on our beaches, we shall fight on the landing grounds, we shall fight in the fields and in the streets, we shall fight on the hills; we shall never surrender.

My parents were doing their best. At Harwich, as at Shoeburyness, the air raids came nearly every night. The beaches were closed to the public and the forces were erecting scaffolding defences to guard against an invasion by sea. Jock's days started at 4.00 am. As well as his day job training army recruits he was put in charge of blocking all the roads in the area, pacifying indignant farmers and encouraging the local civil defence units. He kept trying to get these secondary jobs sewn up so he could delegate them, but each time he got near it the pressure on him increased. He describes his position in his usual understated way:

I always catch a packet every time there is an upheval in this part of the world, then have to spend a certain amount of time getting sundry unsuspecting gentry trained to take over and do my work for me. Just back to a pleasant state of idleness again before the next eruption.

He was working flat out but every ten days or so he and my mother found ways to meet. Occasionally he found the time and petrol to drive over to her, sometimes she came as far as Southend and sometimes they met half way.

I do thank you Pet for a marvellous day. Just set me up again when I had nearly got to the end of my string.

But it was hard for my mother to feel sure that Jock was the man for her. Bobby, the boyfriend she'd had since she was fifteen, was reported missing in France. He was an only child and his distraught parents got in touch with her. "If he gets in touch with anyone it will be with you," they said, "and please will you tell us right away?" Of course she would. She tracked down a fellow soldier from the same regiment who told her that Bobby had last been seen trying alone, and armed only with a rifle, to hold up an advancing German tank. Bobby never came home.

On the 10th June Norwegian resistance ended. Italy too declared war on Britain and France. The Germans were moving across France and Rommel was the first German divisional commander to reach the Channel coast. There, after weeks of intense fighting, his Panzer Division managed to trap the 51st Highland Division, the most professional British forces, along with the French 9th Corps, at St Valery-en-Caux. British destroyers sent to look for them came under fire from German positions on the cliffs and a belated evacuation attempt on the night of 11th June with 67 merchant ships and 140 small craft was beaten off. The Highlanders fought on until they were down to their last few rounds of ammunition but the odds against them were overwhelming. Over 8,000 men of the 51st Highland Division were driven into 5 years captivity as German prisoners of war where they survived on one meal of soup and bread a day. Often it was infested with maggots which they ate for the extra nourishment they gave. Two years later General de Gaulle acknowledged their sacrifice:

I can tell you that the comradeship in arms experienced on the battlefield of Abbeville in May and June 1940 between the French armoured division which I had the honour to command

and the valiant 51st Highland Division under General Fortune, played its part in the decision which I took to continue fighting on the side of the Allies unto the end, no matter what may be the course of events.

On 14th June the Germans occupied Paris and, on 22nd, France capitulated. On 25th June German planes dropped the first bombs on London. Now Britain was on her own. There was a risk the French fleet would fall into enemy hands and on 3rd July Churchill ordered the British navy to attack the fleet of their former ally in the port of Oran. In three days it was totally destroyed. It was a brutal act, but necessary.

One evening towards the end of June my mother came over to Southend to see Jock. He had booked her a room in a hotel where they arranged to meet in the evening. As she waited and waited there was no word from him but in the evening light terrific air raids developed. The sirens wailed and the windows rattled with the noise and vibration from the ack-ack guns. The hotel guests were supposed to go down to the shelters and at one time my mother, who has always hated bangs and loud noises, set out in her dressing gown for the cellars. She decided against it just in case Jock came, but by the time she had to set out back to Harwich for her next watch there was still no sign of him and no word. He had been out all night and unable to get in touch. Whenever they managed to meet he asked:

"Will you marry me?"

And she replied, "I'm not sure".

She was even coming under pressure from her parents who were fond of Jock.

"You're not being quite fair to this chap," Gran told my mother.

Every time she came over to Shoeburyness he

wrote to thank her:

Sweetheart I do thank you for coming. Your visits just tip the scale that balances my sanity and insanity. Shaky sometimes these days. My sweet you have left a sort of emptiness behind you. Like a field might feel when the sun suddenly goes behind a cloud, harmed by the memory of the sun yet with that breath of chillness at its leaving.

But time was moving on. July was passing. Jock hadn't taken any leave since Christmas and he had been working all hours and every day of the week. He was desperate to get away from Shoeburyness. Months ago he had put in an application for two weeks leave in August, the time when his family had always made their visits to Scotland. Now it seemed that he might get it, but the war was building up and still my mother was undecided:

Have you any chance of getting away at the same time? I am being absolutely torn in half over leave as I could not bear it if you were not there and at the same time am longing to see Ayrshire again. That place has somehow got into the bones of me. The smell and the feel of the hills and the heather, the strong quiet folk and the noisy little burns. I have often wondered what it is that draws me to that place. I suppose mostly it is the one place which has always been the same in a wandering life. Must manage to take you there somehow, wonder how you would like it.

Towards the end of July my mother decided that next time Jock asked her to marry him she would agree. They were due to meet in Chelmsford, about half way between Harwich and Shoeburyness. Jock took her to a dining room above a pub near the cathedral where one could still buy a scant meal without food coupons. It was nearly three months since he first asked her to marry him and, as they sat there alone in a huge room full of empty chairs and tables, he was beginning to wonder if in the end she might say no. His voice was querelous as he asked, "Are you going to marry me?" It wasn't quite as she had visualised it and her reply didn't come out quite right either. When he got back to Shoebury he still wasn't certain he had understood:

Darling did you really mean what you said in that little inn in Chelmsford? My sweet I can hardly believe it.

As soon as Gaffer was told of the engagement he sent off a telegram to my mother's parents. It said, "Delighted. Still laughing. Ted."

Jock and Peggy tried to get to London at the same time to buy their engagement ring and have some photos taken, but it was never possible. My father had his head well linked in with his heart, but it was agony to jostle his conflicting priorities in those terribly difficult times. His leave came through, two weeks to run from 12th August, but my mother was called to an officers' training course at Greenwich at precisely that time and Jock went to Scotland on his own. It was his last visit. The white heather, for good luck, he sent my mother is still in the envelope with his letter:

Sweetest this place is just heaven. Bleak cold and raining every hour or so with the cloud cutting off the tops of the hills making all the colouring soft dark green and purple. Feel as though I had been in a desert then some very damp place and just let the whole body suck up moisture through the skin. Sounds horrid but is really glorious. If I do not see you at the end my sweet it will mean 14 days gap which is more than I could stand.

19. A Dichotomy

In the early years of the war the army had a huge shortage of trained men with actual combat experience. Generally only the old soldiers who had fought in WW1 had both. Of the younger trained professionals my father was rare in this way with both his army training and his fighting experience in India. As a result he was valuable to the army, both on the field and in training new recruits.

From Scotland my father listened to the news broadcasts as the Luftwaffer stepped up their attacks on military and airforce bases in the south of England. The Battle of Britain was under way and the Germans believed they were winning. They aimed to wipe out the RAF Fighter Command and if they succeeded...

There, on 20th August 1940 he listened to Winston Churchill's famous speech to the country where he said;

Never in the field of human conflict was so much owed by so many to so few.

And my father was on leave. He felt he had missed out on the first round of fighting in France and now he was away when he was most needed in England. Right from the start this was a parallel strand in my parent's relationship. My father was a professional soldier first and foremost and my mother, who came from a service family too, completely accepted this. The thought of anything happening to him was more than she could bear yet they were both putting everything they had into fighting this war. Since before they met again my father always had the idea that he should be fighting at the front. He felt it was the way in which he could best help win the war, and it was there that ambitious young officers gained promotion. Sometimes in his letters to my mother he mentioned the dichotomy between this wish and his love for her. He spoke with the widely used euphemisms of the time:

My little one I am an ungrateful toad. I heard of a gunner unit not so far from here which is to be shipped abroad in the near future and oh darling I wished it was my own. Sort of madness that seizes me when I think of any other unit which gets the chance of a show. Suppose really it is a sort of reaction against having been left out of the last party. Feeling that as a trained soldier I ought to be in a fight somewhere but they will never let me get at it. My darling do you realise you are intending to marry a bloodthirsty old war bird of the Colonel Blimp type?

Although he realised his ambition might seem bloodthirsty he was young and capable and he was sorry he had been unable to help his colleagues in France in the summer of 1940. He longed to be able spend more time with my mother yet he accepted that it was impossible 'till these Huns have been put back in their kennel'. Like my mother he was trained from his earliest days to do his duty. Yet my father had a further reason for his desire to go to the front. He was following the family tradition.

My father had seven admirals in his immediate ancestry on his father's side. The male members of Gaffer's family were all naval men; both on his mother's and his father's side his ancestors were seamen. His mother's naval family, the Owens of Campobello Island, joined the naval side of the Cochrane line when his parents married in 1873. Both Gaffer and his elder brother became admirals, as was Gaffer's father, and several other close relations. His great-grandfather Archibald was the younger brother of Thomas Cochrane, a naval hero in the Napoleonic Wars.

Thomas Cochrane's exploits were fictionalised in the characters of Captain Marryat (who worked under Cochrane for many years) of C.S.Forrester's Captain Hornblower, Patrick O'Brian's Captain Jack Aubrey and many other 'fictional' naval heroes. His ghost-written autobiography became a best-seller in Victorian times. Many biographies of him have been written and one recent account, by David Cordingly, once the Keeper of the Picture Gallery at the Maritime Museum in Greenwich, is particularly well researched. Cordingly's book makes a very clear and fair assessment of his life and this is necessary as Thomas Cochrane has always been a controversial figure. His daring exploits at sea were matched only by those of Sir Frances Drake and Nelson but Cochrane was often his own worst enemy. He was honest and fearless to a fault. In all walks of life this led to his speaking out against those in authority wherever he saw unfairness or corruption, and this created enemies in high places. Thomas Cochrane was a hero to many schoolboys of the 1920s and a direct inspiration to my father.

My Cochrane ancestors are descended from

Thomas Cochrane's younger brother Archibald who fought with him in his early years when, as captain of the diminutive 14 gun warship the Speedy, with which he harassed the enemy along the Spanish coast. It was Archibald's line which carried on the naval tradition while Thomas's direct male descendants predominantly joined the army. When he was twenty-four Cochrane met Nelson, who was then forty-one. He never had the opportunity to serve under Nelson but greatly admired the older man. Cochrane took to heart the advice he was given on that occasion, "Never mind manoeuvres, always go at them." This suited Cochrane's character and he followed this dictum both at sea, where he found that the well-managed surprise attack was extraordinarily effective, and on land, where the tactic more often backfired; for instance in his outspoken speeches in the House of Commons as MP for Westminster. He was a man of action, a buccaneering hero, but also very careful of his men. He was at his best when he was working independently as a frigate captain where he could exercise his extraordinarily skilful seamanship and imaginative solutions without reference to higher authority. His life story is one of extremes: of daredevil escapades and the capture of many more prize vessels than any other post captain of the time. He was forever outwitting adversaries of many times his own size. He was a fantastically popular naval hero but it was his own big mouth which brought him down and even now his record is controversial. Even now he is often written out of mainstream naval history.

As a coding rating my mother had already been doing cipher work when they were short of staff in the cipher office in Harwich. Now, while my father was in Scotland, she was promoted to 3rd Officer. Half way through her Officers' Training Course at Greenwich her name shot up to the top of all the lists.

Peggy and Jock hoped to meet up as soon as he returned the following week, but it wasn't possible. Back at Shoeburyness the air raid warnings were incessant and the rail lines blocked where bombs had dropped at Shenfield and Rochford. He tried for three days to ring her without getting through.

One night in Harwich my mother lay awake listening to a ringing bell. This had to be the invasion. She wondered what she should be doing. But in the end it was only a particular wind that had carried the sound of a bell buoy over the sea.

Back in Shoeburyness Jock was still trying to arrange a meeting:

By hook or by crook we will be together next weekend. If the trains do not work shall have to get a boat across the river or a plane or something.

Their engagement was announced in the local papers:

I am getting the backwash of the local attempts at humour. Skipped most of same by an air raid which occurred at lunch time causing me to dodge into the town for a meal, the mess being all underground and consequently not functioning.

Then the situation got worse. All leave was cancelled. On 7th September 1940 the Luftwaffer mounted a gigantic raid on the docklands of London, hundreds of bombs rained down on the civilians below. The blitz on London had begun.

The MI5 office at Wormwood Scrubs, where my godmother Ruth was working, was temporarily disbanded. With her War Office pass she made her way up to Scotland to join her husband Lt.Col. Jim Munn, the army officer she met in India when she came out to visit Jock in Peshawar before the war. He had always specialized in intelligence and now he was in charge of training at the Special Operations

Executive at Arisaig in Argyllshire. When Ruth reached him he admitted he had received 'a very odd signal'. It was the coded message which meant the Germans had set out across the channel to invade England. Between the 8th and the 10th September the moon and the tide were right for ships to drift silently across the channel from France. Ruth knew this was the optimum time to mount an invasion and that her father, who was in the Home Guard at Hove, had been put on general alert. A build-up of troops and ships had been observed around Calais. Churchill ordered the RAF to drop a row of flares across the channel to give the impression, at night, that a huge armada of ships was lying in wait. It was an old trick Thomas Cochrane had used although the original idea is attributed to Drake.

But the invasion never came.

20. Wedding

With the immediate threat of invasion my father was moved from Shoeburyness. His next letter, sent on 9th September 1940, was sent from Crook, County Durham. There he was given a troop command and continued to train recruits. He was billeted with a family and the mess was an abandoned empty house with no telephone.

Darling I have longed for you to be here, just aching longing, very selfish of me as I do not know what you could do here all day as I am working from breakfast to supper time and this is a very small place. One shop and a Co-op stores sort of village.

They just had to write to each other, look at their photographs and wait;

My love of course I want to know about your watches or anything else that is happening to you. I wonder if you know how much it means to me to see your writing on a bit of paper and to know that you still love me. It is just everything to me my darling. You are a sweet one my pet to go up to London to have your photo taken for me. Could you do one more thing my darling if you happen to be in town again. Get a frame for yourself and tell the shop to send me same and bill. Think you would go in a brownish leatherish sort of frame that will stand frequent packing and moving. My darling you need not worry about costing me money as I am a cautious old bird and just do not spend anything if I have not got any to spend. And if there is anything in the till it is or will be as much yours as mine. My lovely one it is always worth all the money I have got to see you for five minutes.

By 19th October when my mother got 14 days leave they had been apart three months. Jock was running a course for the airforce at Redesdale in Yorkshire between 23rd and 25th October and they met up in Crook, Co. Durham after that. The delay and the separations were too much for my mother. She was beginning to despair. She was only twenty-one and the world was topsy-turvy. By the time she arrived in Crook she was wavering about her decision to marry Jock.

"We will have to try to unbutton this somehow," she said. "It is just too much to hold this one together. I'm afraid I just can't go through with this marriage."

My father sat looking at her quietly for a time which seemed endless and then he said, "Mmmmm. It's a pity as I'm sure it would have been good." After another pause he said, "Before you go I wonder if you could just sew this button on my jacket for me. You would do it so much better than me."

Nobody could sew on a button more neatly than my mother. Her sewing was the neatest of all at the Domestic Science College where she went for a year after leaving school. She stayed and sewed on his button and of course she agreed not to go back on the engagement. She made her way down south just missing the nightly blitz on

London. My father wrote:

> *Feels like being cut in two when you are away. Same sort of dull aching feeling allied with a sense of something missing. As to the button little one a proper permanent kiss is proof against fire and water.*

It was bliss to be together but she thought that even if they were married they would still have to suffer the agonies of constant separation. Again she felt uncertain. Even in England they would never be able to work at the same place and now every able-bodied person in the country was working for the war effort and, worse still, at any moment Jock might even be sent out to fight abroad. She loved him but she wished that life were simpler. She came up to County Durham again at the end of November when, after her terrible trip up, he stayed up way into the night drinking and talking to his colleagues about world affairs. It was not a good move. After she got back she sat down and wrote a long letter to try to explain her confusion. She wondered whether to burn it but instead she pushed it into the letter box. When he received it Jock realised he was in trouble. He stayed up late into the night to try to save his skin:

> *I suddenly felt that writing to you was more important than all the sleep in the world. My Sweet I am glad that you sent that letter you thought of burning. Darling I did not understand properly when we were together though I might have done if we had been allowed to remain together on Saturday night. My Sweet I know the feeling of struggling and struggling alone in a sort of muddle with only a very muddled prospect in view. But darling one, that is just what we are trying to avoid by getting married that we neither of us shall be alone again even if we are separated. My love I am afraid it calls for a last supreme effort to get over all the muddle of fighting alone before we come together. My darling as you know I am not much of a Christian but I do think they*

have got something when they speak of people being married as being united and becoming almost one person because marriage is really giving all that one is and much much less important all that one possesses to someone else. So that ever afterwards there would be always both of us in anything that happened, as though you were getting an extra brain and an extra limb and giving as much in return. Also darling do you remember saying you often knew when I was going to ring up. Love is a very powerful force and can do odd things with distance.

Have just read this letter over again my love and feel that it has not really made what I want to say clear at all but cannot do any better at the moment. Only wish I could have that weekend again, feel that I could do so much better if only we could be together again. For as usual my love we wasted most of our time by being interrupted and thinking of unimportant things like presents and trains. Fraid that will always be so till we can be married then if we feel like being alone together we can just lock the door on the whole world and let them stew in their nasty muddles till we are ready and strong enough to face them again.

Love you my sweetest more than I can say, Jock.

The wedding date was fixed for 25th January 1941.

My mother's friends egged her on to apply for some leave after the wedding. She cabled a message to her C.O.:

"Submit that I be granted 2 months unpaid leave. Getting married and husband not likely to remain long in England."

She got it. My father saved, begged and borrowed coupons and petrol until he had enough to drive down from Co. Durham to Essex and back. He counted down the days to the wedding.

On Saturday January 25th 1941 my father, again dressed in army riding breeches and high leather riding boots with a long sword hanging to his side, has his arm linked into my mother's for their wedding photographs. Although the weather was freezing the couple look radiant. At the wedding service at the little church at Layer-de-la-Haye the congregation knelt as they sang the second hymn:

> O perfect Love, all human thought transcending:
> Lowly we kneel in prayer before Thy Throne.
> That theirs may be the love which knows no ending,
> Whom thou for evermore dost join in one.
>
> O perfect Life, be Thou their full assurance
> Of tender charity and steadfast faith.
> Of patient hope, and quiet brave endurance,
> With childlike trust that fears nor pain nor death.

Grant them the joy which brightens earthly sorrow,
Grant them the peace which calms all earthly strife;
And to life's day the glorious unknown morrow
That dawns upon eternal love and life.

The words were heartrendingly appropriate. The two handsome young people were in love. They both assumed the conventions of their similar backgrounds with which their own situation fitted as neatly as a white kid glove. My father, five years older, had sowed his wild oats in romantic and dangerous places, fighting the Mohmands, shooting his tiger. My mother was younger and more conventional, a loyal person with a large group of friends, she liked to play second fiddle. They had four adult bridesmaids, his sister, her sister and her two best friends. The two hundred guests were all behind them. There were no niggling little doubts, no skeletons in the cupboard.

In spite of the cold and the rain their wedding was everything a wedding should be. The construct perfectly fitted the situation. It was not just my mother's long white crepe-romaine dress, the Honiton lace veil lent by her grandmother, and the bouquet of white orchids and camellias which were correct for the occasion, the underlying feelings and assumptions of all those present were completely with them. Everyone there was thrilled. Everyone was genuinely optimistic for their future. Everyone was hoping that the wishes expressed in the hymn would be granted. But life in wartime can be cruel.

21. Married Life

After their one night honeymoon Jock carried his bride back to his billet in Crook, County Durham. Their journey was somewhat similar to those he once made back home from Marlborough by bicycle or boat. He picked from his wedding presents those which he considered the most essential; a thick woven car rug, a bitters shaker and a bottle of gin. Then he put the two suitcases my mother had packed so neatly onto the back seat of his 10 horsepower Ford. She climbed into the front seat beside him and they were off.

Flurries of snow began to fall as they drove on and on northwards up the Great North Road into the wind. For months he had been using a motorbike for his work, saving his petrol coupons and scrimping and borrowing to save enough fuel for this journey. They huddled together under the dark green chequered rug and pushed on northwards through the slush and sleet, and into a blizzard, stopping occasionally for a tot of gin and bitters. The snow began to push its way round the edges of the ill-fitting windows of the car and to her horror my mother saw that blisters were forming on the lids of the two new rawhide suitcases they had been given as a wedding present.

    The two months they lived together in Crook was to be the longest they were ever allowed. During the day while Jock was out at work she stayed close to the kitchen range with Mrs Redshaw, his landlady, and sewed from dawn till dusk. One day she sorted their wedding telegrams and photographs and stuck them on the first pages of an album she intended to fill with mementoes of their life together. From time to time his batman dropped by to look after my father's clothes and polish his boots. Every minute of that time is etched into my mother's memory; the time when the batman, who had an awful cold in his nose, pulled aside the pan of boiling stock from the range and sneezed right into it; the day when the snow was so deep on the path from the house that Jock stepped right over the garden gate on his way to work; and the day he dropped the precious bottle of gin and it broke.

    Sixty years later she showed me the gloves he bought her in Newcastle. She went to buy a pair of plain knitted woollen ones but he listened as she gave the size of her hands and slipped behind the counter to bring out a pair of the very best Dent's hand-sewn gloves with rabbit skin backs, leather palms and knitted linings. In her car she still keeps the woven green-chequered rug. It is well-worn now but still quite usable, not yet completely threadbare.

    During the time that my parents were together in Crook the campaign in North Africa was building up.

The Italians under Mussolini had been trying to extend their empire from its base in Abyssinia, Eritrea and Libya. If they could annexe British Egypt it would clear a route through to the oil fields of the Middle East to fuel their tanks and trucks. In August 1940 while my father was taking his last holiday in Scotland the Italians had taken British Somaliland, but in December 1940 the British Western Desert Force opened an offensive against them. In the early months of 1941 the Allies fought back the Italian advances over the North African desert. Five days before my parents' wedding they took the vital supply port of Tobruk and on 7th February 1941 they occupied Benghazi. An area of land the size of France and Britain was recaptured. The soldiers of the Desert Force were professional and they fought valiantly, but at that time it was both under-manned and under-equipped. In spite of this they were approaching Tripoli when Churchill took away the best of their forces in a doomed attempt to save Greece. On 12th February 1941 Hitler came to Mussolini's rescue sending the troops who were to be known as the Afrika Korps out to Tripoli under Rommel. The ambitious German general soon drove the Allies right back across the same stretch of desert until, on 29th May 1941, the Allied forces managed to stop him at the Egyptian frontier.

At the end of March my mother's unpaid leave came to an end. She had moved from Harwich. As a cipher officer she went back to her work in the maze of stuffy tunnels below the Naval Dockyard at Chatham. The nightly blitz on London had ended and though the centres of many industrial towns, Coventry, Cardiff, Birmingham and Bristol, lay in ruins, the worst of the bombing on England was over. Jock was transferred south, first to Angmering then on to army bases at Findon, Lindfield and Hurstpierpoint in Sussex and to Milborne Port near Sherborne in Dorset.

There he worked seven days a week and often from 5am until midnight. He enjoyed the teaching and he did it well. The new recruits listened hard to what he had to say. Their lives depended on it but more importantly, he said, so did the lives of others. He found he could gain their attention to such an extent it was like playing a musical instrument as he tried to mould them into his way of thinking:

So few people outside seem to realise what a great change a civilian has got to go through before he becomes a useful soldier. In essence the change between the mental reaction of "how does this effect me?" in any given circumstance to "How does this effect my unit?"

It was the attitude he himself applied to his work. During their time in Crook Jock began to call my mother Wigget; it is something I never knew until I read his letters. And he took on the traditional male responsibilities such as sorting out their tax returns. My mother thought I would be bored by these letters about such mundane tasks, but I found them hugely reassuring. I liked to think of my father as an ordinary person doing his tax returns, just like the rest of us. I liked these simple letters best of all. It made my father seem more real. He was older than my mother and liked to advise her about any problems she had at work:

Sorry to hear about the head wren that you dislike, the only saving grace seems to be that she knows her job. That is a very great thing these days my sweetest. One can forgive almost anything for that, certainly in these parts. Can imagine your wailings and gnashings of teeth. Sometimes sweetest I wish I could be much more like Wigget and feel things strongly. As it is I become like a creaky old machine as far as anything to do with my job is concerned. Do not seem to mind very much who I work with provided they know their stuff or are under my command. In fact would much rather have an absolute horror who was efficient than the pleasantest chap in the world who was a fool.

Tensions arose inevitably from living and working in a tight interdependent group. Jock was well used to the situation and his naval ancestors too were well known for their understanding of group dynamics. I was amused to find that he himself resorted to precisely the same methods to keep his privacy that I once used at boarding school. He developed a way of shutting himself off from the others in the mess which he called 'oystering' and he advised my mother to do the same:

Only hope is to do my oyster act and just close up and fade out when things get too crowded. Remarkable how like a piece of furniture one can become as far as the rest of the world is concerned when you just do not intend to be noticed or bothered at all. If I get absolutely fed up with my company in the mess I choose a chair where I shall not be tripped over and mentally pull down the shutters. Just sit absolutely still and think of something else. If anyone really wants to get me back to the land of the living they have to shout twice. Once to get me back, the other time to say it again when I can hear what is happening. Usually rewarded by 'Yes' or 'no' and a relapse if I do not want to be pulled out of my shell.

In another letter he said:

My method of getting fed up is usually to retire into a corner with a book and take no further interest in my surroundings. A state of affairs most easily produced by somebody making really thickheaded remarks in all good faith. Can deal with any kind of mistaken or misguided fanatic provided he has sufficient intelligence to uphold his convictions reasonably but a convinced fool is beyond my powers of endurance.

"Does your mother realise how like your father you are?" asked Alec.

My mother has sometimes said that I was so like my father physically that some gesture I made would bring her up short when she had not been thinking of him at all, but I'm not sure if she made other connections. 'Oystering' was neither understood nor condoned in the new family she created. It is interesting how much of one's make-up is genetic. I have always found it easy to understand why adopted children struggle to find their natural parents.

My mother mentioned, I remember, that my father always chose himself the smallest room he could find. At boarding school I always managed to get myself transferred from a dormitory to a tiny room of my own where I could read with a torch under the covers till late into the night. I used various means to achieve this and they always worked within the first week or two of term. Once I organised the girls of my dorm to jump down in turn onto the steel beds from the upper part of a large hanging cupboard. The matron soon moved me out when she found a splay-legged iron bedstead and a hair mattress split from top to toe.

I think my father managed without resorting to such methods, but the staff at his school were certainly more tolerant and intelligent than those at my convent girls' school. After one of his many moves my father described yet another new room in a requisitioned house. It was, he said, 'a typical James abode'. The tiny window was covered at night with battered cardboard blackout shutters and the bare walls were interrupted only by a fireplace on whose mantelshelf he arranged his smaller belongings either side of his photograph of my mother in its folding leather case. He slept on a camp bed under khaki army blankets. The only piece of furniture was a chest of drawers he had discovered and brought in. It was, he said, the usual type: without handles, wobbling on three legs and with cigarette burns on the top.

The situation was just as my mother had feared. Even though they were married it was impossible to be together. As soon as she came off her 12 hour night shift she went straight to the station in an attempt to get to meet Jock in the 36 hours she had before she was back on duty. Sometimes he was able to meet her half way and they spent an hour or two together in somebody's house. "People were very good like that to servicemen during the war," she said. But the train timetables were often interrupted and the stations had no name boards. Often my parents simply couldn't make it in the time they had to spare. Many times my mother would get nearly to the place where my father was stationed when her time ran out and she had to turn back. And, to make things worse, he was still longing to get involved with the real fighting:

Wish they would dump us in Holland to bite the Hun in the pants while he is busy with the Bolshie. Not much chance of that though I fear. Wigget sighs with relief. Restless sort of oaf you have got for a husband my darling.

On 6th April 1941 the Germans invaded Yugoslavia and Greece and eleven days later Yugoslavia capitulated. They fought their way down the Greek mainland and by the end of May they had captured Crete. Chris, my mother's elder brother who was a Lieutenant in the navy, was involved in the evacuation of the island. The lower deck and the messes of his ship H.M.S.Defender were crammed full with exhausted soldiers hastily packed in on top of each other before she made off at top speed swerving to avoid bombs. The news was terrible but when the Bismark, the Germans' new battleship and the pride of their fleet, was sunk in the Atlantic on 27th May, it gave my parents a much needed tonic.

Now the Germans in Italy and Crete had air control of the central Mediterranean and the British soldiers in Tobruk were completely isolated. My uncle Chris's ship HMS Defender was one of eight destroyers, four British and four Australian, who supported them. The destroyers came in pairs leaving Alexandria at 6 pm. with stores and extra soldiers and steamed ahead at 20 knots. They entered Tobruk Harbour and put their load ashore silently in complete darkness before beating it back 300 sea miles to Alexandria to arrive as soon as possible after dawn. Towards the end of June a German aircraft spotted the glow of Defender's wake below them in the darkness and the bomb they dropped beside her broke the back of the destroyer.

A Mother Goes Out With Her Naval Family

Lieut. C. L. Round-Turner, R.N., won the D.S.C. and bar. When he went to Buckingham Palace for investiture his mother went with him. But that's not all. His father, his brother and his two sisters went, too. And they're all in the Navy. This picture of the family was taken after they left the Palace.

My mother as a cipher officer and Grandfather as C.O. at Folkestone Port got news of the sinking immediately. The list of survivors took longer to arrive and the details of their fate came through in code. It was my mother who received the message that Chris was safe. Defender's sister ship H.M.A.S. Vendetta was able to pick up the whole crew and they even made a couple of attempts to tow the damaged destroyer back to port before it began to break in half and they realised it was no use. They torpedoed the remains and sent her to the bottom. But Chris was not out of danger, he still had to make his way home. He travelled on a damaged aircraft carrier round the Cape and over the Atlantic to a naval repair yard in Norfolk, Virginia and went on to Halifax, Nova Scotia from where he made a perilous journey back across the Atlantic in a huge old liner the Alcantara escorting a merchant convoy back to Greenock, where finally he was back in England for the first time in three and a half years.

During their brief times together my parents got closer and closer;

I seem to be six times as much in love with you as I was before that weekend. Didn't think it possible before but it is.

The separations caused by their war jobs became ever more intolerable. By the autumn of 1941 my father, who had always been so enthusiastic about fighting, began to long for the war to end and to plan what they might do afterwards:

21/9/41. I did enjoy our weekend together. Makes me long for the time when this party will be over and we can be together for good. Never thought that if I had the luck to see a major war I should want the thing to end. Surprising how ones opinion changes.

2/10/41. I am getting rather tired of this war. Long for a time when this middle period will be over and we can either get on with it or get it over and I can return to my Wigget and a reasonable existence again.

16/10/41. Darling one, I long more and more for some sensible form of life when I can live with Wigget and grow pigs or something. My sweet I love you so much and we seem to see each other at longer and longer intervals.

Often my father was working in a defended area and it fell to him to enforce the rule that civilian wives were not allowed in. He could hardly bring in his own wife even though she was a WRNS officer. That Christmas he was left in charge of the officers mess of 132 Field Regiment at Milborne Port. It was their second Christmas since they got together, and for a second time they were separated. In his letter to her Jock described a 'slight disturbance' which started on Christmas Eve;

All started by the singing of rude songs followed as it is apt to by such games as pillion polo and cockfighting.

Nobody was allowed to escape and up till 3am anyone who slunk off the bed was discovered and tipped out.

Party reached a climax with, I regret to say, your husband wielding a fire extinguisher on two officers making a spirited scaling assault with ladders on the window of the defending party, the first being pushed slowly in through the window by the second in the face of a bucket of water thrown at the head every 15 seconds.

Below his description he drew a little sketch of the scene. The lower man on the ladder has a balloon coming out of his mouth saying "Get in you fool." Life in the army was like boarding school and my father was growing out of it.

My love our times together are so grand that I am apt to be furious at anything that happens when we part again. Stupid as it is a poor way of relieving the feeling of hopelessness that comes over me when I lose my Wigget again. My darling I cannot tell you how I detest leaving you. Makes me feel like a caged animal without even the satisfaction of iron bars to work on. Darling I do so wish this war would end.

That month, on 7th December 1941 after the Japanese attack on Pearl Harbour, the Americans entered the war. Tobruk was relieved by the 8th Army two days later and that Chrismas Day the Allies re-took Benghazi. But on 21st January Rommel opened a new offensive in Libya.

For over two years my father had made it known to the army authorities that he wished to be sent abroad on active service but ironically it was only now that he was sent for the medical checks which tend to precede such a thing. Four years previously in India he had developed a detached retina. There was no treatment then for that condition and it left him partially blind. As a child I had been told the story of how, in March 1942, the doctor who examined him exclaimed, "My dear boy you are completely blind in one eye!" In spite of this two weeks later in mid April he was passed as medically A1.

Medical Board consisted of three decrepit old birds who I think would have marked anything suggested by the patient on his papers. On being told firmly that as far as I could see having a blind spot in the right eye had no effect on my ability or otherwise to do my job they eventually agreed and inscribed it as such on the records.

This was confirmed by the War Office. If only...I have always thought. If only those doctors had been stricter. Then when my parents met in early May they both had news. My mother said,

"I have got something to tell you." And Jock replied,

"I have got something to tell you too."

They discussed who should tell their news first. In the end they tossed for it and my mother won the toss.

"I'm going to have a baby," she said. It was marvellous. Now she was pregnant she would be allowed to stop work and she could come to live with Jock. Then he told her his news,

"I've been posted abroad on active service."

Their timing could not have been worse.

The doctor had worked out that the baby was due a week before Christmas and they decided that if it was a boy they would call it Thomas and if it was a girl it would be Jane. He wanted a girl like her. She wanted a boy like him. At the end of May 1942, my mother took a month off work to be in Nottingham with Jock. While she was there Rommel opened up his second Libyan offensive.

"If anything happens to me," my father said, "just forget our life together as if you were turning over a page in a book. Get on with your life as if I had never existed."

My mother didn't reply. The thought was too terrible to contemplate. She left it till the last minute to leave Nottingham, on June 21st when Jock had to leave for a training exercise. That day Rommel took back Tobruk and once again the Allies were pushed eastwards back into Egypt where they managed to hold him at the narrow point between the little railway halt on the coast at El Alamein and the impassable Quattara Depression forty miles to the south. The fighting that summer was the most awful of the whole campaign and the 8th Army suffered more casualties in these battles than in any others in North Africa.

"Do come and see me off if you can," she had said.

"I don't think I'm going to be able to," he replied.

But my father managed to get his whole troop to the station. When her train was still standing at the platform waiting to leave she spotted him over on the other side. As he rushed over to say one last goodbye he was wearing battledress and a strange flat cap she had never seen before. But he had to go back. She leaned out of the window of the train taking in every last glimpse of him as he walked back down the platform. But he didn't look back. At last, as the train picked up speed, she forced herself back to her seat.

He was gone.

On the 14th July 1942 immediately before boarding ship Jock posted off his last note from England:

My darling I have found that I have grown to love you even more than I thought was the top limit before the last month. Do you realise my sweet the last month has been the longest time we have had together except the first two months after we were married...I have got out of the way of sleeping on a camp bed. Seems a poor substitute for a comfortable bed with Wigget. You have made me soft my love. Love you my pet more and more every day, a fact which is becoming an absolute obsession to me.

It was grand to hear your voice at 6 o'clock this evening. Will remember it till we can be together again.

That time would never come.

22. Round the Cape

My mother had no idea where her husband was going and, although he may have had his suspicions, nor did he. Details of troop positions and movements had to be kept strictly secret. 'Careless talk costs lives' was the saying of the time.

It was too dangerous for a troopship to steam down the Mediterranean and this time Jock's journey by sea to Suez took nine weeks. His ship formed part of a convoy of transport vessels escorted by destroyers and corvettes which went down the west coast of Africa, around the Cape, and up the far side of Africa to Egypt, sailing around the coastline Gaffer's grandfather on his mother's side Captain William FitzWilliam Owen first surveyed over 100 years earlier. First he passed the Azores and the Cape Verde Islands to Freetown, Sierra Leone. There they were not let ashore lest they caught malaria or yellow fever so the troops sweltered on board for several days like hot sardines as the ships re-fuelled. My father's 28th birthday came and went; he only remembered it two days later as they continued on past the Island of Fernando Po where Owen once set up a colony for the release of rescued slaves. There was very little to do on board. Now he had all the time in the world to spend with my mother but she was miles away:

Wonder if you have got any of my letters yet. This is the fourth since we parted. Also wonder how soon I can hope for a letter from Wigget. This is the longest spell I have ever been without one, expect Wigget has been the same. Love you darling always.

The first three letters he sent never reached her.

Although the War Office kept this to themselves many letters from the troops abroad never reached home. Sometimes the mail ships were sunk in enemy action. My parents always dated their letters and now they began to number them as well to check the ones which never arrived.

If ever he had a moment to spare back in England, apart from the times he tried to visit my mother, my father busied himself with knocking up small sheds or with his water divining. My mother told me how, during 1941, they went with Gaffer and Ga to have drinks with a neighbour in Hawkhurst. She had a large garden and was a keen dowser. Various people at the party showed an interest and she showed them how it was done. My father had a try and to his surprise it worked for him. He became interested, bought books about it and tried out different sticks. Sometimes when they were together after that he would say, "I think we'll have to move from sitting on this wall, I can feel water rushing underneath." And my mother would tease him about it.

He got quite good at his dowsing and at the Brackens, Ga's old house near Ascot which is now the offices for a German technology firm, he could tell the depth of the water below the surface and that it had too much iron in it to be any use for drinking. My mother sent a dowsing rod off to him in the desert, where it would have been useful, but it never reached him there. Quite recently I lent his old books to someone I know who has the gift and later I apologized for 'those funny old books', but my friend rejected my apology, "They are the best books I have ever found on the subject," he said. "They gave me real encouragement." I have seen that a few people can dowse, finding water and even the foundations of long demolished buildings, but it doesn't work for me.

On board for nine weeks, and without my mother, my father read any books he could find and stayed up late at night discussing world affairs. Some of the men put on plays and tried to get him to act but, like me, he was no good at it. My mother had shown him how to darn a hole in his socks and now he had plenty of time to practise;

Have achieved one thing have darned a stocking with Wigget's mending outfit. Made what I thought was a very fine darn till I turned it right side out and found that in spite of playing about at the turning game I had darned it with the tag ends on the outside. Am at the moment almost watching my stockings with hopes for another hole to try again. One point of finesse does one have to finish off the ends or can they be left like the loops?

Gaffer always used an orange to darn a sock when he couldn't get hold of a darning mushroom (sailors used to get very good at this kind of thing) and now Jock found that this method was a great improvement on using the left fist.

At the Cape the men were allowed ashore and he bought my mother a pair of silk stockings. In England neither silk nor the newly invented nylon stockings were obtainable as the material was needed for parachutes. Months later she received the precious stockings in a packet without any note or detail of its origin, which the censors would not have allowed.

As he continued up the far side of Africa my father was running short of books and sometimes he just sat on board watching the flying fish and thinking of my mother at home. He looked at the latest photograph she had given him and he found little things she had wrapped up neatly and packed into his case:

My love I have just opened my ink bottle and found it all packed in soft paper. You are a darling. Must have been using the other bottle all the time up to now. I feel like rummaging all through my kit and finding all the Wiggetries at once but am being strong minded at the moment as they will last much longer if I wait and just come on them as I use the gear. Promise myself a field day if I have to store a box anywhere. Shall go through it for socks folded Wigget fashion first.

I was ashamed when I read this. I never liked the scrupulous way my mother did her packing. It reminded me of being homeless, of always moving on. Yet now I found that my father had loved that homely ability. For him it was like opening a Christmas stocking. Knowing that he had loved my mother so much made it easier for me to love her too. And, now that the ice was broken, she was being so much more open with me about these times. She was even quite interested in my project.

PORT TEWFIK, 11TH AUGUST 1942. BATTLE OF ALAMEIN, 23RD OCTOBER-3RD NOVEMBER

On 14th August 1942 Jock's ship docked half way up the Suez Canal at Port Tewfik. He went ashore and sent tiny photographically reduced military airgrams to my mother and to Gaffer and Ga. Every piece of mail was read by the censors and all offending passages were obliterated but my father's letters are unmarked. He was always careful not to mention anything remotely tactical. Now he said;

As you may guess from this airgram I am in a Port unspecified and am anchored ashore to stretch the legs and sample the local alcohol. Apart from that there is very little I can say without infringing the Official Secrets Act. On the whole am being looked after exceeding well.

The troops were put up in camps near Quanassin and rigorous training began with strenuous PT first thing in the mornings followed by route march practice:

Still living in comfort and getting fat on it though a little question of PT in the very early morning has been mooted and seems an imminent danger.

They learned to judge their direction using the position of the sun by day and the compass and the stars by night. The place was swarming with flies and many suffered from upset stomachs which they were the first to call gyppy tummy. Often it was dysentery. He went into Cairo where he searched fruitlessly for his friend Buster and went to a dance. He was getting lonely.

Spent a somewhat expensive evening in the local town last night, prices well up to English standards. However it was worth while once. My sweet I do miss you. Was missing you terribly last night as was sitting back watching the dance floor and sipping a glass and kept on thinking of things that I wanted to say to Wigget and of course could not.

Through my research I had become quite knowledgeable about the war. It amused me how many men were happy to talk to me about it, how much they knew and how little, as a rule, the women knew. I had been just the same, but worse, I hadn't wanted to know. Now I wanted to find out everything, to imagine it how it really was.

I worked out that it was five days after my father arrived in Egypt that Winston Churchill came out to size up the situation. He had changed the leadership in North Africa, appointing General Alexander as commander of the entire Middle Eastern Force with Lieutenant-General Montgomery, who arrived at the same time as Jock, as Commander in Chief of the 8th Army. At last he had decided to give his generals in North Africa his full and unequivocal backing. Now he was determined to drive Rommel back once and for all.

To capture the imagination of the troops Churchill squeezed his portly figure into a boiler suit and on his feet he wore evening pumps embroidered with his initials, the left shoe marked 'W' and the right marked 'C'. From his mouth hung an immense cigar. With his hand he gave the two fingered 'V for Victory' sign.

Montgomery too was a master of communication. His first priority was to raise the morale of the troops and immediately he set out to visit all the formations of his army. He too wanted to get the attention of every soldier so he too went out of his way to amuse them. Every day he wore a different hat; sometimes a beret, sometimes a wide-brimmed Australian bush hat, they were always decorated with a selection of shiny badges from the regiments serving under him.

Montgomery took his time to prepare for the battle which would turn the tide of the war. He planned every move in minute detail leaving no stone unturned. He was determined to push Rommel right back out of North Africa and he knew this would be no easy task. He had Churchill's complete confidence and he insisted that he was given the best troops and the latest weapons. He built up a force hugely superior to Rommel's in numbers and, in spite of considerable pressure, would not allow himself to be pushed into battle before he was ready. Time was on his side. He was a master of the set piece battle whereas Rommel's skill lay in pushing through a fast and unexpected attack. On the full moon of 30th-31st August Rommel's army moved forward in an attempt to catch the 8th Army unprepared, but they were expecting his attack and pushed him back. It was a huge boost to morale for the Allies. Now Rommel just held his ground. For months the two huge armies faced each other at Alamein and Rommel used the time to reinforce the minefield which lay between them on the narrow neck of desert running between the coast and the impenetrable marshy sand of the Quattara Depression to the south.

Two and a half more months were to pass before my father was given his new appointment. He had taken a cut in rank from major to captain to come out to North Africa and now he was longing to get the job done so he could get back home to my mother. Although the delay was due to Montgomery's determination to plan everything to the last detail, it was desperately frustrating for him.

My darling one, Again can think of very little to say that does not infringe the censor and his merry bunch.. I think I can go as far as to say that I am sitting around in base depot waiting for someone to be shot or otherwise get written off before I can step into his shoes. A situation which I find has its disadvantages as this is one of the most expensive spots I have ever met in my experience. Hence I go down on my little prayer mat every evening and say please God post me away from Base Depot to some unit in the desert. The Hun seems to have failed in his latest push without killing off any Battery Commanders so I shall continue to sit and shall go on doing so until a pair of dead man's shoes become vacant.

Twelve weeks had passed since he set out from England and three since he arrived in Egypt and still not one of my mother's many letters had reached him. There were all kinds of methods of sending mail but none of them seemed to work:

Still no mail...Will try another cable next time I go anywhere near the city. Try Marconi as opposed to GPO see if that is any better. My sweet I do wish you were here. Just the way that things happen that the first time since we have been married that I have practically unlimited time to spend with Wigget she is thousands of miles away.

As luck would have it my mother had now given up her job and she too had time on her hands. My father was on reduced pay, there was still no sign of a job and he began to fret:

If, as I suspect, I am being soaked a Major's tax on a Captain's pay I shall only be dragging down about ten pounds a month, most of which you will need at home...Have still got about two quid left of the money I brought from England which I am hanging on to to last till I start to draw some allowances to live on or alternatively begin to earn some money again. The latter seems to be fading further and further into the future.

He thought that his friend Buster, who had once shared his boat and helped him build the swimming pool at my grandparents house in Hawkhurst, was in Cairo. Buster had been out in North Africa for some time but now he couldn't find him anywhere and it turned out he was back in Europe. Now he experienced for himself the conditions his friend had described:

I understand now Buster's strictures on the local fly. If you try to take an after lunch siesta you either have to keep awake and swat flies or else half awake and twitch, a restless proceeding either way but one which provokes uncontrolled mirth in the onlooker. The sight of someone lying on a camp bed with apparently St Vitus' dance controlled by half a dozen determined flies is rich.

It was 20th September before a brief telegram from my mother finally got through to him. The relief he felt shows immediately in his reply:

My darling one, Thank you for the cable it is grand to hear even the odd twelve words from you. I am sorry I have been so peevish but it really it is only cos I love you so much and am just existing in hopes of a letter, have nothing much else to think of these days until I can get a job again. The airmail stuff arriving now was posted about the middle of August, Ordinary mail heaven knows, don't think I have seen any for anyone since I have been here..

He dreamed that, once the war ended, he might leave the army and set up as a farmer in Scotland or Rhodesia:

Am beginning to work out the possibility of tobacco farming in Rhodesia as a means of earning the family bread and butter after the war. What do you think of that as a suggestion? Am pumping any South African I see in these parts as to probable costs, it might just be possible...

He never got to know what she thought about it and it was I, not my mother, who went to live in Africa. Zambia, where my first husband and I lived when our two children were little, was previously Northern Rhodesia. I loved it there.

My father and mother had terrible trouble with the mail and he got more and more frustrated:

"There are two high spots of the day when there might be some mail from my darling, but usually have to look nearly a dozen times a day just in case I might have missed a letter or because the pile looks different as someone else has upset it looking for theirs. Notice the disgraceful effect of continual lack of work. Get an odd job of bottle washing every now and again for which I am very thankful and sit about reading most of the rest of the time. A demoralising existence but should not have the effect on

me that it has. There is very little I can say without worrying the censor and his minions except that I love you more than anything else in the world and shall go on doing so always and always...

In every letter he declared his undying love, and always at the end of the letter, so his feelings didn't distract him so much that he could say nothing else at all. My father so much wanted to get on, there seemed no end to his frustration:

Have reached the limits of lunacy. Was going into the local town with one Eric Harbin, a chap in the same state as myself posted from being a Battery Commander in England to unwanted dogsbody here, with two specific objects in view; to badger the paymaster on my part and to visit a particular shop on his. Half way there in the train we both discovered that we had not got the essentials of the job, I the papers I wanted to wave in the paymaster's face and he the address of the shop. Having laughed that one off we got out at the next stop and walked across to the other side only to discover that we had got out at a one eyed little halt where the trains only stopped once an hour. Having seen three whistle by leaving us standing we attacked a greasy mechanic who was messing with the signals and persuaded him to take the fuse out of one and so stop the next train, which he duly did, quite how the system started again I do not know.

Myself I am surprised how many trains were passing by on that track and an hour doesn't sound too long to wait, but anyway they arranged it otherwise. Through an ironic twist it was Eric Harbin who took over as commander of my father's battery as it fought its way up through Sicily the following summer.

In Cairo many of the troops socialised, drank too much and flirted with the ladies as they waited for the battle to begin. Alcohol was the mainstay of social life in the desert but my father, who was normally quite a drinker, was trying to keep off it in order to save money. With the baby due at Christmas he became more and more worried about his financial situation. He had no idea how little my mother and I would have to live on once he was gone.

Have been cudgelling my brain as to how to avoid spending any money on alcohol and yet not be a complete wet blanket on any party I happen to be in. Have found one solution in a species of local absinthe which costs about 10d a tot for the whole evening.

Still only the occasional telegram got through from my mother and, as the end of September approached, he began to have real regrets:

Am beginning to realise just how much of a fool I was to volunteer for this game. Still I should have been dragged out eventually if I had not which would have been rather ignominious.... I alternate between periods of intense frustration when I am convinced that the powers that be think I am quite worthless and I rage at having not a thing to do to prove anything else and periods when I go into a sort of stupor...One of these days we shall be able to chuck the army and live a rational existence.

At last, on 2nd October, he was offered a job. He didn't take it but it made him feel a little better:

Was offered an anti-tank Battery yesterday and refused the job preferring to wait for field or horse artillery. Shows I have not been thrown completely on the dust heap

In the run up to the Battle of Alamein he found himself a 'temporary messenger's job driving a staff car for about twenty hours a day going from one dump to another all round the base area'. Three months after he left England, and twelve days before the battle began, my mother's letters at last began to arrive:

I have started to get your letters to wit two postcards and an air graph written at the beginning of September. My darling it is grand to hear from you again, puts a different complexion on life altogether...Wish I could see any signs that this sort of party would not occur every generation.

My father always referred to battles and wars as 'parties' in his letters and I found that both the War Diaries and Jack's diaries do the same. I was puzzled and it took me a bit of time to realise what he was talking about. The language of war is peppered with euphemisms. In the 'party' the 'softening up' happens first and the 'mopping up' later. It is a language of concealment. Although my father uses the euphemisms current at the time he also had a way of showing that he saw the reality which lay behind it. When he said "I am sitting around in base depot waiting for someone to be shot or otherwise written off before I can step into his shoes" it was, unfortunately, the truth of his position. The reality was unthinkable yet, if they were to lead their troops into battle, army officers had to face it. The tension this created led to a black humour filled with irony and understatement for which my father was well known. He used humour to show that he recognised the horrors of war and to encourage his men not to panic and to enable them to move forward in a practical way.

As a child I often heard people refer to my father's cynical jokes and perhaps that was why I was happy to be called a cynic too when I was young. Now I would be considered cynical, no doubt, for questioning the use of the words 'party', 'softening up' or 'mopping up' to play down the realities of the battlefield; but he was clever, I think, to use humour in this way.

Three days before the battle began my father found his friend Buster who all this time had been back in England, he discovered. Simultaneously he was given another temporary job. They managed somehow to fit in one last supper together. Buster never saw his friend again and, although he was my Godfather, I don't think he ever came to see me. I guess he didn't want to be reminded of my father and of what, by then he knew, came next.

1992-1998 THE SEARCH II

23. Windlesham

As I stood in the War Cemetery at Alamein after the service in October 1992 I looked westwards across the desert and wondered about my father's last journey. I would like, I thought, to follow the route so I could try to feel for myself what it was like for him and the other soldiers of the 8th Army in 1942. But it wasn't possible. The road from Alamein led along the Mediterranean coast westwards over the Halfaya Pass into Cyrenaica, the fertile and hilly eastern end of Libya. My father crossed through Cyrenaica and on over 1000km of desert into Tripolitania, the other fertile area at the western end of Libya adjacent to Tunisia. During the five years which followed our trip to Alamein these two entries into Libya by road were firmly closed to simple tourists like me, and no planes flew in or out of the country owing to the American air embargo. But from time to time I carried on my research in England.

One bleak November morning Alec and I got up early. The night had been windy and wet but now an unusual stillness had fallen over London. At the end of our street some small ornamental pine trees each stood in its own little pool of water. The surface of each pool was scattered with pine needles and the gutters next to the pavements were brim-filled with deciduous leaves from the plane trees which lined the road. It was Sunday and the streets were empty, but as we hurried along towards the underground station the distinctive smell of dope smoke wafted towards us. Perhaps the man who appeared had been up all night. He glanced shiftily in our direction but he had nothing to fear from us. We were on a different quest.

It was Remembrance Sunday and I wanted to go to a service at the church at Chavey Down near Ascot where Ga had lived as a child and then to walk the five miles or so on to Windlesham where Gaffer's family once lived. My father had known these places as a child when he visited his two sets of grandparents there. We arrived a couple of minutes late for the service at the modest brick-built church of St. Martins at Chavey Down and took the very last two places left. Almost immediately I was fighting back my tears as the lady lay-preacher recited the verse from Laurence Binyon's poem, so familiar yet still so terrible;

They shall not grow old, as we that are left grow old.

It is always hard for me to think of my father dying at an age so much younger than my own. The lady lay preacher read out the names of the twelve young men from the small parish killed in both world wars. The second name was Ga's brother William, killed in France in WW1, and I was thrilled to find that he was still remembered in this little village after all these years.

"Now we will all say the Creed and confirm the belief which holds us all together in one Communion..."

Does it hold us together, I wondered, or does it divide us? One hundred and fifty people were shoulder to shoulder as they recited the Nicean Creed, but could I believe any of it?

"He was condemned under Pontius Pilate, crucified, dead and buried..."

That I believe. But I couldn't be sure about the rest. In the midst of that friendly and well-meaning crowd I was engulfed again by the sense of isolation so familiar to me as a child. It seemed an eternity since I had been able to believe these things they professed to know.

The service was crisp and intelligent and when it was over the preacher stood by the door and shook our hands warmly. She even found time to introduce us to the local historian who, to my amazement, knew all about Ga's family as if they had lived there yesterday.

"Your grandmother was pretty as a picture on her wedding day." she said. "I have a photograph of their wedding in 1908 in my book about Chavey Down. Your grandfather was dressed in full dress uniform with a tall hat and a double row of brass buttons down his jacket. Fourteen midshipmen from his ship formed an arch of steel with their swords and your grandparents walked underneath it. Did you see the marble plaque on the back wall behind your heads?"

We hadn't, and now we looked at the simple white plaque and read the inscription to Ga's father, brother and her nephew, Ruth's younger brother;

In memory of Sydney King George a generous donor of this parish who died on January 18th 1926 and of his son Captain William King George, killed in the great war in 1915, and of his grandson Acting Pilot Officer Geoffrey Clive King George RAF killed flying 2nd April 1936, aged 21 years.

The historian went on telling us about Ga's parents' contributions to the little church, amongst them the pews where we had been sitting and a pre-fabricated 'iron room' which had arrived on a horse-drawn cart. Ga's mother was an early suffragette, it seems. She also organised annual parties for the Sunday School children.

"She gave them a wonderful tea with strawberries and cream! She organised games and races and the winners were given silver sixpences. Once they held a tilting tournament. Two sets of horses and riders fought long and hard through several bouts until finally they both fell at once. Another year there was a brass band. One hundred and sixteen children went to that party, it was the highlight of the year for many of them. We are so sorry to have lost touch with the King George family. They did so much to help our little community. It was a terrible shock to the whole community when Mr King George died in January 1926."

Judging from my father's letters at the time his grandfather's death was sudden. He and Suzanne were staying at the Brackens that winter whilst Ga went to visit Gaffer who was stationed out in the West Indies. No illness is mentioned in the letters but suddenly Uncle Mac took the children up to Scotland where, only a few days later, they heard their grandfather had died.

I said that I was really glad I had come, that I had enjoyed the service, and I explained that unfortunately there are very few of us left.

When Ga's father Sydney King George lived here he had six children. Ga, his only daughter, came second. He had four grandsons and three grand-daughters. But two grandsons were taken to Australia after their father was killed in WW1 and the two remaining grandsons (my father and Ruth's brother) were also both killed in their twenties and none of the three George granddaughters (Suzanne, Ruth and Ruth's sister Rhona) had children. It was unlucky. So apart from some Australian second cousins (who I have never met) I am the only descendent of my generation from that family.

"And do you have any children?" asked the local historian anxiously.

"Yes two, luckily, and several grandchildren," I replied.

After the service we set out to walk to the Brackens

where Ga's family once lived. On the way we discussed the sermon. I was puzzled that its two messages seemed to contradict each other. Firstly the lay preacher told us about St. Martin; he who had split his cloak to share it with a beggar. That Sunday by chance was also the name day of St. Martin, the patron saint of the church. He was born into a military family, she said, and when he grew up he followed the family tradition and went into the army. As time went on he found it increasingly difficult to equate his Christian ideals with his profession in the army. He thought about this and became one of the first recorded conscientious objectors.

The lay preacher then went on to the subject of Remembrance Sunday. She took a text from the gospel of St.John where Jesus said at the Last Supper:

"This is my commandment, that ye love one another, as I have loved you. Greater love hath no man than this, that a man lay down his life for his friends."

The lay-preacher used this passage to stress that those who gave their lives in the service of their country were showing the greatest kind of love which could be given. The greatest sacrifice one can make for the sake of another person you love, she said, is to give up your life. She discussed the concept of sacrifice and explained that Jesus had told his disciples at the Last Supper that through the sacrifice of His life they would be saved. Apparently St John had doubted this at the time and I too found it hard to follow the reasoning.

Alec suggested that in Jesus' time, as well as folk memories of human sacrifices made to propitiate pre-Christian gods, the Romans still sacrificed animals. Three centuries later animal sacrifices were still made in Roman temples and in the arena I had seen at Lepris Magna. I thought it was about time we thought about this again.

"Sacrifice is a barbarous old idea," I said, "and by now we should have dropped it. I don't agree with the sacrifice of humans or animals and also," I went on, "the Ten Commandments say quite clearly 'Thou shalt not kill'."

I was getting back to the position I always seem to arrive at in the end.

"I think that St. Martin arrived at the right moral position when he decided to be a conscientious objector," I concluded.

We had been absorbed in our discussion and now we found we had arrived at the entrance to Ga's old house, the Brackens, on the London Road. A small lodge building at the gateway was empty so we walked boldly on up the driveway. The massive trunks of giant American redwoods blocked the light on either side of us and way above our heads their great branches were monstrous, prickly and black against the deep grey sky. When Sydney King George, his wife Pattie and their six children moved into this house in 1891 these trees must have been small. Maybe they planted them. Perhaps when my father knew them they were still quite a normal size.

The old house looked unloved and neglected. The German electronics firm using it had divided the inside into tiny offices with walls lined in wood-grain Formica. Round the back a window lintel was supported with acro-props. The old tennis courts were used as a car park and the apple trees in the orchard were loaded with unpicked fruit. We walked into the woods where as teenager Ga once hid presents for her friends to find in treasure hunts. The path led on into a dark place inside ancient rhododendrons, their inner branches knotted and knarled. We emerged into the light onto an unkempt lawn. I had seen photographs of Ga and her brothers playing croquet on that lawn. In those days it looked so trim but now it was uncut and full of weeds. To the south the grass fell down over a ha-ha and continued on through a distant field gate into the woods.

On 11th January 1926, only a week before his grandfather died, my eleven-year-old father wrote enthusiastically to his parents in the West Indies:

"I am trying to build a little house in a tree, it has got a nice sort of fork where three branches go out of the trunk at the same height so it makes a nice flat place for the bottom and the three branches make good supports for the walls and they provide twigs if you climb a little higher and if you go down there is ivy and stuff to fill up the cracks. I have made a rope ladder so it is very easy to get up and down to fetch things."

Alec and I slipped away and walked out again onto the London Road where incessant and uncaring cars rushed by. To the east the housing estates on the edges of Bracknell had pushed out to within half a mile of the old house but to the south a large swathe on our map was coloured green with darker green trees extending all the way down to Camberley. To the south-west blue flags on the map indicated golf courses. We weren't following the dotted line marked 'national trail' leading to a heritage centre, tennis centre and leisure pool as we wanted to walk the other way, down to Windlesham where Gaffer's family once lived. We had been invited to tea by my father's first cousin, Gaffer's niece Moll, who still lives in a cottage in the grounds of the old family home.

We turned right into the Swinley Road. It was not pedestrian-friendly. We passed a windowless corrugated metal building behind a high fence marked 'Danger, Keep Out' and after half a mile the road was crossed by a railway line which doubled as a fire break in the woods. We leaned over the bridge and looked back over the woodlands behind the Brackens. My father had walked down there as a boy;

"We had a fairly long walk in the morning right down at the bottom of the garden beyond the railway line and we saw a blackcock down there".

As we strained our ears for birdsong a rusty-saw noise came from the trees, craaak-craaak, and a single magpie flew out. One for sorrow. We walked on past an Industrial Park and another micro-processing firm. Now the footpath ended and the verge was littered with flimsy plastic hub covers, coloured silver to imitate chrome, which had flown off the cars which shot by.

Cutting down through a housing estate we slipped through a snicket at the end and found ourselves in a vast plantation of pines. A distant drone of traffic signalled a busy road but inside the wood we could have been the only two people in the world. We walked down a long clearing, a firebreak between the trees which extended line upon into the distance like an army. A misty purple light seeped between their trunks and only bracken grew at their feet.

This land had been wooded from ancient times. It was once the kings' hunting ground and was named Swineley Forest after the wild swine which lived there. Between the wars the Forestry Commission cut the remaining deciduous trees and planted pines. How Uncle Mac used to hate those pines for the reduction in plant and bird life they caused! But we enjoyed the peaceful surreal atmosphere as we trudged on mile after mile. At last the firebreak came to an end and we found ourselves amongst the bright green hillocks and winding tarmac driveways of a new golf course where small groups of people were intent on their game. There were always golf courses on this land, even in my father's time:

"I caddied for Uncle Mac and Uncle Jack and we went nearly right round the golf course and I carried the golf clubs nearly all the way and they began to feel very heavy before I had finished."

Then we scrambled out onto another road and made our way towards Windlesham House. Until recently this was a country lane but now its banks were cut through on either side with ostentatious new gateways. Their massive gateposts were studded with digital security buttons and on top of each a camera sat like a vulture. When dark-windowed cars approached the cast-iron gold-ornamented gates opened mysteriously in response to an inhuman signal. Set back behind short driveways stood large modern houses in a variety of applied styles: 'Mock Tudor', 'Mock American Prairie' and 'Mock Medieval Castle'. Here every man used his money to live separately in his own fortified island. What would my father have made of all this? Did he give his life so we who came after him could live like this? I am not sentimental about the old times when so many of the rich exploited the poor but we modern folk don't seem to have got things quite right either.

When we came to the flimsy willow fence around the garden of Windlesham House it had many gaps and we climbed in easily from the side of the road. Inside huge untrimmed trees towered above us, their dead branches hanging, jagged and rotting, waiting for the winter winds to dislodge them. Our feet sank into deep mounds of leaf mould as we broke our way through the undergrowth to a rough open space dotted with dozens of small oak trees which had grown from acorns over the forty-five years this land had lain neglected. Finding no sign of Windlesham House we sat down amongst the fungi springing from a rotten tree trunk to eat the picnic lunch we had brought.

We couldn't find the old house so when we had finished our sandwiches we crossed back over the road into a 20 acre stretch of common land called Admiral's Fields.

A small engraved sign by the cricket pavilion read "This Field of Remembrance is maintained by the people of Windlesham as a memorial to those who gave their lives in the two World Wars." The traces left by my father's family are so strong, and so consistent, I thought. I was glad to see groups of people with dogs walking there, their children crowding onto the slides and swings. The Admiral could have been Gaffer's elder brother Archie, who handed over the land, or his great-great uncle Admiral Edward Owen who first bought Windlesham House in 1834, or any of the Cochrane admirals.

I was interested in Edward Owen who originally bought Windlesham House in 1834 and converted it from a wayside tavern. He was born illegitimate, the son of an immensely capable and courageous naval officer and his housekeeper. Edward lost both his parents by the age of four and experienced his first sea battle at the age of six. William FitzWilliam, his younger brother and our ancestor, had an equally difficult childhood, yet both brothers fought in wooden ships throughout the Napoleonic Wars. Both became admirals and Edward was knighted.

William was an early mapmaker. He made the original hydrographic surveys of the Great Lakes of Canada, the Owen Sound and the entire coast of Africa. He was also an early fighter against the African slave trade. Only William had children and Windlesham House was passed on to his grand-daughter Cornelia, Gaffer's mother. The two seafaring families, the Owens and the Cochranes, joined when Gaffer's father, a lieutenant at the time, docked his ship at Campobello Island of the coast of Maine and won the hand of Gaffer's mother Cornelia. This island had been granted to Edward and William's father, the one they hardly knew, in 1775 and he set up a feudal colony there. I remembered the firm tick of the clock in the Morning

Room at Gaffer and Ga's house in Hawkhurst where David and I once played the pianola. Its brass plaque said that it was presented to William FitzWilliam Owen in 1837 by the people of Campobello.

We walked down a beech walk which led, way below, to a pond in a clearing in the woods. Alec had heard a story about the young wife Edward Owen had married quite late on in life. After his death she became rather paranoid, the story goes, and she thought her jewellery had been stolen and thrown into this pond. Her ghost is said to haunt the place and Alec wanted to check this out. I tried to pull him back as he approached a family walking nearby.

"Don't go upsetting the local people with those ghoulish tales," I told him.

But I couldn't stop him. The family he approached with his query looked sensible but their response surprised me:

"Oh yes," replied the mother, "there is definitely a ghost." She indicated her teenage daughter and continued, "Geraldene saw her when she was five. She rushed back to us and said she had seen a 'shouting nun' beside the pond. We couldn't see anything and told her she was making it up. But later we heard the story of the ghost of Lady Owen. We are sure that it was her."

My father was the only male descendent of the Owens to reach his generation and finally the end of the line.

"How lovely to hear from you," my father's cousin Moll had said when I rang, "I think I last saw you when you were a baby."

Now, although she was ninety-one, she welcomed us with tea and delicious scones she had made herself. Her cottage, once the laundry for Windlesham House, was neat and cosy and she was in excellent health and spirits. She only sometimes had a spot of bother with her feet, she said, and when she heard we had walked from Chavey Down she took an immediate and practical interest in the comfortable shoes we were wearing.

She explained how, after 118 years in the family, Windlesham House was sold when her father, Gaffer's elder brother Archie, died in 1952. Her mother felt she could no longer keep the place in good order. But the old house fell into the hands of a developer who left it empty while he tried for 20 years to get permission to build up to 500 houses on the land and, when unsuccessful, sold on to others with the same idea. After the house was listed arsonists burned it down. The land had recently been sold to a further developer who planned (she showed us a cutting from the local paper) to build an ostentatious palace with a copper-domed cupola. Moll didn't seem bothered by the building plans, only by the deer which came over the fence from the wild land beyond to eat the plants in her garden.

I wasn't a baby when I last met Moll. I must have been about ten when Gaffer and Ga took me to visit her and her husband who was still alive then. As a young man he had left the navy to work in Old Shanghai where his job was to keep the great rivers of China dredged and navigable. He and his first wife spent WW2 in the same Japanese prison camp as the writer J.G.Ballard but unfortunately, soon after the war ended, his wife died of cancer. He met Moll who was working as a nurse in Hong Kong at that time and they came back to live in her little house in Windlesham. When I visited as a child I was so excited by his collection of Chinese gadgets: traps to catch several mice at a time without hurting them; race-tracks used by fleas in a 'flea circus'; an opium pipe which doubled as a walking stick, and many more. I wanted to show them to

Alec but Moll had given them away to a relation.

I told Moll that I was interested in the Owens but she replied with a laugh and a toss of her head, "Oh we never took much notice of them. It was the Cochranes who interested us more!"

24. To Libya

During the five years which followed our trip to Alamein the two road borders into Libya, through Halfaya in Egypt into Cyrenaica at the eastern end of the country and at Ras Ajdir from Tunisia into Tripolitania at the western end were the only roads open into Libya. Owing to the American air embargo no planes flew in or out of Libya but there were occasional ferries into Tripoli harbour from Malta. Very few Europeans went into Libya during this time and although I often searched the shelves of our local bookshops for travel guides to Libya, I never found any until 1997 when the new Lonely Planet Guide to North Africa had a small section on the country. The guide book had details of how to find the Libyan Interests Department in the basement of the Saudi Arabian visa section in Portland Place, London.

The door was un-numbered and un-named and the paint was flaking off the front elevation like dandruff. The building was a picture of decay amongst its immaculate neighbours. In the entrance hall two uniformed guards allowed me to go on down a flight of stone stairs to the basement where I found a scuffed Formica-covered counter and, on it, a small plastic bell.

The man who emerged told me that visas were not issued for tourists to go into Libya. So nothing had changed. I turned to leave but he must have seen the disappointment on my face. He told me to wait a second and returned with a business card. As he pushed it into my hand he said, "These people might help." The card gave the name of a tour company in Marylebone Lane, only a few streets away. The tour company had two expensive archaeological tours to Libya. I stood in the dark little shop and considered the problem. I may have put my hand to my head as my father had in the middle of the parade ground in India. I was visualising a bus-load of hot and impatient archaeologists and wondering if I could ask them to wait by a piece of unmarked desert just inside the border while I wandered around to see what I could find. It didn't sound practical. But when I admitted my reason for wanting to go the receptionist went into a back room and fetched her supervisor, who silently took a compliments slip from the top of a pile and wrote on it a name and telephone number.

"You will need Lady Randell," he said.

A few days later I realised it was February 13th, the date of my father's death. When I had a peaceful moment I tried her number. The number I dialled took me straight to Avril Randell in the kitchen of her farmhouse in Norfolk. I was thrilled by what she told me.

"Getting into Libya now is really no problem," she said, "and there is nothing dangerous about it providing one observes the local courtesies such as ankle length skirts and long sleeves for the ladies!"

Although the British Legion found it impossible to get war veterans into Libya it appeared that Avril Randell had found a way. She had already taken two groups of war veterans over the Halfaya Pass from Egypt into Cyrenaica at the eastern end of Libya to visit the war cemetery in Tobruk. I explained that I wanted to go over the western border from Tunisia into Tripolitania, the eastern end of Libya (the two cultivated parts of the country are separated by 650 miles of desert) and she said that she was planning a trip into Libya over that border so she would keep in touch.

"Now I must go and feed my daughter's hamsters," she said. "Cheerio!"

Suddenly there seemed to be a glimmer of hope but I was careful not to set my heart on it in case the trip fell through. I did some more research. First I looked for the map which went with the map reference K0103 which I had from the War Diaries at the Public Records Office. The PRO had six million maps, they said, but no index. They were referenced by a WWII card index to which the original code references had been lost. The gigantic task of re-cataloguing was in progress. In WWII, as the troops moved forward, they often stuffed the old maps into their kit bags for interest's sake. If they made it home they put them into their attics and forgot about them. Many army maps from WWII were coming in only as the war veterans died. There was no central collection point. The maps could be handed in to any museum, map library or regimental club in the British Isles. A week later I discovered the map I wanted was one of only three North African maps held by the Imperial War Museum. It was encased in plastic and headed PÌSIDA. It was cracked where it had been folded, had a pale ochre water stain over one area and a collection of darker grey damp spots by the left hand margin. It had been reproduced by the Army Survey Company from an Italian map and printed in November 1942 soon after the Battle of Alamein.

I wondered who had held it in their hands on the battlefield and longed to lift its wrapper to touch it as if that could bring me closer to its past, but the librarian must have sensed this as he hardly took his eyes off me. He insisted on my using yet another layer of separating talc and a soft lead pencil before he would let me do a tracing of the area around the Libyan/Tunisian border. I could hardly see through all the layers to do my drawing. A note at the base of the map explained that 'K' indicated the general area, '01' was the distance eastwards from the relevant grid line and '03' the distance northwards. With this I found K0103. It was about 2km from the Tunisian/Libyan border at Ras Ajdir.

I wanted to try to visualise the place where my father was killed. I wondered if it had been cultivated or built over in fifty-five intervening years. I tried to find someone who was crossing into Libya on that border road from Tunisia through Ras Ajdir who might have a look for me. Twice I found a Libyan who was going that way and gave them a copy of my little traced map, but neither man got back to me. I was thrilled when Avril rang to say that she herself was going along that route on her way to Tripoli and that she would look for me, but at the last minute her plans were altered and she made the journey to Tripoli by sea from Malta.

In the spring of 1998, Avril rang again to say she hoped to go that way again later on that year. She was planning to lead a trip into Libya this way in 1999 and this was a recce for that trip. I saw an opportunity and made a cheeky suggestion.

"Can I come with you on the 'recce'?" I asked.

"Yes. I expect so," she replied. "Why not?"

I told my mother I might be going to Libya. Immediately she sent me a bundle of fifty letters my father had written to her from North Africa. It was unlike her to be so open with her personal letters and I was touched.

I rang the Commomwealth War Graves Commission. Again they told me their records showed that my father had no known grave and that his death was recorded on the 31st column of the War Memorial at Alamein. Now I thought I would press them a little further. I wrote them a letter enclosing Melia's sketch of his grave, the details from the War diaries with the map reference and a photocopy of part of the map from the War Museum. I told them I was going to go to Libya to look for myself and asked them if they could possibly do a little more research before I left.

I went to a camping shop and bought a special compass adjusted for North Africa, but resisted the new fangled Global Positioning device for £100. I bought myself a modern nautical map of the coast at Ras Ajdir from Stanfords the map shop in Covent Garden and asked a retired sea captain if he could do me some compass readings from the landmarks used for ship's sightings, one of a white tower, another of an oil refinery and various oil derricks out to sea.

I was still unsure if the trip would really happen but when Avril suggested I apply for a visa it seemed I might be in luck, but I was baffled by the very first question on the green visa application card which came through the post. It asked if I had ever been to Jamahiraya. In a lifetime of travelling I have been to many strange places. I couldn't remember Jamahiraya, but it was hard to be sure and I hoped I didn't have some stamp on my passport incompatible with entry into Libya. But when I rang Avril she corrected my pronunciation and told me that 'a Jamahiraya' is a cross between a democracy and a republic. In this case it meant Libya, she said, and I had started at page three. I turned the card this way and that until I twigged that as Arabic is written from right to left the visa card was designed to fold the other way. The 'back' page was the front. There I found the Arabic heading with an English translation in capital letters. THE GREAT SOCIALIST PEOPLE'S LIBYAN ARAB JAMAHIRIYA.

The trip went ahead. The day before I left I bumped into a journalist friend and told him I was going to Libya to look at the place where the 8th Army passed and to see if I could find my father's grave.

"How do you feel about it now you're actually going to go?" he asked.

As a child I was taught to keep my emotions strictly under control, even to deny them. This is a facility I still possess. But at times in my life the stronger emotions have broken through - love, for instance, and now grief. As an adult I have learned to respect and follow these feelings. The tremendous, and to me totally unexpected, love I felt for my two children when they were first born, and for Alec as soon as I met him, are emotions which I have allowed to form my priorities and to guide my life. Now I was allowing the outburst of grief I felt when I first saw the sketch of my father's little grave under the camelthorn bush in the desert to lead me on this quest.

But I am a practical person and I knew it was unlikely I would find the place where my father was buried still untouched after half a century. On this occasion I was calling up my childhood skills of control. I wanted to get closer to that place to help me come to terms with what had happened yet I didn't want to raise my hopes only to have them dashed later.

I met Avril for the first time at the Tunisair check-in desk at Heathrow Airport. I found a neat, petite and immaculate lady. Her trouser suit, socks, shoes, hair and straw hat were all matching in pale cream and her hat was topped with a cluster of red poppies. I pushed my scruffy ruck-sack in at the check-in desk and wondered how we would get on in our week together.

Ten years after Alec and I first flew in to Tunisia Avril and I made the same journey from London Heathrow to the Island of Djerba. There we were met by Fatma, a pretty plump Libyan lady who gave Avril an effusive welcome and me a big smile. She wasn't shrouded in robes like most Arab women but dressed in a tightly-fitting western-style bright blue shoulder-padded trouser suit. Her bangled wrists glistened. She was co-director of a Libyan travel firm in Benghazi, she explained, and she was to be our personal guide. She directed us to a big shiny black chauffeur-driven Mazda. We shook hands with the chauffeur, who was dressed in robes, and Avril whispered in my ear,

"He's the secret policeman."

They whisked us off to a comfortable hotel where the following morning the shower water was hot and breakfast was served with good coffee. This is stylish, I thought, as we climbed into the Mazda and the chauffeur drove off at breakneck speed.

In 1998 the air embargo on Libya was still in place and there were only two entrance points into the country, by its road border with Egypt at the Halfaya Pass into Cyrenaica in the east and the other from Tunisia through border at Ras Ajdir into Tripolitania in the west. Since Alec and I came this way in our tinny hire car ten years earlier the road from Djerba to Ras Ajdir had been widened and resurfaced with money given by the Libyan government. Now we flashed through Zarzis and Ben Ghadames and past the area where we looked at the wrecked tanks. The tanks had been tidied away and the piles of rubbish by the road had gone too. There were roundabouts with shiny abstract stainless steel sculptures and tourist markets selling brightly glazed pottery. As we approached the frontier young men jumped into the road in front of our car shaking bundles of Libyan bank notes they were selling at black market prices. Stalls beside the road were selling plastic bottles full of Libyan petrol. Then we were going through the five police posts which led up to the border.

The frontier was busy with Tunisians who were

pushing their battered old cars across into Libya. They took them only as far as the nearest petrol station where they filled up and drove back to Tunisia to siphon it out and repeat the process. Petrol is cheaper than water in Libya but you are only allowed to export it in the tank of your car. The border police seemed intrigued that we were English. England had just beaten Tunisia 2-1 in the World Cup so in jest they threatened to cut our throats. The black shack where they threw the passports over the heads of the waiting crowd had vanished and the new Tunisian frontier building was smart and built in concrete. The cars were divided into two queues, Tunisian and Libyan. The Libyan cars, like ours, were big, smart and shiny and kept their engines running. The Tunisian cars were old and battered. Their engines were turned off as they were engaged in the petrol-fetching game.

I tried to lift my mind above the hum and bother of modern life. I was wondering how you know precisely where a border lies if you want to make a measurement. I leaned over to look at the kilometre counter behind the driver's wheel. I jotted down the mileage but it didn't seem to have the tenths of a kilometre marked.

We all had to get out so our faces could be compared feature by feature with our passport photographs and we drove into a shed so the customs officers could inspect our baggage. This might have added 100 yards to the measurements, I reckoned. Then there was one more barrier across the road and we were away. Already two kilometres were added since I first read the milometer. I was thrilled to find there were no buildings to the south of the road, in fact the land looked uncannily similar to Melia's sketch, which was in my ruck-sack in the boot of the car.

The landscape flashed by and I was trying to think

clearly. How far should we drive before stopping? Melia gave the measurement to the grave as 'approximately three kilometres from the border'. The War Diaries said '200 yds to the east of kilo 2'. There were no sign of any kilo markers next to the road and I was wondering which measurements I should use. Both were contemporary with my father's death. Judging from his letter and handwriting Melia was a careful and caring man and as it was he who did the sketch I knew he went to the grave himself. Perry recorded the information from a third person who made the measurement, but it was the official measurement and Melia said that his was approximate.

The register clicked over. Three kilometres were added to my original figure. I asked the driver to stop and he did so immediately. I was relieved to find there were no buildings or even fields to the south of the road, just scrubby desert extending out to where, in the distance, the iridescent pale turquoise of a salt marsh shone in the sun.

Avril, Fatma and I got out of the car and stood blinking in the light. Now I needed to walk to the south - but how far should I go? Melia, who wrote the letter to my mother and did the sketch of my father's grave, said the grave was about 300 yds south of the main coast road; the regimental war diaries gave the measurement as 200 yds. south of the road. In addition Alec had made me promise faithfully that I wouldn't leave the well trodden tracks as the land might still be mined. He didn't want to lose me the same way that I had lost my father.

Close to where we stopped there was a sandy track leading southwards towards the salt marsh. So I paced southwards down it with what I hoped were yard-long strides and after 320 steps another track crossed, running east/west parallel to the road. Avril and Fatma caught up with me at the junction of the tracks. Avril handed me a tiny wooden cross with a red poppy on it. So this is the form, I thought. I felt I was probably too far to the east so I turned and walked back towards the frontier along the track parallel to the road.

I walked alone. There were no buildings and the land was not cultivated. In fact it looked eerily similar to that in Melia's sketch. After a couple of hundred yards I stopped and looked around. The sandy landscape lay flat, empty and silent. To the south electricity pylons marched westwards parallel with the coast road and with my track. Beyond them the salt marsh glinted in the distance. So it was here that it happened. It felt good to be here. It was not elation that I felt but the quietness of centring as if the clay in my hands had lost its wobble. How odd that I have always loved these treeless desert places All my life I have sought them out. It is the wide, dry, open, lonely places which pull me.

I would have liked to stay longer, to wander around for the rest of the day and get to know the place and to let its atmosphere seep right into me through my skin, but I was conscious that Avril, Fatma and the chauffeur were all waiting and I didn't want to test their patience. There was only one large camelthorn bush in the area just a few yards to the north of the track so that one, I thought, could stand in for the bush where my father was buried all those years ago. I only needed to walk a little way off the track to get to it, so I hoped I wouldn't get blown up. I planted my wooden poppy cross near it and although I am a heathen I said a prayer for my dead father.

Now I thought I would test the position on the nautical map with the compass to see if I was anywhere near K0103. To the east I could see the oil refinery at Bu Kammash. It had three tiny white towers on the distant horizon. I could see the oil derrick out to sea but I couldn't see Rass Taguerness, Rass el Ketef or Marsa al Birayqah for which I also had the co-ordinates. I raised the compass to eye level and squinted along it at the Bu Kammash oil refinery as the man in the camping shop had taught me, but the bearings were way out. I repeated it for the oil derrick with the same result. To make the readings correct I would have to be at least a mile further south, down by the salt marsh, but that would never be two to three hundred yards south of the road. Something seemed to be wrong with the compass bearings. I couldn't understand it.

So I hurried back to re-join Avril and Fatma. When I reached them Avril handed me two little plastic packets of desert sand she had filled from the place. I liked the idea. I decided I would give one packet of soil to my mother and keep the other for myself. We drove on a few miles to the next little settlement on the road. It wasn't the village in the background of Melia's sketch; there were only some modern factory buildings in that position, but Fatma seemed to have an idea. She wanted to talk to the people in the village to see if they had seen my father's grave. She asked the chauffeur to stop the car and we walked along a dirt road into the village. Barefoot children ran up to us. As far as they were concerned we might have arrived from the moon with Fatma in her bright blue trouser suit and rattly bracelets, and Avril all cream-coloured in her poppy hat. The children led us to three old men who seemed to have all the time in the world to talk to us. Fatma began to ask them questions and told me their replies. They didn't remember the grave, they said, but they remembered when the English came by. The Italians came through first and the English came along behind and chased them out. They liked the English because they chased out the Italians. I am glad we are in favour, I thought, whatever the reason. And I was interested in Fatma's method. It was sensible to talk to these people who live nearby to see what they remembered from the war.

In Libya it is only the old men who know about WWII. They know what they remember. In Libyan schools history begins in 1969 when Gadafi seized power, so younger Libyans know nothing about history before that time, except about Abdul Muktar, a Libyan revolutionary hero who, with a small group of men on horseback, stood up to a huge force of Italians with tanks.

A crowd had gathered around us. The three old men wore long robes under beautiful ancient embroidered waistcoats, tatty with wear. On their heads they wore small white embroidered cotton hats. One had bare feet. Fatma asked them about Pisida, but they were puzzled. This is Bu Kammash, they said, we don't know Pisida. Perhaps Pisida was an Italian name, they suggested. They told us that the mines were cleared from that bit of land by the border in the 1980s. Should we believe them?

When we climbed back into the car Avril handed me a cardboard roll. She had told a war veteran who came on her trip to Tobruk about my quest and he gave her something to give to me. I looked inside and there was a map. The heading said Pisida. Avril's 8th Army friend had stuffed it into his rucksack when he passed through and brought it back to England. When I looked at it I realised it was identical to the carefully preserved map I had seen in the Imperial War Museum. Comparing this old plan with my new nautical map, I could see that the old men were right and that Bu Kammash was the new Arabic name for Pisida.

This was my lucky day.

TO LIBYA

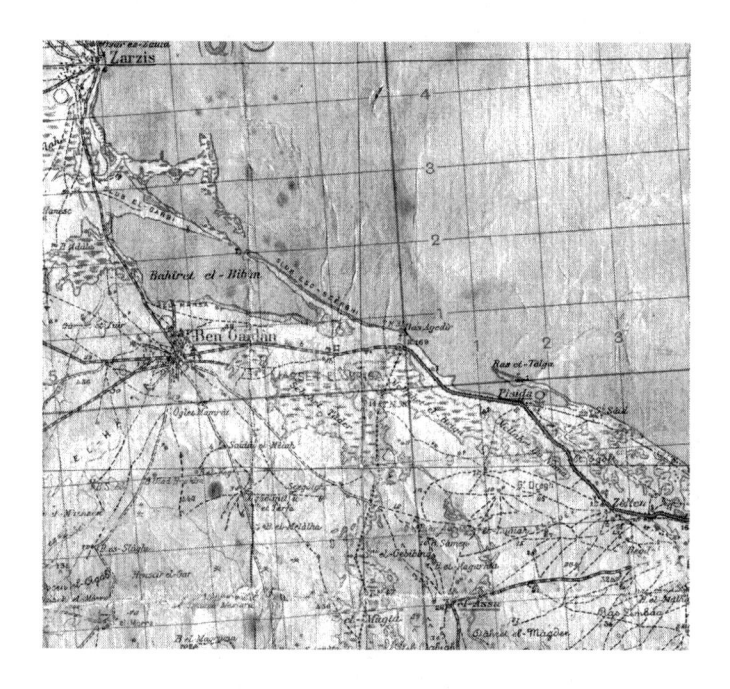

25. The Only Tourists in Libya

For Avril this trip was a recce to plan a tour she intended to make the following year in 1999. Previously she had made two trips with war veterans over the eastern border from Egypt into Cyrenaica and down as far as Tobruk to visit the battlegrounds and war cemeteries there. The trip she was planning would come over the western border into Tripolitania to visit the WWll war cemetery outside Tripoli and the battleground of the Battle of the Hills to the east of Tripoli. She wondered what else there might be of interest in Tripolitania and she hadn't yet made up her mind whether she should try to take the veterans across the desert as far as Benghazi at the western end of Cyrenaica. We might try that out and see, she said.

I think that Avril and I were the only tourists in Libya at that time. Certainly we saw no others. We had crossed into a secret country. Everywhere we went we were treated as honoured guests. We had gifts showered upon us. We were offered more, and larger, meals than we could possibly eat in huge empty restaurants. Piles of food were displayed on tables curtained with ruched bows and draperies in dark red satin. We were served by countless waiters, three or four to each of us. We were quite separate from the ordinary people and they, in turn, took little interest in us. There was none of the tourist-hassle, the haggling or begging which is standard in Tunisia or in Egypt and the people looked well-off. Much of the oil wealth had been shared and schooling and health care were universal and free. A huge pipeline was under construction to bring water from an oasis way down in the desert to supply the coastal towns of Tripoli and Benghazi.

Nothing had prepared me for the extraordinary wealth of the Roman ruins we found in Tripolitania. After Libya came under Italian control in 1914 the Italians wanted to display the glory, culture and wealth of the Roman Empire. With this in mind they ordered the excavation of whole cities in North Africa which had been buried for thousands of years beneath the sand. With the defeat of Italy during WWII this effort was abandoned and, only now that American sanctions had started to bite, Colonel Gaddafi, the Libyan leader, had begun to wonder if a limited amount of tourism might be beneficial to the country. It is possible that Avril and I were the initial guinea-pigs for that idea. To interest the tourists Gaddafi was looking again at his Greek and Roman ruins.

When we walked down into the ancient city of Sabratha so much of it was still there. It seemed that the Phoenicians, Greeks and Romans had just slipped out for a cup of coffee from which they might return at any time. Their ghosts were all around us. The thought crossed my mind that the living on this earth are greatly outnumbered by the dead. Our guide looked like a Roman himself as the warm soft wind from the sea caught up the folds of his long white robes.

The theatre had curving stone seats for 5000 but we were the only people there. Three tiers of galleries formed a backdrop to the stage, which had been recently boarded for modern performances. The seating was steeply angled so that a whisper from the stage would carry by direct sound to every seat. Beyond the stage the blue Mediterranean lay calm and clear. It glistened between the Corinthian columns carved from grey-green streaked marble and through the perfectly formed semicircular arches at the back of the stage. At the side of the stage, where stairs led down into the orchestra pit, a notice was legibly carved in Latin on a tall stone tablet. It gave the name of the Roman patron who commissioned the theatre and the date of his donation, just as nowadays we are told of modern business sponsors for art exhibitions and even the weather news on the TV. It was its crispness which was striking. The letters could have been cut out yesterday except that now you would never find a stone carver to produce such immaculate work. Their original quality had been preserved as, after the towns were abandoned following the terrible earthquake in AD 365 the desert sand blew right over them. Sabratha and Leptis lay beneath the sand for over a thousand years before the Italians came to dig them out.

Leptis Magna was founded three centuries earlier than Sabratha in the 7th century BC. As we walked down the ceremonial steps into the city the stone-paved central street stretched long and straight ahead of us into the far distance where, through the triumphal arch of Septimus Severus, we saw its two sides join at the point of the perspective. At intervals the street was intersected by others at right angles. The city was built to a grid-iron plan, on which the plans of so many modern cities, including New York, are based. Septimus Severus was a local boy who, in the 3rd Century AD., became Emperor of the whole Roman Empire. He commissioned magnificent buildings in his home town of Leptis but died on a visit to York, we were told, of a cold. In the first centuries of the millennium this city stood at the centre of the known world. Its harbours joined the Roman Empire with trade routes stretching southwards across the Sahara through the trading post of Timbuktu to collect the riches of sub-Saharan Africa. Grain, olives and citrus trees to feed Leptis grew on the fertile fields of the surrounding plain and the terraced hills to the west of the city.

We joked as we sat on the Romans' communal

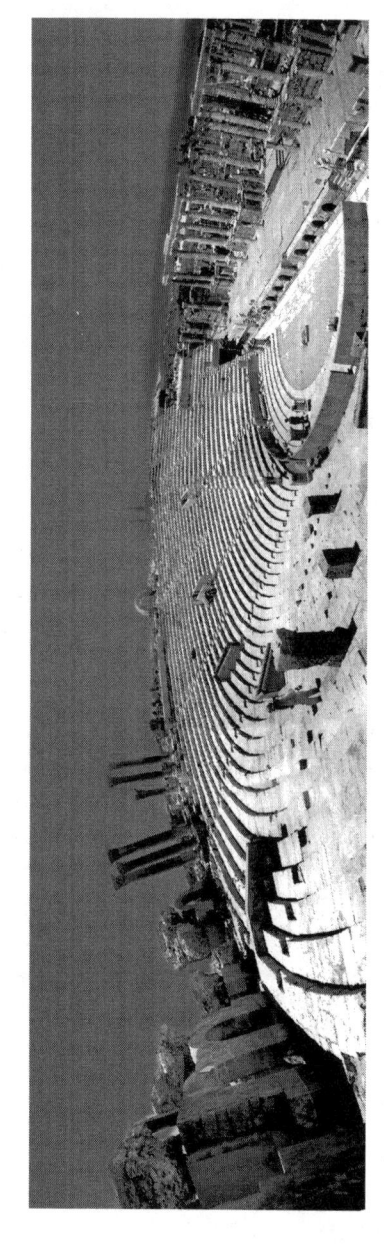

Avril in the theatre at Leptis Magna

loos, and sized up their hot and cold plunge baths, steam baths and swimming pool. Leptis lay at the foot of a wadi, a fresh-water gully where the winter rain ran down to the sea. From there fresh water for the city was taken by aqueduct to a series of reservoirs and cisterns to supply the fountains and baths of the city all the year round. The overflow went out into the neatly delineated harbour which now, like the boating lake at my grandparents' old house in Hawkhurst, lay silted. We looked at the remains of a lighthouse on one side and of customs houses on the other. Wherever Avril walked our 'chauffeur' followed her as closely as her own shadow, but luckily he wasn't concerned about me. We walked along by the beach beside the ruined tracks of the Italian archaeologists' railway. To our right the waves of the empty blue Mediterranean broke over three gigantic and intricately carved Corinthian capitals lying amongst the rocks on the shore. To the west the bay curved out with the modern city of Al Khoms in silhouette. My father drove through Homs, as it was called then, only three weeks before his death on the afternoon of 20th January 1943. He was on his way to fight in the Battle of the Hills. He was given a Military Cross for what he did that night.

    The custodian at the Leptis site museum came with us as we looked around. He lifted the lids of the Roman carved stone and alabaster funeral urns and showed us how they still contained the original human bones. A row of lidded Roman glass urns, each about one foot high, stood empty but perfectly preserved without a chip between them. The custodian explained that the stone bodies of the memorial statues which the Romans made of their important citizens were made in advance, with every detail of their clothes realistically carved to show their position in society. Detailed pieces, the arms and private parts, were carved separately and fixed on later with bronze rods. Only after the man died (and all the statues were of men) a stone head was carved from the death mask and mounted in a hole on the neck of the statue.

I found a model of a huge stadium. "What is this?" I asked. Fatma had no idea but our 'chauffeur' knew and he said he would take us there. He spoke five languages, I had discovered, including Greek. No ordinary chauffeur. He was a charming man even if he was from the secret police. To get to the stadium he drove off the road, and up a track, and through fields of skinny sheep and along where the bottom of our car hit the ground until he stopped by a small thicket of trees. Three men lounged in a hut but they took no notice of us.

I hurried out in front of the others between the trees and as I came into the open a gigantic hollow extended below my feet. I had arrived at the top storey of a colossal Roman circus and was looking down over circular stone seats built for 16,000 people. As I walked down and down the small stone steps carved in beside the seating, the roars and cheers which once echoed round this strange inward-looking space were sounding in my head. I went down to the place where once those sentenced by the magistrates to damnatio ad bestias were tortured and mauled by wild beasts before the gladiators finished them off. It was here that men slaughtered antelope, wild ass, wild boar and enraged bulls, here that they arranged for pairs of chained bears and bulls to fight each other and that gladiatorial duels were fought. The others didn't like the feel of it, they said, and they stayed up at the top. After all these centuries they could all feel the atmosphere of this place where, so long ago, so many young lives were lost.

From the base of the amphitheatre four huge arches led to where pitch black circular tunnels encircled the arena below the seats. One led out into the daylight and through a massive standing arch towards a hippodrome by the sea shore. A WWII concrete bunker clung to the top of the wall. So they did come here. The whole stadium had been buried but now the sand inside it had been dug out. If this desert sand could quickly blow up and bury the

largest structures on earth and preserve them perfectly for hundreds of years, how easily it could blow over a small human grave and bury it for ever.

Outside Tripoli we visited the Allied War Cemetery. If my father's body had been moved from Pisida this is the place where it would have been reburied. The War Cemetery lay behind the Italian civilian cemetery. We walked in through its crumbling stuccoed entrance. When I looked around me I feared the worst. Holes gaped in the ground where table tombs were smashed and the bones of the unpopular Italians scattered. Catacombs stood empty. Broken stones, glass and human bones lay around all over the place amongst parched and straggly grass. Just a few tombs remained untouched with the name of the dead Italian carved neatly and their photographs still behind glass in ornate oval frames. Had these few performed some special service to the Libyans in life? Or was it just by chance that they had been left to rest in peace?

Then we passed through a second gateway into a different world where neat rows of white stones stood upright amongst bright green grass, spiky as a punk haircut. In the distance a gardener was standing, the water arching from his hose. This was the Allied War Cemetery. In spite of the embargo the Commonwealth War Graves Commission had continued to provide money for the upkeep, which was immaculately done. It was a peaceful place with mature trees and a central war memorial.

Avril had a list of names to find and as we walked up and down the rows we found them all. We stuck poppy crosses by the stones and took a photograph of each for their relatives back home. I would have been pleased to find my father in this place so I searched around in the most likely places. I found the graves of others killed that day, the day before and the day after.

But not my father.

26. To Benghazi and Back

Avril decided to drive over the thousand kilometres of desert separating Tripolitania from Cyrenaica. We set out early from Tripoli and after Zliten and Misrata, the last towns in Tripolitania, the palm trees ended and the two-lane tarmac road stretched out for miles in front of us. Here the desert had reclaimed the land right up to the coast. Hour after hour we hammered along accompanied by an incessant bleat-bleat-bleat, a signal that we were exceeding the 150 km. per hour speed limit. The wandering camels had no road sense. They swung their legs rhythmically forward and sometimes moved sedately out in front of our driver who slammed on the brakes and several times missed them by a whisker. The only other traffic on the road were oil tankers and once a convoy of a dozen low loaders each carrying a long section of concrete pipe 10' in diameter for building Gadafi's ambitious Man Made River, designed to bring water from an oasis way out in the Sahara to the coastal towns of Libya. Regular camel carcasses beside the road told their own tale. Fatma had only one cassette tape of a vapid pop song which she played over and over to cover the bleating speed signal:

You should have seen the look in my eyes, baby, I just want to keep on loving yoooooooooooo After all that we've been through I will make it up to you I promise yoooooooooooo...

In the back of the car I began to feel car-sick. The dried-up wadis were bridged by treacherous single track wooden bridges covered in shingle and on either side the road was potholed where the winter floodwater had overflowed. We skidded to a halt before each bridge. Battles were fought by the 8th army at these wadis. We crept forward over Wadi Zem Zem and the wadis Ouesca, Chebir and Tamet. Then we were off again, hammering on eastwards towards Benghazi stopping only for the occasional police post, meandering camel or large pothole. We crept gingerly across the wooden bridge at Wadi Matratin and flashed past the place seven miles to the west of El Agheila where my father was camped when I was born on 31st December 1942. To the south of the road there were pylons now to take electricity from one end of the country to the other, but beyond them the crusty surface of the desert stretched unchanged and infinitely onwards. Only clumps of dry camelthorn grew here, their shadows tucked tightly below them. Groups of skinny camels meandered between the spiky bushes. Late that evening we arrived in Benghazi. We were exhausted after driving all day but we were given a huge supper and shown to a bedroom on the 17th storey of a modern hotel overlooking Benghazi harbour.

  The war had extended into North Africa in September 1940 when the Italians began to pour troops into their colonies in Libya and Ethiopia. Mussolini wanted to enlarge and consolidate his empire by conquering Egypt, thus gaining control of the Suez Canal and access to the oil fields of the Middle East. The British Western Desert Force under Wavell were badly outnumbered, but they made valiant attempts to resist their advance. Several times the Allied troops took Tobruk and several times it was retaken by the Germans and Italians. Once the Allies crossed across the desert and almost reached Tripoli but again they were pushed back.

  Only in 1942 Churchill decided the Germans must be pushed out of North Africa once and for all and built up a huge army at Alamein under General Alexander and Montgomery to make sure of success. After the allied

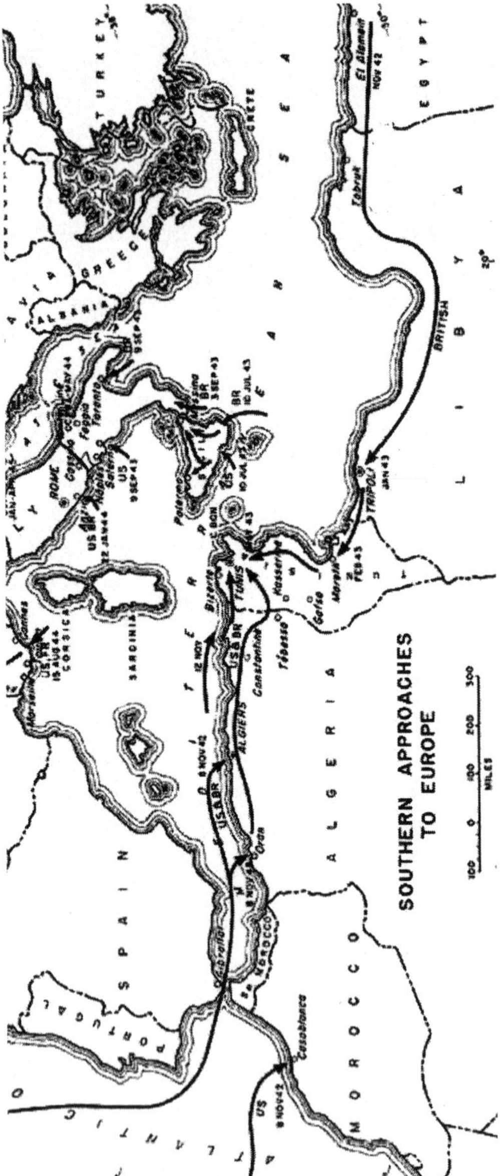
SOUTHERN APPROACHES
TO EUROPE
MILES
SPAIN
PORTUGAL
MOROCCO
ALGERIA
LIBYA
EGYPT
TURKEY
GREECE
ALBANIA
CORSICA
SARDINIA
CRETE
Casablanca
Oran
Algiers
Constantine
Bizerte
Tunis
Kasserine
Gafsa
Tébessa
Mareth
Tripoli
Tobruk
El Alamein
Palermo
Salerno
Naples
Rome
Taranto
Foggia
BRITISH

victory at the Battle of Alamein in November 1942 the defeated German Afrika Korps and their Italian allies under Rommel retreated across this desert land. The British 8th Army under Montgomery followed in hot pursuit. At the same time the British 1st Army and the Americans landed in Morocco. The aim, which succeeded, was to catch the entire Axis army between British 8th and 1st Armies 'like a rat in a trap' in Montgomery's words.

In the winter of 1942 the British 8th Army, my father with them, spread themselves out southwards from the coast road over the desert to try to avoid mines and attacks from the air. The wadis were boggy from the winter rain and the military transport stuck repeatedly in glutinous soft sand. Petrol was in very short supply. My father had heard someone on the radio describe the land as 'hummocky, bumpy poached-egg country'. He explained to my mother in one of the letters she had lent me:

The hummocks are clumps of camelthorn, a little bush about a foot high and olive green or olive brown, which burns with a very intense though short lived flame. A great cause of exasperation to cooks as with great labour they collect a large pile with intent to cook a meal and find that the whole pile goes in about two minutes having also, unless in skilled hands, burnt the pan and left the dinner uncooked. However since the dinner almost invariably comes out of a bully beef tin that is of no very great moment.

Convoys coming across the desert make rather a remarkable sight with the whole landscape covered with vehicles as far as the eye can see in any given direction, each with its little plume of grey dust coming up behind till the bulk of the area is shrouded in a sort of Scots mist. Stopping in the late afternoon when little pin points of fires spring up all over the place as a mug of tea is brewed and the tin openers are plied, the place bedding down except for guards almost immediately as there is nothing else to do and no light to do anything by.

Supplying the armies over these distances was a logistical nightmare and the length of the supply lines was critical. The farther each army advanced the more extended their supply lines became. Food, water, fuel and ammunition all had to be brought over enormous distances. It was critical to both sides to take and keep the supply ports of Alexandria in Egypt, Tobruk and Benghazi in Cyrenaica after which there was no good harbour until that of Tripoli in Tripolitania.

The Germans had superior guns and tanks. They also had tank transporters which was a crucial advantage over the long distances and wide open spaces of the desert. The Allied Air Force was superior and this was to prove decisive in the desert where ground cover was minimal. The shortage of fuel and water was always a problem. The few water wells were often contaminated by oil, or by dead animals, and both sides blamed the other for this.

After a trip to find a battlefield from Wavell's time way out in the desert at a place called Beda Fomm, Avril and I turned round and set off back across the desert to Tripolitania. We left Fatma in Benghazi and travelled with our same chauffeur and a young Libyan called Tayseer who had lived in America as a child and spoke perfect English.

We dashed back along the coast road in the June sunshine stopping only at the occasional police post. These were normally red and white striped corrugated iron huts with searchlights mounted on their roofs. They flew the plain green Libyan flag. Armed policemen looked at our papers time and time again before they lifted their barrier, usually a long pine trunk like an old-fashioned telegraph pole, weighted on the short end and hinged from a concrete-filled oil drum. Once we stopped when one of our tires shredded, but a man at a tin shack by the road changed it for us in minutes. Once there was such a strong smell of burning rubber in the car that it began to bother even our chauffeur. Often we stopped when camels, donkeys or goats wandered onto the road in front of us. We flashed past my father's camping place outside El Agheila and rattled over the wadi bridges. We had as much bottled spring water as we wanted to drink. My father wasn't so lucky:

> *Getting up about an hour before dawn does not feel too bad till an icy little wind springs up just as the first lightening of the sky happens. Usually tries to cut my face off just as I am finishing shaving, teeth cleaning and washing in half a cupful of cold water. I bless my cut-throat razors on those occasions as they seem to manage to make short work of the whiskers no matter how unprepossessing the circumstances.*
>
> *Shall remember the desert for odd things always: Lying in a cocoon of ground sheet and gas cape while the rain pelts onto the ground sheet, wondering how long one can go on waiting for a pause before making the first movement to get up, which lets in a flood of water from above and below. Temporary discomfort made up by the water to be collected from the tops of trucks and other odd places.*

That afternoon the air-conditioning system on our car packed up and it began to heat up. Finally after 1000km the countryside became more rolling and when we came to the ridge where the pure desert ends we stopped and looked down into Tripolitania, towards Misurata, Garibaldi and Zliten. In the last of the light we drove through the choppy landscape where my father fought the Battle of the Hills and there, near the modern city of Al Khoms, we stopped for a minute at a roadside stall and bought the sweetest honey I have ever tasted, collected from wild bees. It was already dark when the hydraulic brakes on the Mazda packed in but the 'chauffeur' drove on, braking on the clutch. We reached Tripoli that evening before the restaurant closed at our hotel. Our 1030 km. journey from Benghazi to Tripoli had taken only eleven hours. My father and the 8th Army took more than eleven weeks to complete that journey.

To find Wavell's old battlefield we had asked an old Bedouin to come with us in a long journey out into the desert. Inspired by this and by the way Fatma had asked the old men at Bu Kammash (as Pisida is now called) I made a list of questions I wanted to ask there at the way back. There we drove off the tarmac onto the dirt road amongst the mud houses of the old quarter. A different group of old men appeared immediately. They were all dressed in cotton robes and tatty embroidered waistcoats like the first ones we had met. Some were barefoot. I had made a list of questions and our new guide Tayseer asked them, and translated the answers for me.

"Is the border in precisely the same place as it was in 1943?"

"Yes."

"I have heard that there were two roads running towards the border in 1943, the present coast road and one running parallel to the south of it which is still there as a track. Is this right?"

"Yes. The track to the south was built by the Italians in 1927 to take a railway. The railway was never built that far at the time but it should be built in a few years time. Then the railway will run all the way from Cairo to Tunis." It seemed a good idea in terms of transport, but I hoped the new railway wouldn't pass right over my father's grave.

"Are the coast road and the track to the south of it in the same positions now as they were in 1943?"

"Yes."

"Has the area within 3km. of the border on this side been completely cleared of mines?"

"No, but the mines are ineffective now." I was not reassured by this reply. It was not what we had been told a week earlier. Besides when WWII mines are occasionally still found in England the whole area is evacuated. After years buried in our damp soil they still explode.

"Do people walk over the entire area now?"

"Yes. Animals were hurt in the 1940s and 1950s but none since."

"Do you think it is safe to walk over this land right up to the border and southwards from the road right up to the salt lake?"

The men were beginning to fidget. Why should they be made to feel responsible if some silly tourist wants to blow herself up on a mine? After a pause one of them said,

"It is always best to take someone with you who really knows the land. You should talk to Mr Ramadam-el-Assy. He is old now but he has been a shepherd here since he was a boy. You will find him at his house at Ras Ajdir."

We thanked the old men and left the village. I looked out of the car window as we drove past the place where I had planted my poppy cross by the old camelthorn bush. It was odd how that place looked exactly like Melia's sketch while on either side the landscape was different. We had to pass through the first frontier barrier to get into the border village of Ras Ajdir where we found Mr. Ramadam-el-Assy's house quite easily. It was modern and looked well organised. We spoke to his son but Mr Ramadam was out. I left him a photocopy of Melia's sketch to see if his father remembered it and our new guide Tayseer promised he would drop in on his way back across the frontier and see if he could talk to the old man. He gave me his phone number in Benghazi so I could ring from England to check the result. I tried many times but I never managed to reach him again.

Now we had crossed that first frontier post the police wouldn't let us go back to have another look at that patch of land where my father was buried. We were right into the customs sheds with all the performance that went with that. Before I knew it we were back in Tunisia and the money touts were jumping in front of the car and waving Tunisian notes at us. The black market was flourishing right in front of the police station, but nobody seemed to be bothered. I said I was sad to leave Libya and Avril agreed;

"Me too," she said. "The men are more handsome there!"

It wasn't exactly my first concern. I had discovered the land where my father was buried still quite untouched and I knew I must come back with Avril the following year to take a more careful look at it.

When I got home from my first trip to Libya there was a letter waiting for me from Liam Hanna the Director of Information at the Commonwealth War Graves Commission. He apologised for the delay in replying and said:

According to our records graves in the vicinity of Pisida, up to the border with Tunisia, were concentrated into the Tripoli War Cemetery after the war. We have no record of recoveries at the map reference given (K0103). However we do have a record of two graves very close to this spot (at K0204) which were not recovered, having been washed away during the rainy season in 1944. It seems possible that your father's grave may also have been lost in this way.

I looked at my map of Pisida. K0204 fell to the north of the coast road. My father was killed to the south. The two points were about a kilometre apart.

Then I took my photographs to be developed. I

pieced together my photographs of Sabratha and Leptis Magna to make panoramic views of the Roman theatres and the circus. They looked impressive even in London where panoramic photographs are ten a penny. With them were the four plain little photographs that I had taken when I went off on my own along the track just inside the Libyan border.

These were not the sort of thing which would interest anyone else and I went into my sitting room to

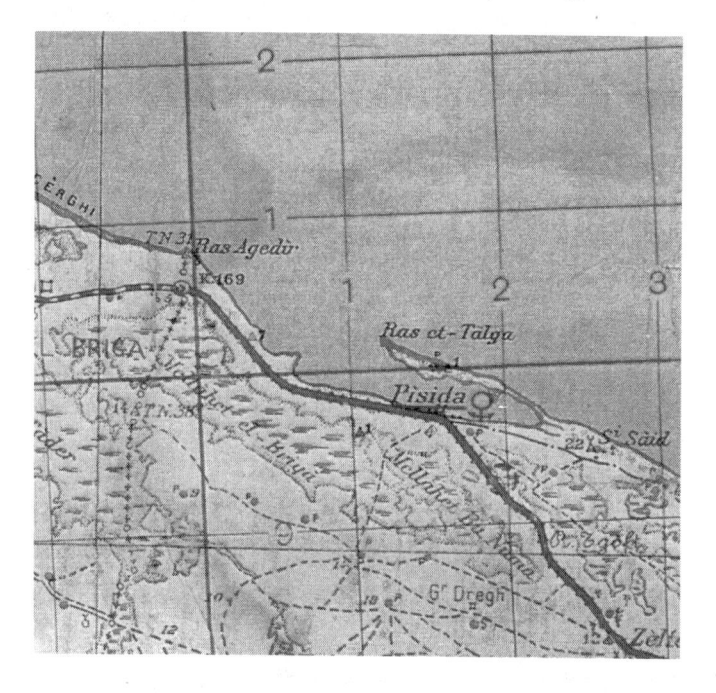

look at them carefully on my own. I sat in front of the window and spread them out on the floor with the map of Pisida and Melia's sketch of my father's grave. I wanted to look at them together.

The first of the photographs looked southwards towards the salt marsh shining with its iridescent light in the distance. The wires from the electricity pylons crossed across the sky above the bleak, flat, sandy landscape.

Then I looked at the other two photographs. When I was at that place Melia's sketch had been inside my rucksack in the boot of the car and, though I had noticed the general similarity between the landscape in the sketch and that which surrounded me, I hadn't been able to compare them in detail.

Now I saw that the camelthorn bush where I planted my poppy cross was the only large old bush in the area, just as it had been in Melia's sketch. I had turned round and as I took the photograph I was looking back the way I had come. To the left of the track as I looked eastwards I saw there was only one large camelthorn bush and, as I looked closer, its shape seemed spookily similar.

In that strange dry country where writing carved into stones two thousand years ago is as crisp and clear as if it were done yesterday was it possible that the same old camelthorn bush could last for more than fifty years? Around the outside of the bush thick bunches of dead dry old branches rose in bunches, but in the centre it was still alive and fresh young green shoots were growing there.

Now, as I looked from the photographs to the sketch and back to the photographs a strange feeling began to creep into the pit of my stomach. Could it be that this was the very same bush? Could that same bush possibly still be alive after all these years?

The sketch (see page 23) was done from a position to the north-west of the bush. I wished I had taken a photograph from the same viewpoint as that of the sketch, low down to the north-west of that bush. I imagined Melia squatting down to rest the paper on his knee as he made the sketch. But, according to instructions, I had been careful to stay close to the track for fear of mines. My photograph was taken from a position to the south-west of the bush and I was standing up. The track in my photograph seemed to be in the same position in relation to the bush as that in Melia's sketch.

In the sketch the earth is piled over the body in a long low hump. The head is at the east end pointing towards the camelthorn bush and my father's tin hat is placed on top. The sketch was done around midday and I could figure out the orientation from the sun shadows to the north. When I looked carefully at my photograph I could see a slight long hump coming outwards to the west from that bush and in the centre of the hump, where maybe once there was some extra moisture down below, another smaller bush once sprouted, and then later died. Was I imagining things? It looked so terribly similar. It had been a bit cloudy that day at Pisida but it was around midday when we were there; perhaps around the time of day that my father was buried and Melia did his sketch. The shadow from the bush would fall in the same direction. There was no sign in my photographs of the little village in the background of the sketch, but maybe those buildings were temporary dwellings built by nomads who later moved into more permanent brick-built village houses.

I am not someone who is normally fanciful but I began to be a little haunted by the similarities between my photograph and Melia's sketch. Was it possible that I had stumbled across the very place where my father was buried? I shared my thoughts with my mother. She looked at my photographs and she cried. My mother is a very brave person. I had never seen her cry since the day of the Memorial Service in Chichester when I was six years old. As she wiped away her tears my mother told me that the following year, when I went back to Libya with Avril's tour, she would come with me.

1942-1943
MY FATHER'S STORY III

27. The Battle of Alamein

My father waited three months for the Battle of Alamein to begin and finally it was a starter's pistol which broke the silence. At 9.40 p.m. on 23rd October 1942 the Battle of Alamein started by the light of a full moon, exactly as planned, as if it were a running race. Many soldiers wrote vivid contemporary descriptions of the battle.

Captain A Grant Murray of the 5th Seaforth Highlanders, who was out with a patrol covering the start line, described how it began:

Suddenly the whole horizon went pink and for a second or two there was still perfect silence and then the noise of the 8th Army's guns hit us in a solid wall of sound that made the whole earth shake. Through the din we made out other sounds - the whine of shells overhead, the clatter of the machine guns...Then we saw a sight that will live forever in our memories - line upon line of steel helmeted figures with rifles at the high port, bayonets catching in the moonlight and over all the wailing of the pipes...

As the kilted pipers of the Highland Division went forward on foot with their infantry their wild-sweet music could be heard shrill and high above the crash of shells.

The twelve day battle was a killing match, a World War 1 battle of attrition. The Germans had laid half a million mines in their 5 mile deep minefield between the sea and the Quattara Depression. The Allied infantry were sent out in front of the tanks to break their way through it on carefully taped routes. The newly invented mine detectors had arrived but many were faulty. Most of the troops still used the old method of poking the ground with a stick or bayonet. Wave upon wave of infantry went forward under enemy fire. The tanks followed through the gaps they had made. Contemporary accounts give a graphic picture:

> *Once the shells started falling there were times when it seemed they would never stop. Men suffered the most appalling injuries. They would be lying on the ground, crying out for help, covered by a mixture of blood and sand - hardly recognisable as human beings. It was night time and with the sand being churned up by the shelling it resembled an impenetrable fog. Vehicles were burning fiercely, many with the crews trapped in them. The battle had to go on despite the carnage, and the stretcher bearers were being killed too. One could only utter a few words of comfort that 'somebody will be along shortly.' This was real warfare - no holds barred. It was man against man and deadly machine against machine.* (Lt. Leslie Meek)

> *When some hundreds of guns are firing at once, the high shrill sound grows until the whole sky is screaming. When the first shells land the earth shakes, clouds of dust and smoke arise and the immense crash drowns the approach of the shells which follow. The uproar swells and fades and swells again, deafeningly numbing the brain. Through it comes the enemy's reply, the crump of mortars, ripping through everything the crack of bredas, the viscious pup-turr, pup-turr of the German Spandau machine-gun.* (Alastair Borthwick)

> *The night quickly became obscured by sand, smoke and cordite. We were on a compass bearing and could only follow the man in front. As we took casualties their loads were distributed amongst the rest of us. The platoon sergeant at the rear carried an amazing eight belts of ammo...Several positions in front were manned mainly by Italian infantry. We gave the Jocks supporting fire as they went in with the bayonet.* (Pte Jeff Hayward).

All the way the steady, remorseless taking of position after position stumbling into enemy machine-gun and mortar pits, passing over the bodies of Germans and Italians lying dead in their holes. (Lt. Felix Barker)

All around bore evidence of the terrible struggle - enemy guns and vehicles lay scattered, the twisted pieces of metal smoking and burning furiously. The night was brilliantly lit by moonlight. We marched on, most of us unshaven for days, we could smell the stench of the dead. (Capt. Ian Cameron)

Veterans of the battle speak of the horrific screams of the tank crews trapped inside as tanks burst into flames or 'brewed up' as the troops called it with grim humour. Contemporary photographs show corpses with their flesh burned to the bone. It is difficult to tell, from my father's dead pan description, the part he actually played in the early days of the battle:

Roughly I have been collecting up all the trucks, ammo etc. for a unit which was wanted quickly, and clearing up the mess they left behind.

Six days into the twelve day battle on 29th October 1942, my father finally received his posting. He got the appointment he most wanted in the re-formed 51st Highland Division. As the Battery Commander of 491 Battery of the 127th Field Regiment R.A. he had charge over around 150 men and eight 25 pounder guns. The Second-in-Command of the regiment was killed and William Melia, the man who later drew a sketch of my father's grave, was promoted to fill his post, leaving his Major's post for my father.

The 51st H.D. had been re-formed in June 1942 under the command of Major-General Douglas Wimberley two years after its disastrous capture at St Valery-en-Caux. Once again they faced Rommel. The gutsy Scots soldiers were determined to restore the reputation of the division under their new leader. But at Alamein many of these soldiers were new to the battlefield so Montgomery placed them between the 9th Australian and the 2nd New Zealand Divisions, both veterans in desert warfare.

Douglas Wimberley, commander of the Highland Division, was very tall, lean and tremendously energetic. He was cheerful, but a serious soldier. He rode along on his jeep with his long legs tucked up under his chin right in front of the troops. He set an example by being calm and unflurried. In spite of his English surname he always lived in Scotland. He was accepted as a true Scot. He wore on his head the 'bonnet' of the Camerons and was given the nickname of 'Big Tam' or 'Tartan Tam'. After the war Gaffer went to visit Wimberley at his home in Scotland and found he remembered my father well.

Towards the end of the Battle of Alamein when Wimberley saw the tanks coming out of action loaded with the dead bodies of his highlanders, he telephoned General Oliver Leese and said, "Surely it's not necessary to continue like this?" The 51st fought valiantly at the Battle of Alamein but the cost was high. They had 2827 casualties, more than any of the eight other divisions fighting there.

As my father began to push his way through to the front to find his new regiment he was only now beginning to get the letters my mother posted soon after he left in early July. He replied immediately:

Have been posted at last and shall be on the move again. Posted to 127 Field Regiment. Also got my rank back again so the stranglehold on the purse strings is removed. My Sweet your estimate of £30 at Xmas seems extremely low are you quite sure you are not being over economical? The whole object of my various enquiries on the money front was to make sure that you had enough. I can always get along out here on next to nothing by cutting off alcohol and if necessary tobacco and living on army rations. Anyway anything that gets as far as the bank at home is all Wigget's as I pare off what I want before it starts...I have just had a bunch of sea mail letters nos. 2, 3, 4, 5 and 7, one and six not appeared dates 17th July to 31st July...Sweet I do love you more than anything, one of these days when Huns and Japs have ceased from troubling we can be together again and never be separated any more. A grand dream wonder how far off it is. Would make the period in between seem still more pointless however if we knew the answer to that. How odd it would be if we could tell exactly what was going to happen to us in the future, Would be rather hard to keep up any interest in the game at all if we knew that.

Yes.

On the twelfth day of the battle the Germans finally retreated. Wimberley was bandaged on both knees, one wrist, one arm and both ankles. His desert sores and abrasions were painted with gentian violet.

28. Alamein to El Agheila

My father reached his new regiment on the last day of the battle of Alamein, 4th November 1942, the day Rommel gave up and ordered his army to retreat.

Back in Britain the people were desperate for good news. The bombing had eased a little but food and clothes were scarce and rationed. The people were sick of gas masks and air-raid shelters. As soon as he heard of the victory at Alamein Churchill ordered that the church bells ring out in celebration all over the British Isles. They had been silent since the retreat from Dunkirk two and a half years before. Alamein, together with the victory at Stalingrad, finally turned the tide of the war against the Germans.

After the battle four crack German divisions and eight Italian divisions ceased to exist as effective fighting formations. Nine generals were taken prisoner, along with thirty thousand others. A large number of enemy tanks were destroyed, and huge quantities of guns, transport, aircraft and stores were captured. For the troops at the front line there was no time to celebrate their achievement. As Rommel turned to retreat Montgomery made an attempt to cut him off and capture the whole Axis army. He sent the veteran New Zealand 2nd Division round to the south on a 'left hook' through the desert in an attempt to overtake the Axis troops and block their retreat. The New Zealanders set off on 5th November in perfect weather and went way down into the desert but on November 6th and 7th the rain bucketed down. The fine desert sand turned glutinous and the New Zealanders' tanks and armoured cars sank deep into it. Gravelly, dried-up wadis, which had previously formed discreet hidden roads, turned into impassable running streams. The Germans were given a crucial twenty-four hours to get away. The long chase across North Africa had begun. The goal was Tripoli. For three years it had been the target of the 8th Army and when on 8th November the 1st Army landed in Algeria the race was on. The 8th Army were quite determined that they would get to Tripoli first. They wanted to chase Rommel out of Africa forever.

Rommel made good time out of Egypt over the land which had changed hands so many times in the last two years. They retreated through Fuka, Sidi Barrani and over the Halfaya Pass out of Egypt and into Cyrenaica, the Eastern end of Libya. Rommel's army moved back over relatively cleared ground, but as they went they laid mines and booby traps, dug anti-tank ditches, demolished buildings to block the roads, and shelled and sniped at the Allied troops who followed. As the retreat continued the German supply lines from Tripoli became shorter all the time but those of the Allied forces, supplied through Alexandria, grew longer.

Petrol was so scarce that many of the Allied troops advanced on foot. The men had plenty of bully-beef, only an occasional luxury back in England, and thick army biscuits, but they felt hungry for much the time. Sometimes they advanced all through the night. Contemporary news footage shows lean, fit young men giving everything to the chase.

The huge army was spread out over the desert driving over the rough rocky ground amongst the camelthorn bushes. It moved forward at 80 miles per day. There was a shortage of tank carriers so many tanks had to be driven as well. In army language they 'dealt with pockets of resistance at various points'. On 7th November my father found time to write again:

> "Have had a rather hectic last few days. Have now joined my unit and taken over a battery. Am still rather in a state of not knowing what they can and cannot do and trying to play ball in the party at the same time. However am shaking down and chasing the cobwebs out of the brain. As you will have gathered from the news we are on the move. I personally have not seen much of the Hun beyond the odd stuff left behind and a few bombs, the blighter is running too fast. Am at this second living in a German built hut, very well built too, hence the opportunity to write as it is blacked out and we can use a light after dark. Have spent quite a lot of today going through odd German and Italian papers picked up about the place and sending them back to the intelligence boys. Have also seen some quite useful stuff lying about for the salvage experts."

The front line forces relied on the BBC for up to date news of progress on other fronts. Knowing this the Germans put out radio signals to jam the air waves and the trick was to find the lesser known BBC broadcasts at odd times to avoid it. My father had a radio in his armoured car, which he called his tin can. He made it his job to get information so he could contain the wilder rumours which were apt to circulate. I was reminded of the times when I sat with Gaffer and Ga in the drawing room at Hawkhurst as they slowly turned the Bakelite tuning knob on their big brown pierced-fronted valve wireless, searching the air waves for a clean message from London, Paris, Brussels or Hilversum. Even now the thought of its woo-oo-oo-oo-eeee interference shrieks catch my imagination.

The wireless brought the welcome news that the American and British 1st Armies had landed in Morocco and Algeria and were making their way eastwards towards Rommel from the western end of North Africa. It was Montgomery's aim that these two Allied armies should catch the Axis troops 'like a rat in a trap'. My father approved of the tactics:

It sounds as if someone has at last got his thinking cap out of store, only hope we have got enough stuff to put it through. The old Pessimistic James. There are so many damn fool optimists about that I have to do something to try and redress the balance.

My father was coming home as fast as he could. He couldn't wait to get back together with my mother; sometime, somewhere. He was only hoping to be able to bring his men safely back to England. By the 12th November they were in Cyrenaica on the road to Tobruk. They stopped overnight in an area recently vacated by the Italians.

Their lines were in an indescribable state of filth with all their little creeping and hopping friends still in occupation. Had a disturbed night last night, was to be seen standing stark naked on a hill top waving my blankets in the breeze to get rid of uninvited guests.

In WW2 the Italian army still operated a decadent elitist system. The officers led relatively luxurious lives and, I am told, even had caravans of prostitutes following them around. This was at the expense of their men, many of whom were peasant recruits with no understanding of the standards of personal hygiene needed in the desert. Positions vacated by the Italians were often infested with lice. Both the German and the Allied troops tried to avoid them.

On 13th November the Allies re-took Tobruk. As soon as the harbour was cleared of wrecks the supply ships could dock there by-passing the long trek by land from Alexandria. On 15th November the Martuba Airfields were re-taken. Jock was getting back into his work:

I have got most of the dust shaken out of the old top storey but shall probably find there are still odd patches of rust to exorcise.

But he was still bothered by insects:

We have moved to a cleaner spot since I last wrote. Had one very disturbed night as saturated my bed with anti-louse powder. Net result that the inhabitants crawled up from the depths in single file and took off on coming to the face.

Now it was only five weeks until 18th December, my mother's due date. My father thought he was bringing in a Major's pay (although in fact he never in his lifetime did) but he was worried about the arrangements for the money reaching their bank account in England.

On 20th November Benghazi was re-taken. Once they had cleared the harbour of wrecks the allies could begin to use if for supplies, but petrol remained scarce. Rommel had retreated to El Agheila, a position he had managed to hold against the Allied forces on two previous occasions.

On 24th November my mother started a longer four-day journal of a letter describing her life at home, where she was living with her mother at Layer-de-la-Haye outside Colchester. She sent it by a different method, called A.M. Her beautiful forward-sloping writing is tightly packed into fourteen sides of airmail paper which formed a solid little pillow in the envelope:

Darling one – Have just finished supper and am sitting by the cosy stove in the dining room and am going to enjoy myself writing to James. Can't remember if I ever told you that for a fuel saving effort we now use the dining room as a sitting room as well – we put away the big dining table and only use the one that was once an altar - pushed it up to the far end across the room and then we've got a sofa and a chair or two down the fireplace end. As a matter of fact it's a good idea because this sort of stove is the sort that burns very little and you keep it going day and night and the room is always beautifully warm for meals as well.

Have now embarked on a khaki pullover for Indian prisoners which Mama and I are knitting between us... Spent the morning mending. I turned out my chest of drawers yesterday and found all the things which wanted mending and it was a mountain about the same size as the one we turned out for you before you went abroad... should like to get it all dealt with before Thomas arrives as I shan't have a great deal of time then I reckon!

I met one of the people in the village whose husband is in the M. East somewhere. I asked how he was and she said she'd had a letter about a fortnight ago from him. Also I heard yesterday that Jenny's husband had sent an airmail card and that somebody else in the village had heard from her son so I hope that I may get a letter from you one day soon my darling though I know that all these people have been moved back to somewhere where they can post a letter whereas my James, if he possibly can, will be moving in the opposite direction I'm sure, knowing the nature of the creature!

Here I went off to ring up your family to congratulate your Pa on getting mentioned in dispatches. He hadn't heard anything about it... he told me he had been up to London for the day and forwarded an airgraph from you sweetheart and it arrived this morning. I can't tell you how lovely it is to get it – I could hardly sleep for thinking about it coming! Anyway it arrived safely – one written on 2nd November saying that you were having a Riviera style holiday with sea bathing and giving me your new address and I see my darling that you are a Major again which is very exciting! Congratulations my sweet and I see also that it's a field regt. you're in which is what you wanted isn't it so that's very lucky – was terribly afraid that having turned down the other offer you might have got stuck for want of anything better turning up! My James doesn't often get had for a mug but it seemed a bit risky...oh darling – its made so much difference getting a letter – I really feel a different person – at least I've gone a little further nearer being my real self only shall never be completely that till my James comes back again... tomorrow I have to go to the doctor which is a bore but I suppose I shall only have to go about once more after this before 'Thomas' puts in an appearance. What a thought – I hadn't really realized that it was quite as close as that. Oh darling I do wish you could be here with me because I can't help having a bit of a dentist pain but it won't take long I 'spect I'll forget all the horrid part the moment it is over!...I do so hope it will look a bit like you sweetheart – a little somebody that belongs entirely to us and that reminds me of my James to look at would be lovely to have to keep me company till my darling comes home again...I love you darling one always and always and one day we'll be together again – lots of kisses for James – Wiget.

In North Africa winter was approaching, the weather was cold and wet and there was no moon at night. The Allied troops drove on through minefields and wet salt marshes where the vehicles became bogged down and had to be dug out repeatedly before they could continue. Living conditions were basic:

Am at present sitting in a hole in the sand writing on a map board balanced rather unsteadily on my knee. This letter has been interrupted five times so far. Main cause of complaint at the moment in this part of the world is the cold. I have taken to living in Pa's leather woolly waistcoat which I find very comforting, sometimes with my long smelly fur coat over the top, net result a most curious and unsoldier-like figure.

My father's 'fur coat', which Jack Swaab remembered on our first visit to his house in Wimbledon, was a shaggy Afghan sheep coat that he bought in Peshawar before the war. After my father was killed it was sent home and my mother kept it close by her in Reeves, the cottage in Layer-de-la-Haye where she and I were then living. Eventually it became infested with bugs and, having no way to get rid of them in those days, she had a ceremonial burning. Now she told me how she wept as it went up in flames.

In North Africa the troops were advancing over comparatively clean desert but the going was not easy. The sand was soft, wet and deep where it was not held by the roots of the camelthorn bushes. Mail came through to the front in fits and starts:

Seems very strange to get your news in jumps backwards and forwards, as the airport cards set up a lot of problems by referring to sea-mail letters written weeks before and arriving months afterwards. I think I know nearly everything you have written by heart as it goes around in my pocket. An active Wigget writing industriously for the time I have been away had just about filled the big pocket in front of my battle dress trousers.

Water was desperately short. When it rained by day the troops sometimes stood out in it naked to get clean. After a night of rain my father collected water from the canvas roofs of the trucks and shared it around for washing.

The outfit is gradually getting 'desertised'. We are now able to get along quite happily on half gallon of water per man per day which took a bit of thinking out at first. I personally work it out as half my tin mug-full for washing, shaving and teeth cleaning per day, 3 pints made into tea for drinking and half a pint for cooking, mostly in breakfast porridge. We get a windfall every now and again when it rains as it has done for the last two nights. Collected about 12 galls from a canvas roof which gave most of the place a 'bath' standing up in half a basin of cold water.

They reached Mersa Brega, about 30 miles from El Agheila where Rommel was making his next stand. Again Montgomery sent the New Zealand 2nd Division round into the desert to try to outflank the Germans with a left hook and cut them off. The Highland Division advanced along the coast road. At the last moment Rommel realised he would be trapped and retreated. He largely escaped the outflanking movement which again came too late.

On the morning of 13th December the Highlanders entered Mersa Brega and went on to El Agheila. They found both towns deserted but thoroughly booby trapped in a most unpleasant way. Abandoned cars and jettisoned field glasses were wired to mines. Dead men lay about. At the time it was said that some of these bodies were mined so that when the soldiers went to bury them the mines exploded, killing them as well. There were many casualties. Yet the North African campaign is said to have been the last to keep vestiges of chivalry in modern warfare. The desert was an ideal battleground. Both armies were professional and well led. This is warfare as good as it comes.

Twenty Axis tanks and five hundred prisoners were taken but many more escaped. It was a mercy for my father that the Germans

ran from El Agheila without us having to butt our heads into that position.

A violent sandstorm blew up and a wall of sand a hundred foot high advanced on the troops. It was followed by torrential rain. In the next 300 miles across the desert to Buerat the Allies had to cross four large wadis, named Tamet, Chebir, Quesca and Zemzem. These were places where the winter rain had created canyons through the desert as it made its way to the sea. Rommel positioned his defences at ZemZem. Beyond that he planned a major stronghold at Buerat.

In Benghazi the wrecks were now cleared. Supplies were beginning to come in. The next useful harbour was at Tripoli, 650 miles westwards across the desert and now in German hands. Montgomery was afraid that if he took his army any farther he would be unable to supply and feed the troops and would be forced to retreat. He decided to make camp seven miles to the west of El Agheila to gather his resources before the final thrust through to Tripoli.

29. Christmas and New Year's Eve 1942

My father's battery waited three weeks in the encampment at El Agheila. There Montgomery learned he had been promoted to general and Douglas Wimberley was awarded the DSO. Those who had been lightly-wounded at Alamein returned to their units and new men came to take the positions of those still in hospital or killed. Preparations continued and the troops occupied themselves with inter-unit football matches, exercises and assault practice. Montgomery circulated amongst them, carrying out inspections and watching them shoot. Shoes and badges were polished and the mail came through. The desert was sometimes unbelievably beautiful and my father commented;

Tonight produced the 'green flash' argued about in the Times correspondence columns every now and again, The sky was royal blue with crimson lake clouds, one with a green bar across the edge, It was quite astonishing, but here it only produced the remark that 'it looks like another freezing cold night'.

Back at Layer-de-la-Haye my mother was preparing for the arrival of the baby, but her feelings were elsewhere. On 16th December she started another four-day twelve-side letter which she again sent by A.M. This method was cheap, but very slow. These letters sent by A.M. never reached my father.

I machined up the hems of six nappies too this morning – Mummy got them for me in town yesterday with six of the remaining eight coupons and they were Utility ones and evidently they arrive in the shop in a long roll with a mark where to cut them off for the right size – then they cut them off and sell them to you with raw edges and you have to hem them up! I'm quite certain that a man worked out the coupon values for things and allowances for coupons because they give you fifty coupons for the infant's clothes and as it requires at least four dozen nappies at a coupon each the fifty wouldn't go far. I suppose one might manage with three dozen but the washing would be perpetual. I was lucky and got some butter muslin ones which weren't couponed but they aren't making them any more. ..Finished a second pair of gloves for Thomas which has finished up all the oddments of white wool now and started on a pair of socks for you out of some thick wool I had. It may not be quite enough for the complete pair but I will finish the toes with a different shade of khaki if not and I dare say they will be just as warm and I know my James won't mind a bit of Wigitry about his toes!

I love you darling – I wonder if you realise my darling quite how much I love you? – there's one thing quite certain I could never tell you in words even if I took a lifetime over it. The thing which will always mystify me is why I didn't realise it sooner – it took me such a long time to realise that it would be a good idea to marry James and once I had realised it I could never understand why I had taken so long.

She finished her letter on 20th December. Her supposed 'due date' on 18th December had come and gone, but it was lodged in my father's mind and on that day he wrote:

Wonder what my Wigget has been up to. These last two days you have seemed very close my love. Have a feeling in my bones that you have relapsed into a nursing home to deal with Thomas or Jane. My darling be careful of yourself as you are so very precious to me.

At Layer-de-la-Haye they got together a wonderful Christmas supper on Christmas Eve, so that their two faithful helpers could have the following day off. They ate pork with brussel sprouts, roast potatoes, apple sauce and stuffing followed by Christmas pudding and custard:

wish the Germans could have seen it as it would be excellent propaganda.

After the meal my mother started another marathon twelve-side letter:

I miss my darling very very much it being Christmas – not that we have ever spent Christmas together as far as I recollect have we? But perhaps next one we will have together – do you think there is a hope my pessimistic old darling?! Just when I was going to sleep last night darling you seemed awfully close and I think you must have been thinking of me too – don't know what the time would have been with you exactly but I don't suppose time makes the slightest difference to the war in your part of the world! It was lovely to feel my James so close. No sign of Thomas sweetheart – I wish he'd hurry up although, poor little creature, it was only the doctor who thought he would arrive a week ago – I never thought he'd come so soon – and neither did the doctor last time I went so I really don't know why I'm fussing...I really don't mind now if 'it's' Jane. I've made myself imagine a rather nice little Jane with James' blue eyes and my black hair and she's very wicked and very attractive and my James finds her amusing – so that I won't be heartbroken if it isn't 'Thomas' after all!

On Christmas Day 1942 the Quartermaster managed to produce some roast pork and even a slice of turkey for Christmas evening dinner at the camp outside El Agheila. After the meal my father sat with his men around a small camp fire and they even started to sing, but just as things were getting going the rain came down and put an end to it.

I wonder what kind of Xmas my Wigget had this year. Ours was slightly spoilt by a very wet night which washed me out of bed in the early hours of the morning. Had provided for air attack by raindrops with a ground sheet and a gas cape, but was torpedoed by submarine attack in a flood of water rushing down the hill side I was sleeping on...The King's Speech on the wireless in my tin can was interrupted by some blighter doing a bit of buzzing and the occasional wave of atmospheric and/or Hun interference. However I managed to get the gist of the thing and wondered if Wigget was listening too.*

She was listening and also wondering the same about him. On 26th December she continued with her long letter;

I was happy all day yesterday because the postman brought me a letter from you – a recent one came very quickly dated Dec 10th. I have wanted one so very much for days and days and it arrived as a Christmas present – the very best one that could be imagined! It said you'd walked a hole in your heel though my darling – I am hoping it is better by now but I rather mistrust my old rascal – I'm afraid he won't do anything reasonable about it and will get khaki dye in it or something – I am hoping that some medics will have spied him limping about and demanded to see the damage. I expect a ruckle in your sock started it off when you didn't have time or inclination to remove your boot and straighten same – am I right?

She suggested he should carry more clean socks and wash them more often, but realised there might not be water to spare! Her Christmas present from him was the stockings he had bought in the Cape and sent off the previous July:

Oh I meant to tell you sweetheart that I got my Christmas present from you out again on Christmas day and gloated over it! They are lovely stockings my darling and now I shall preserve them for a terribly splendid occasion – I can't think anything short of James coming home will be nearly important enough! At this rate Thomas will have to be a New Year present from us to each other sweetheart – in fact if he doesn't hurry he won't get in to 1942 at all!

My father was still at this camp outside el Agheila when I was finally born on the evening of 31st December 1942. That morning the earliest spring flowers burst into bloom in the desert. One soldier gathered more than forty different species from the damp ground of a single wadi.

I have always known that my birth was not easy. Even now a look of horror and pain spreads over my mother's face when she speaks of her thirty-six hour labour.

"The doctor had to unwind the cord and then he pulled you out with forceps," my mother told me. "It made your head a funny shape, your chin was pushed right in and there were dark purple bruises up either side of your face. You looked very strange. But I didn't know anything about it. By the time you arrived I was right out of it."

My mother had no idea what was going on. She was alone, scared and in pain. There was no chance of her feeling any control over her body, no chance that she felt, as I did when my children arrived, that this was a wonderful and exciting natural event. But now that I am able to put my birth into the context of that time I realise that the emotion she still feels about it relates to much more than the physical pain of childbirth. That whole time in her life is inextricably linked to my father's death.

I have always felt guilty about it. I had understood that it was my fault that I wound my head up in the cord and made everything so difficult for my mother. Now I am glad to find not only that the same thing happened to my father when he was born, but also that it doesn't prolong the labour. The danger is not to the mother but to the baby who can be strangled unless the cord is cut as soon as the head is born. I was very relieved to discover this.

On new year's day my father described what he

had been doing the previous evening:

Am still waiting anxiously for a telegram from Wigget's Ma as to the little Wigget's birthday. I did not after all manage to sit up till midnight last night, Arranged for the enthusiastic Scots to have a mug of tea laced with rum to see the New Year in and trickled quietly off to bed.

He might have stayed up had he known. On new year's day my mother wrote a postcard (which she had bought in advance) showing two hands holding up a baby. The caption coming out of the baby's mouth says "Well! This is a funny ole world – but I likes it!"

On it she wrote:

Darling heart, Mummy has just written you an airmail letter to tell you about our daughter but this is just a line in real Wigit writing to show my James that I'm very well and to tell him that I love him terribly and that the little creature is an absolute angel and terribly precious being a little bit of my James!

She didn't let on what she had been through any more than he did with her. They were both being brave and trying not to bother the other. But her card never reached him. It would be 26 more days before he even received Gran's letter to give him the news and by then he had only 18 more days left to live.

30. Jack Swaab

My first letter to Jack Swaab in March 1988 arrived on his seventieth birthday. As a present for his eightieth his younger son had his secretly-kept war diaries typed out and five copies bound. Jack wrote a small foreword and lodged a copy in the Imperial War Museum. He had never offered to show me his diaries and I was always too shy to ask him outright if I could see them. I felt rather sneaky as I borrowed a typed copy of the transcript from his son - who didn't mind a bit and was delighted to lend it to me.

Jack was four years younger than my father Jock, and very different. Jock was down to earth and he knew how to live off the land: but Jack made an unlikely soldier. Jock was naturally brave, rugged and practical: but Jack was an intellectual. Jock was brought up in a service family: but Jack had signed up because he believed in the cause of that particular war.

From school Jack went to Oxford University but was sent down. He has never told me why, but I suspect it was for the same reason that he sometimes got into trouble with the army authorities, for his irreverent attitude and insubordinate tongue, or for his way with the girls. After working as a newspaper reporter he started at London University where he was doing well (he would have been a gold medallist the principal told him) but war was declared and he enlisted as 928547 Gunner Swaab.

My father was in charge of Jack's unit at the army training camp in Milborne Port in Dorset. There Jack was scornful of the petty rules. He was made to polish not only the front but the back of his cap badge. His toothbrush had to be perfectly aligned on his barrack room bed. But Jack admired my father. My father was brought up with the knowledge of how to live in a small group and how to lead them fairly. Jack liked my father's tolerance, his humour and the way he could distinguish the important from the trivial.

In 1942 Jack volunteered for service at the front. He was sent out to Cairo. One of the first letters my father received when the army stopped at El Agheila was a letter from Jack, sent from Cairo. He asked my father whether a place might be found in his regiment. My father replied;

Dear Jack,

I have taken over 491 Battery in this part of the world. I can hold out no very great hopes of hooking you in. The Highland Division is apt to be a bit of a closed book to the Sassenach. Usually they wait patiently for one of their own chaps to return from hospital. So far the regiment has been extremely lucky in the Officer Casualty line, only one fatal and I have filled that vacancy with my own body. However one of these days fortune may not be quite so kind and we may have a bottle washer's job vacant.

> Great relief in this part of the world that the Hun evacuated El Agheila before he was seriously attacked. Might have been a sticky party if he had really hung on to same.
>
> If you really have ideas of mixing with the 51st you will have to get rid of that metropolitan air of yours! Englishmen start at a disadvantage and Londoners at a greater one and as for newspaper reporters –.
>
> Seriously I will do what I can but do not hold out any hopes as the lads of the village do not take too kindly to imported English officers, apt to be treated as foreigners for some considerable time which does not always help the war effort.
>
> You are a young clown - why did you leave your last job to go playing with AOPs and the Middle East? Highland Division is convinced it is going home straight, Huns or no Huns, which may make Cairo somewhat of a backwater. Do not get into more trouble than you can help in your present location with the local flossies who do mostly have the clap. The beer is bloody which is better than here where it is non-existent.
> Yrs affec, J.O.Cochrane.
>
> P.S. The proper mode of address is 'dear Major' but do not let that worry you unduly.

Jack received the letter in Cairo on 23rd December and the very next day his posting came through to my father's own battery. On 29th December he set out from Cairo on his way to the front.

After an uncomfortable and dangerous six-day journey Jack reached my father's battery on the morning of 3rd January 1943. He arrived in the middle of a sandstorm. The sand stuck to his eyes, ears and mouth. Jack found my father 'the same as ever and pleasantly unimpressed' by his arrival. Lunch consisted of two cold sardines and a cup of tea each in their 'Officers' Mess', a tarpaulin over a large hole dug in the ground with planking for tables. Later that day as the sandstorm increased the whole Officers' Mess was carried away by the wind.

Towards evening the wind died down a little and Jack found himself a small tent for the night. His eyes were bunged up and sore with sand and he wrote up his diary in the flickering candlelight. His pen picked up the grains of sand on his paper and scratched it as he wrote:

It is odd to be in Tripolitania lying utterly alone in a little oasis of light in the darkness with the wind blowing outside. I think I can hear the sea, just over the ridge to the north of our bivouac area. A dog barks.

That night and the following day the gales in the Mediterranean caused havoc back in the newly captured harbour of Benghazi. The waves smashed the breakwater and heavy seas broke into the inner harbour. Ships tore loose from their anchors and crashed into each other. The men of my father's battery felt the consequences over the next ten days as the supplies coming in through the port dropped from 3000 to 400 tons a day. The whole 8th Army was thrown back on supplies from Tobruk.

Jack was attached to Battery H.Q. At first, as my father had anticipated, he felt lonely, but he sewed the Highland Division sign on his army uniform and it made him feel he belonged. He began immediately to record his first impressions of the other officers of my father's battery. About my father he says:

Jock, his usual saturnine and unruffled self presides, dropping an occasional crack.

Jack was initially (but only in his diary) quite rude about some of the officers:

Gegan like a fat cockatoo. Forshaw too cocky by about eight months.

By the time I knew him Jack said that he couldn't believe how hard he had been, at first, on the fellow men of his battery, who later he began to respect so much.

My father, on the other hand, never commented in his letters about the men with whom he lived so closely sharing hunger, thirst and danger. He knew how to keep a group pulling together in these circumstances. He was a professional through and through.

For the first few days Jack was careful not to talk too much and to be respectful, but he couldn't keep it up for long. Soon he began to establish his role in the group as the court jester. Jack had written a skit on the 'Convoy Cutey' and when he docked in Durban the piece was used by Moira Lister on the radio there. She sent the script in to the South African Broadcasting Company who later sent Jack some royalties. Now he tried it on his new battery. My father's comment was, "H'm, a bit better than your stuff used to be," and Jack had the feeling he was amused.

The following day the wind changed. A southeasterly brought the sun and swarms of flies. The flies had multiplied and grown fat where three years of fighting in that part of the desert had given them so many dead bodies and latrines to feed from. They tormented the soldiers who sometimes made fantastic fly traps, but the flies returned persistently to attack their eyes, mouths and nostrils. The bites left painful sores which sometimes took weeks to heal.

Because of the supply problems caused by the storms which had wrecked Benghazi harbour Montgomery at first wondered whether to postpone the advance across the desert, but then he decided to stick to his original plan. He knew there was a risk that they might not get through to Tripoli before supplies ran out, thus forcing a retreat. The sea was still rough and at night the men lay in their dugouts and listened to it booming against the shore.

After Jack's arrival my father's battery stayed one more week in the camp outside El Agheila before they set out on their dash across the desert to Tripoli. Jack began to settle in. He gave Sandie Cowie, my father's cheerful Command Post Officer who wrote one of the letters to my mother after my father's death, one of his bars of chocolate. He was amazed at his delight. He had never experienced the battlefield and was quite looking forward to it:

I think I am going to be rather happy in this battery. Jock says we shall be going into action very soon and I am rather pleased at the prospect, though perhaps that is foolish.

The soldiers had their money changed to British Military Currency, which Jack found 'rather natty', but in the desert money had ceased to have much meaning. The Arabs bartered eggs for tea and sugar and among the troops. Cigarettes were the usual currency. My father commented about this in a letter he wrote to Ga:

Money in notes out here has no importance in popular opinion. I think you could leave practically any sum about with perfect safety, a very good object lesson in the intrinsic value of same as, not being able to eat it or drink it or smoke it, it is only rather a nuisance to carry around; until a canteen appears when it immediately assumes a value once more. I have taken to buying up the complete stock of any canteen that comes our way and rationing the contents, otherwise the first arrivals buy it out complete, very largely for the joy of for once having something to spend their money on.

The populace is causing me a lot of work at the moment by wanting to remit sums from its pay to wives and families. A period of not being able to spend anything will come as a windfall to all sorts of harassed wives at home. I am the only loser as I have to fill in countless forms in order to effect the transfer.

It's a funny life this. One's values change completely. The most important thing in life at the moment is apt to be the existence or non existence of a mug of so called tea. It is usually brewed with salty water from a mixture of tea leaves, sand and odd unidentified foreign bodies. Next most important thing is the chance of a bathe which is reckoned purely as a substitute for a bath, the latter being of course quite out of the dreams of possibility. However we manage to keep fairly clean somehow, there being not much beyond the greasy parts of trucks to get dirty on, and even grease yields to treatment when rubbed in clean sand.

The other odd thing is that in spite of eating enormously most are always hungry. I think it comes from eating concentrated food, as it is nearly always bully beef and biscuits, which nourish the body without filling the belly.

My father's watch stopped working in the sandstorm the day that Jack arrived. There was an amateur watch-mender who he hoped might fix it, but for now he could only tell the time by 'stomach clock and asking'. This was to cause him a few problems over the next few days.

All and every day bombers and transport planes flew over travelling westwards. Jack recorded Hudsons, P12 and P14s, Dakotas, Tomahawks, an odd Spit Vc, a Lysander or two, Mitchells, Marylands, Baltimores, Bostons and Bombays. As the men waited for their orders to leave they listened to the faraway sound of the Allied bombs dropping. Jack had been told that they were bombing Mussolini's Marble Arch built on the boundary between Cyrenaica and Tripolitania.

The mail and newspapers came through. The daily '8th Army News', the '8th Army Weekly' and the 'Crusader' were all published in the field. The 'Egyptian Mail' came through from Cairo, but by the time it arrived the men had picked up all its news on the radio.

Jack had brought with him from Cairo a little hoard of '555' cigarettes. Now fifty of them vanished from his kit and he blamed his batman. Montgomery had reduced the cigarette ration to the troops to make space on the supply ships for more essential supplies. 555s were rather sought after. They were much better than Two Aces, C. to C. (for Cape to Cairo but nicknamed 'Cough to Coffin') or Victory V's. The 'V' cigarettes were very bad, Victory V became the trade mark for a large number of goods and was always a sign of the lowest quality. Jack reckoned that boxes of 'V' matches contained a proportion of about two good ones to eighteen duds and noted that even the good ones flared up high and dangerously then burned with a sulphurous glow. 'V' ink was a greenish-grey liquid with lumps in it.

On sunny days the men went swimming in the nude. The white skin from behind their shorts looked like swimming trunks. One day my father found a large German petrol tank full of petrol and brought it back for use. Jack was pleased to be in my father's battery. He noted:

Jock is very decent to me. I like serving with him as much as I knew I should.

My father's letters home were often written under very difficult conditions. Once he mentioned that he was sitting in the corner of a wireless truck so tightly wedged between two other men that only one could move at any one time. He was constantly interrupted by orderlies asking questions or handing him piles of papers. The day after Jack's arrival, when I was four days old, my father was worrying about the baby. He wrote again to my mother:

Your Ma's cable must have got lost on the way. I am beginning to wonder what has been happening to my poor darling....

Am rather shocked to hear that you only received one letter from between 28th Oct and 1st Dec as I must have written between ten and fifteen during that period, wonder if any of the wanderers will turn up eventually...

Am only hoping and praying that my not hearing anything is mail getting lost and not anything that has happened at home...

the last news I have had was dated 14th Dec and I feel there ought to have been a cable somewhere but that it has not fetched up as yet...

You do seem extraordinarily close sometimes my sweetest most at odd times when I wake up in the middle of the night. Funny feeling as it is not like a dream in so much as I know you are not there yet I can almost feel you beside me and sometimes when going to sleep I can feel a Wigget's good night kiss. A lovely feeling as it is not a dream. I am still where I know I am, I can still feel that the ground is hard and the blanket is damp, but somehow Wigget is there too...

He received another belated air letter which had chased him across the desert, but still no telegram about the baby. He often mentioned that he noticed:

If I say how much I love you at the beginning of a letter it drives everything out of my head so nowadays I am cautious and do not say a thing about that until the last few lines. It looks then as if it was put in as a conventional ending but I think that my Wigget will know that I still love her and if I put anything at the beginning of a letter I just have to close down. The only real point in being here at all is as a means to being with her always and always with no interruptions.

On 8th January my mother wrote a densely packed airletter from the nursing home on Colchester where I had been born. In those days it was the practice to stay two weeks in the nursing home and in the eight days since my birth she had not even been allowed out of bed:

I've never been in bed so long before without putting even one foot on the floor. I ought to get up the day after tomorrow for a bit. Have just had my supper and must go off to sleep in a moment or two until woken up at a quarter to ten to feed the 'inf' – otherwise I find I get very weary as it is half past five every morning we are woken in order to feed the creature at 6 am.

Family and friends visited her and brought lovely scented winter flowers from their gardens. Ga visited with Aunt Suzanne. My mother had heard that Peter Sedgewick, (who as a small boy had played horses with my father) who had been reported missing, had been discovered, wounded, and was in hospital in W.Africa. Her previous letter had told him of a friend from Harwich killed.

Then, in spite of their firm agreement that I should be called Jane she began to wonder whether to christen me 'Janet' after her mother, my Round-Turner Gran. My mother has never been good at making decisions, especially on her own.

31. Dash across the Desert

On Monday 11th January 1943 the advance across the desert began. At first light my father and his battery set off by truck from the camp outside El Agheila. The warm spell was over. Now it was cold with intermittent rain. My father was driving and Jack travelled in the back. The whole army spread out over the desert in brigade column. The relics of former conflict lay about, a petrol tin, a crashed plane, a burned out tank and amongst the debris the occasional clump of desert honeysuckle with sweet-smelling purple flowers grew up. At 8.00pm that evening they stopped near Mussolini's 'Marble Arch' and ate cold tinned Machonochie. It fell to the bottom of their stomachs like lead.

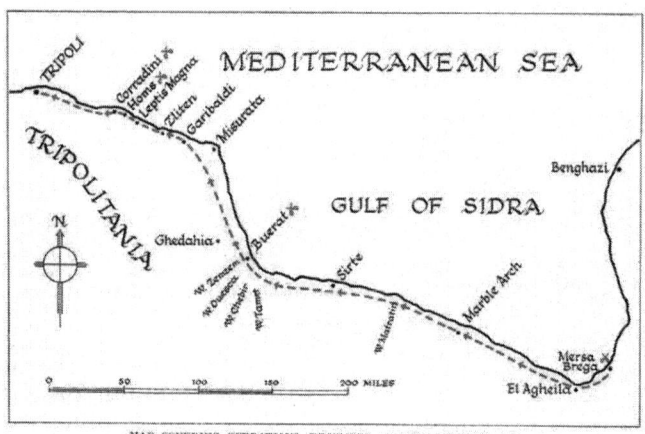

MAP COVERING OPERATIONS, DECEMBER 1942-23RD JANUARY 1943

On the morning of 12th January they were up at 5.30 am. in bitter wintry weather. All day the whole army with nearly 500 tanks moved westwards towards Tripoli. A sharp cold wind blew the sand up into a dense dusty cloud around them. They drove 106 miles that day reaching Wadi Matratin, the first of the large wadis, and managed to cross it without getting bogged in the marshy ground where the grass and scrubby plants grew. It was dark by the time they arrived at Sirte, in the middle of the desert where, half a century later, Avril and I visited Gaddafi's new marble government compound. Late into the night they listened to the tanks as they rumbled and clanked their way forward.

On Wednesday 13th January they drove on through blinding sandstorms over the undulating desert landscape. The next enemy position was inland from Buerat at Wadi Zem Zem, beyond the smaller wadis of Tamet, Chebir and Quesca. That evening they stopped at Wadi Chebir and listened to the bombs exploding in the distance. Wadi ZemZem was boggy and impassable in some places with rocks and high cliffs on which Rommel had positioned his artillery. Germans and Italians manned the ridges. It was said that they had 300 guns behind barricades of barbed wire. The land in front was heavily mined.

On the afternoon of Thursday 14th my father's battery was due to move forward 16 miles into battle position. The 51st Highland Division was to go straight down the coastal road while the 4th Light Armoured Brigade looped inland to the south. For Jack it would be his first experience of fighting:

I feel a subdued excitement but at times a feeling as in the dentist's waiting room, "for God's sake let it begin and get it over!" But I'm not afraid - yet.

The ration was half a gallon of brackish water per man. Salt had been added to the water in a vain attempt to cover the bad taste. Some soldiers shaved with the dregs of their tea. My father could have used the water-divining rod my mother had sent, if only it had reached him.

That afternoon a sandstorm blew up, but in the evening the wind settled. As dusk fell the ridge to the west formed a dark outline against a red sunset. From behind the ridge came the rumble of guns and bombs. As the last fires died down the whole army was in darkness, but the red tips of cigarettes glowed across the desert as far as the eye could see. A machine gun was tapping to the north. The gunfire and the sound of shells went on all night.

In spite of his short-sightedness and the blind spot in his right eye my father was a Forward Observation Officer. On Friday 15th January he attended a conference called by Douglas Wimberley which took place among the sand dunes in Wadi Tamet. Wimberley explained in army terminology the details of the plan for the attack on Zem Zem, which was to start that night. There were to be four phases. In the first, codenamed 'Silk', contact would be made with the enemy, then in 'Satin' the enemy positions were to be captured, 'Cotton' related to the advance through the enemy positions and 'Rags' to action by the engineers in following up behind the fighting troops making the coastal road suitable for the wheeled vehicles which followed. As Winberley explained the plan, with the help of models built in the sand, a group of enemy planes made a low-flying attack strafing the men with machine gun fire. If they had known how close they were to wiping out a vital tranche of the leadership of the 8th Army those enemy pilots might have come in for a second attempt. But luckily they never knew. The officers scattered instantly and no-one was hurt.

That day, back home by now, my mother wrote an airmail letter. Although my father thought my name had long since been decided my mother really needed him at home to reassure her that she was making the right decision. Now she was unsure:

I shall ask Arthur Hichens, who married us, whether he will christen the 'inf' when I hear from you whether you approve of 'Janet Margaret'.

I have to go and see the doctor again...Must thank him for all he has done as it makes me mighty grateful when I think that if he hadn't been clever the 'inf' mightn't have made the grade at all and then I don't know what I should have felt.

That afternoon, as my mother was worrying about my christening, my father went forward to recce the enemy positions at Zem Zem. He borrowed Jack's watch and Jack made a note in his diary:

I could hardly refuse him but it's bloody being without it; also there's a good chance it won't reappear as he's gone forward with the other two F.O.O.s. It's the last time he or anybody else has it.

My father detailed Jack to help Sandy Cowie, his Command Post Officer. It was Jack's first experience of battle and he noticed that it was only when a shell came close, with its spiteful whistle and bang, that the more experienced men lay down on their faces:

One hour to go as zero hour is now 22.30. The ammo - 160 rounds per gun - is stacked and we are working hard in the Command Post against the clock. Somewhere a few thousand yards ahead Germans and Italians know something is in the wind but not that an hour from now a curtain of steel and an armoured wall will move in to destroy them. The enemy guns are nervously banging away all the time. We are completely silent.

At 11.30 pm that night the Allies responded. By midnight it was over. At 2.30 am. the men of my father's battery were waiting for orders, but he was still out in front. At first light they moved on and at 8.30 am they were firing again. There was frantic hurry everywhere and the sky was full of planes. By 13.15 no water, petrol or ammunition had come up. The smallest amount of each was vital. The men were tired and many were irritable from lack of food and sleep. They came up through a minefield where several Scorpion tanks lay blown apart and through deep enemy trenches where the flies buzzed mercilessly. At 5.30 that afternoon before my father rejoined his men, and returned Jack's watch. He said nothing of what he had been doing out in front through the night. At 8.30 that evening as Jack was writing up his diary by moonlight they received their orders along with the official news:

We have just received orders. Rommel has retreated fast and this time we're not sending armour but 152 Brigade and all the Divisional Artillery with mediums, bofors and what have you. It means driving all tonight, all tomorrow and maybe tomorrow night. We have no food in hand and hardly any water, a bottle full each. We have had at most four hours sleep during the past three nights.

That night the men of my father's battery snatched a couple of hours sleep before forming into several enormous columns flanked by armour for the drive towards Tripoli. Jack was impressed to see the army stretching for miles across the desert, but as they moved forward part of a column two miles to the south of them was blown up by mines. When it was his turn to drive Jack nearly went into a badly marked minefield. It was a lucky escape.

The following day the men moved so fast that they got ahead of the Allied air cover and German planes flew over, but they were not attacked and later 12 Allied fighters flew over in the other direction. The water was contaminated with petrol. My father had a poisoned foot. Jack had lost a filling from his tooth which made it difficult for him to eat the army biscuits.

It was bitterly cold as they drove through that night. They moved forward in ghostly white columns of guns and vehicles which bumped and shook as they drove through the wadis. They held a course guided by the stars, steering a little to the left of the plough. Many vehicles broke their springs. Those which broke down irreparably were pulled by others until nearly every sound vehicle had two or three trailers in tow.

At 10.00am. on the morning of 18th January they reached the ridge that marks the end of the desert. Just as Avril and I had done they stopped at the edge and looked down over the fertile plain of Tripolitania stretching towards Misurata 10 miles ahead. Jack managed to get together a breakfast for the officers of the battery of hot porridge, bacon, beans and tea. Sustained by this they drove on until 5.30pm when they ran out of petrol. By this time they were dog tired and hoped to settle in for the night. Jack noted:

My eyes were hot and if I sat still I had that horribly exhausted feeling when your hands seem to dissolve and grow large.

But they never got to rest. Montgomery had come right forward and was issuing orders directly to Wimberley. The 51st Division were still not moving fast enough, he said. My father's battery was ordered to drive on another 55 miles to Zliten, but they had no petrol. Three hours later when they were still waiting for petrol an enemy fighter plane flew over and strafed the standing army with machine gun fire. Their nerves were jangling. Jack had squirreled away a little hoard of cigarettes and he gave my father eight. As they moved away a fiendish cold wind got up and the rain began to come down hard. As dawn broke they were still driving and a glorious sunrise lit up clusters of white-painted farm buildings along the Mediterranean coast. At last they were out of the desert. They could have a look at Mussolini's empire.

That night my father's battery set up camp on an Italian farm near Zliten, about 90 miles east of Tripoli. Its former owners had fled leaving a very well tended vegetable garden which was immediately looted by the men. Jack was disgusted to notice that some of the officers joined in the looting and he still had the energy to drive off one man's truck to teach him a lesson. That evening they brewed a supper of bully stew followed by stewed apricots in syrup and listened to the BBC from London. It told them that the 8th Army was 50 miles from Tripoli in the Zliten area. Jack wrote up his diary:

That's us; it's funny when you hear it on a No.11 set from thousands of miles away. Plane overhead so I must put my torch out. No air-raid warnings here...

The men took off their clothes for the first time in a week, crawled into their sleeping bags and instantly dropped asleep. But after only two hours, at 11.30pm on 19th January, they were woken by an unwelcome cry, "Prepare to Advance!"

Forty minutes later in the moonlight they set out from Zliten. They were hallucinating from lack of sleep but Jack still kept up his diary:

Sometimes when driving I nod off over the wheel and I hear all sorts of conversation and see strange images and colours. Then suddenly a real voice with very rapid crescendo breaks in and I wake with a horrible start. At first it was hard to distinguish which voices were real, but now I know, and a second subconscious leans happily back and listens.

After the end of the desert the Italians had built a splendid road, straight and wide with well-grown palm trees which rustled in the breeze on either side of its broad avenues. The Italians had left and as the 8th Army approached they found the enemy had planted the road liberally with mines. They had to keep their wits about them and drive onto the verges to avoid being blown up, but through it all Jack wrote up his diary:

There was something depressing about driving by moonlight past the white villas of Mussolini's Imperial dreams. The thing looks as if it has been jolly well done and the gardens are well stocked and tended, though the Arabs and soldiers now trample them at will....

They drove all night by the light of a full moon, and when it went down they carried on in the darkness for two hours before a golden sun rose over the Mediterranean and they finally set up camp outside Homs. They were close to Leptis Magna though they may not have known that. This was no time for sightseeing. Arabs rushed up to exchange eggs for tea, so that morning they had bacon and eggs for breakfast. But it was a dangerous place to be:

A mine has just exploded loudly up the road...and another! So now on to Tripoli, but one man won't go, I saw him lying by his shattered jeep early today. He looked quite peaceful lying there curled on his right side and I suddenly understood Sassoon's line "When you lie like that you remind me of the dead". He seemed so utterly lonely lying there.

32. Battle of the Hills

Between Zliten and Tripoli the coast road leaves the sea to skirt round to the south of the ancient city of Leptis Magna and the modern town of Al Khoms. It was called Homs in 1943 when my father was there. After this the road crosses a rugged range of hills running right down to the coast. They are the tail end of the huge range which forms the Atlas mountains. As he retreated Rommel left his rearguard amongst these hills to make a last desperate stand to preserve the city of Tripoli with its deep-water harbour from the advancing 8th Army.

Rommel's first position was a fort code-named Edinburgh Castle on the first sizeable hill beyond Homs. When my father came that way on 20th January 1943 the Germans were raining down shell and mortar fire from the fort both on the only road to Tripoli and on the little town of Homs. Between Homs and 'Edinburgh Castle' they dug a huge anti-tank ditch 20' wide, 20' deep across the road. It was many miles long, extending to the south right into the desert and to the north right down to the sea. Eleven miles further down the main road past 'Edinburgh Castle' is a second rocky hill called El Nab. This was Rommel's second defensive position.

My father's battery provided the artillery support to a specially formed unit codenamed 'Hammerforce' led by Brigadier Richards, the popular and experienced commander of the 23rd Armoured Brigade. This brigade using Valentine tanks fought time and again with the Highland Division, so often that it almost came to be seen as part of it. Hammerforce was made up of forty tanks of

THE BATTLE OF THE HILLS. 20TH-21ST JANUARY 1943.

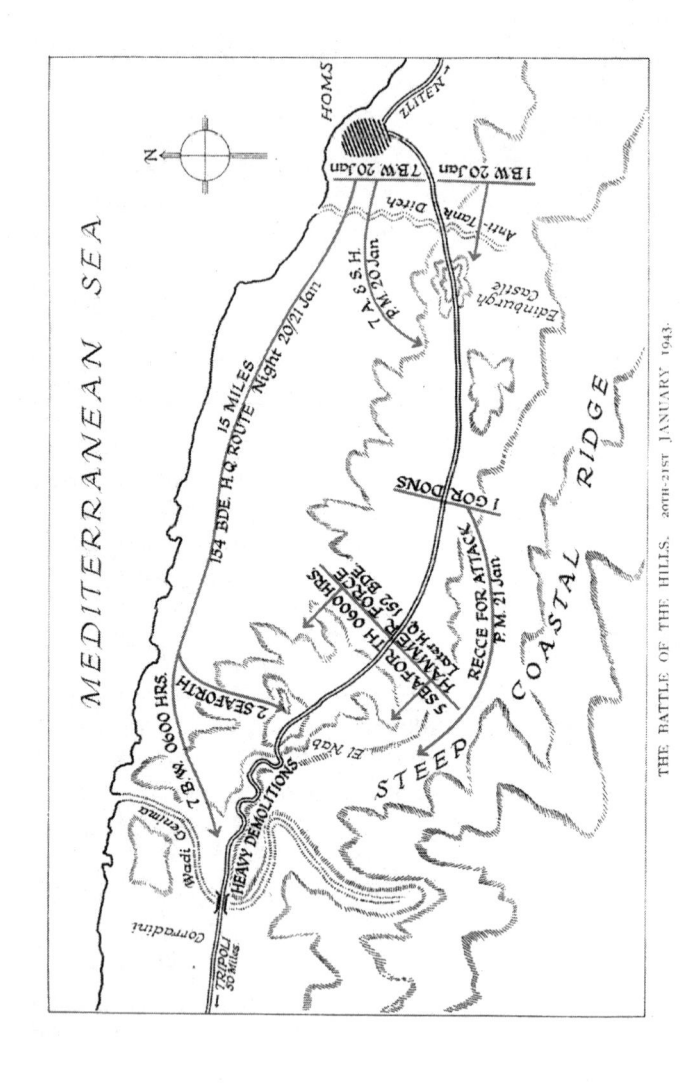

the 23rd Armoured Brigade, the 61st anti-tank regiment, the 5th Seaforth Infantry and 'C' Company of the 2nd Seaforth, one Company of the 1/7th Middlesex machine-gunners, some sappers, an ambulance unit, and part of my father's artillery battery which was supporting 'C' company of the 2nd Seaforth Highlanders. It was quite normal for a special force to be made up to suit a particular battle and for an artillery battery to be temporarily attached to a different infantry battalion.

At 11.00am. on the morning of 20th January 1943 all non-essential vehicles were drained of petrol to get my father's battery mobile and around midday he set off for Homs. Jack and some others were left behind.

The plan for the Battle of the Hills, as Wimberley explained to the officers of Hammerforce at 2.00 p.m. that afternoon, was as follows:

First the stronghold at Edinburgh Castle would be attacked by the 1st Battalion of the Black Watch. The battle was taking place as he spoke.

Secondly, that evening, there was to be an advance along the coast under cover of darkness. This force, under Brigadier Stirling, was made up of the 7th Black Watch and 'A', 'B' and 'D' Companies of the 2nd Seaforth Highlanders.

Thirdly, as soon as Edinburgh Castle fell, the 'Hammerforce' column under Brigadier Richards was to pursue the enemy along the road to attack any further positions they might hold including the rocky outcrop El Nab.

As Hammerforce entered Homs at three that afternoon they found it smashed and deserted. An additional outflanking force had been sent to attack Edinburgh Castle from the rear and by five it was in Allied hands. At five-fifteen Hammerforce moved off from the east of Homs in 'an eleven mile cavalry charge' through the unoccupied trenches and low hills along the route of the road. Radio communications were bad in that hilly country and the maps were poor too. It was heavy going over the ancient terracings and as soon as the tanks left the road they were bogged down. They were relying on the full moon to see their way but when darkness fell it was hidden by clouds.

The anti-tank guns and the sappers went first along the road followed by my father's artillery battery and the infantry. They advanced quickly until eleven that night when they came face to face with the enemy. The Germans were entrenched in the hills either side of the road in front of the outcrop El Nab. They stopped the advance of the Hammerforce troops with heavy machine-gun and mortar fire. Company Sergeant Major Durrand, who was up there with my father, later described the attack:

50 yards from the top every bloody thing in creation opened up on us. Point blank it was. There were 3 machine guns dug in on top of the hill and the Boche were heaving tattie-mashers at us too. There was a sniper out on the right. It was still dark and he was shooting at the noise. We got down. The first burst had killed six or seven and wounded two or three.

The two armies were face to face and so close that the Germans were throwing grenades. My father was awarded a Military Cross for his part in this battle and the citation tells the story:

The Infantry were held up by heavy machine-gun and mortar fire so Major Cochrane went forward. Finding that he could not get good enough observation from the ridge occupied by the forward infantry he went forward to a higher ridge in front and stayed there observing all night despite heavy enemy fire.
When daylight came on the following morning Major Cochrane found that he could see deep into the enemy's position by standing

up on the forward ridge. Despite heavy enemy fire he conducted many shoots in this manner and among many other targets obtained direct hits on the enemy anti-tank gun and mortar, both of which were causing casualties to our troops. His coolness and complete disregard of heavy close-range machine-gun and mortar fire and his efficiency in dealing with the targets he saw evoked unstinted admiration from the infantry he was supporting.

I suppose, since his M.C. citation says so, that my father did stand up on top of a forward ridge in front of the front line infantry completely disregarding the heavy machine-gun and mortar fire. I would prefer to think that he was lying flat on his face as Jack Swaab told Gaffer when he wrote to him two months later. Jack checked the details with Gunner George Reynolds, my father's acting Observation Post Signaler. He said that the two of them crept forward in the darkness to see if they could see what was going on until my father discovered he was so close to the enemy he could hear them speaking to each other. Rather than retreat they lay down flat where they were, my father a little bit forward from Reynolds. He listened to the sounds and, although he couldn't see them he judged the positions of the enemy from the sound of their voices and guns. Reynolds then relayed the information back to the forward infantry on a remote control wireless set. When the full moon came out from behind the clouds my father was able to see quite precisely the positions of the enemy mortars and machine guns. Following his directions the infantry shot over his head at the targets he described. For five hours through the night the two of them lay out on that ridge with machine-gun and mortar fire wizzing overhead in both directions. Once when the infantry got no reply on his wireless they assumed my father had been killed. But later they discovered he was so exhausted he had temporarily fallen asleep in that position.

It was a heroic thing to do. My father was given a Military Cross and Reynolds a Military Medal with immediate effect. The medals were recommended by Brigadier Elliot the Commander of the Royal Artillery and my father's citation was signed both by Elliot and Montgomery. The army authorities were delighted that my father behaved in this way. I would have preferred him to be more cautious.

By the morning of 21st January some of the Hammerforce troops were fighting face to face with bayonets. The attack very nearly failed. There was no way for the stretcher bearers to get through to the wounded. It was a nasty business.

That same night on the far side of El Nab another confused and bloody battle was taking place. Brigadier Stirling of the 154 Brigade set off along the coast with a force made up of the 7th Black Watch, the 7th Argyll and Sutherland Highlanders, followed by 'A', 'B' and 'D' Companies of the 2nd Seaforth with their supporting artillery. They were unable to get their vehicles, tanks and heavy weapons across the huge anti-tank ditch which Rommel had prepared outside Homs, so they marched sixteen miles over the muddy terracings of the hills in the darkness carrying only small arms. Their aim was to re-join the main road beyond El Nab and to cut it off at Corradini where there was a road bridge over the Wadi Genima, thus trapping the German rearguard.

Unfortunately, as their maps were very poor, they thought they had reached Genima when they came to a wadi half a mile short of it and began to advance up the wrong valley. The 7th Black Watch, who were leading the advance, looked back from a crest and saw enemy transport advancing along the road. They opened fire, but then suddenly they saw that the vehicles were British and stopped firing. The tank and several anti-tank guns immediately turned round and fired back at them. Too late they realised their mistake. The tank, guns and vehicles had been captured from the British but they were now being used by the Germans. Many of the Allied troops were by this time out on an exposed forward slope. Some were overrun by the enemy. There were heavy casualties.

At the same time the 'A', 'B' and 'D' Companies of the 2nd Seaforth advanced from the sea up the wadi which led towards El Nab. The land was so rough and communications so poor that they spread out in small groups. Some men were even acting alone. Their attack on the rear of El Nab came as a complete surprise to the Germans, who were concentrating their fire on the Hammerforce troops to the east of the outcrop. The battle went on all night and into the following morning.

At 11.30 am. on 21st January the Germans put up a smoke screen. The smoke could equally have covered a retreat or an attack but mercifully when it cleared the troops found that the Germans had left. As they made their way up the road towards Corradini they were blowing huge holes in the road and after they had crossed the Wadi Genima they blew the bridge behind them.

At 1.00 pm. Brigadier Richards gathered the Hammerforce together and ordered them to continue along the road past Corradini to take the airfield at Castelverde. The road had been so effectively destroyed that it took the force nine hours to cross the Wadi Genima. The 1st Gordons were sent forward to reinforce the brigade and to help them mend the road.

After a good night's sleep back at the camp Jack began to feel lonely and a bit disgruntled. Field Artillery was overloaded with officers and there was very little opportunity for promotion. He had only had a taste of the battlefield at Zem Zem and he was raring to go:

I hear we are missing quite a decent little scrap the other side of Homs and wish to God we could go up there where something is happening.

Jack's wish was granted almost immediately. He was asked to take a couple of petrol lorries and some ammunition up to the battery, by now 15 miles beyond Homs. He started out at first light:

Went right up to the front past the two enormous craters the Boche had made by blowing bridges in front of Homs. I went on through hilly country with many gullies and ravines. Masses of tanks were there, about two hundred of all types. I passed an 'S' minefield with about four violently dead Tommies and a leg with a gaiter and boot attached lying about. I reached the Battery at about 06.15 and got back about 23.15 chiefly by getting the Military Police to get me through by means of some vague talk of 'Brigadier's priority'. Luckily the moon was very bright as all the armour was coming the other way. Enormous Shermans loomed out of the dark amid clouds of dust and low slim Crusaders snaked noisily out at us.

For my father and the Hammerforce troops there was no time to rest. They pushed on all through that day and the following night as well. At 7.00am. on 22nd January then occupied the airstrip at Castleverde without opposition. The Valentine tanks went forward while the rest of the force worked at filling the roads which the Germans had smashed so comprehensively behind them. At 4.00pm that afternoon the tanks came to a place where they could go no further. Then the others, with my father's battery amongst them, were ordered forward into the attack again. All through that night they made their way on towards Tripoli, for so long the goal of the 8th Army.

In the first light of 23rd January 1943 my father drove through the fringe of orange groves on the edge of the city, past the empty red-roofed houses so recently abandoned by the colonial Italians with their gardens overflowing with flowers, along beside the tramlines and between the factories and past the shuttered shops of the Via Roma. At 5.30 a.m. they arrived in the central square, the Piazza Italia. Everything was quiet. The German and Italian troops had left and the Italian civilians had gone with them. The Arabs were hiding. The shops were looted or barred.

Some armoured cars from the 11th Hussars had already reached the city by the desert route but they had avoided the fighting so the Highland Division discounted this. 'C' Company of the 2nd Seaforth, the tanks of the 40th Royal Tank Regiment who were acting as taxis for the 1st Gordons and my father with part of his battery were the first fighting troops to enter the Piazza Italia. Wimberley arrived soon afterwards and immediately asked the Gordons where they intended to paint the HD sign. The re-formed 51st Highland Division had adopted the sign, where the second vertical of the H is used for the upright stroke of the D, from the original 51st Highland Division of WW1. They painted the sign everywhere they went and it led to their nickname the 'Highway Decorators'. The Gordons replied that they had no paint, but Wimberley produced some from the back of his jeep. He told them he would like the sign above the entrance door to the Miramare Theatre, a magnificent Italian theatre built to house 2000, and just around the corner from the Piazza Italia. They painted the largest HD anyone had ever seen and it was bright red.

That morning, at my Round-Turner grandparents' house at Layer-de-la-Haye, my mother sat up in bed after her 6 am. feed. She was writing to my father;

I have just listened to the news and wonder if you too are approaching Tripoli.

He had already arrived.

The biggest bit of news ever which you may or may not know already is that I love you always and always and I want you home again more than anything. Do you remember today two years ago my darling? It was the day you were trying to get here from Crook and got held up by the snow and the bus that got stuck and then you had to sleep at Huntingdon in a chair! And you rang me up in the evening to say you wouldn't be able to get here till tomorrow – my poor darling – you did have a couple of perfectly beastly journeys down and up to Crook to fetch your Wigit. Hope you thought it was worth it my sweetest! Personally I don't know now what I'd have done if you hadn't – the thought of not being married to James now is quite unthinkable – but I don't want to think that thought so that's all right!

A guest at the house left for about ten days freeing up a bedroom:

It will be 'a good thing' as then I can get the young woman organized – at present Mama has her at night as she was being so difficult screaming for hours that I got all upset and couldn't feed her properly and so Alice had her for a few nights and got very weary and then Mama has had her for about three – she is OK now and doesn't scream thank heaven but she was being underfed evidently as I rang up the Matron at the Nursing Home and said 'What shall I do with her – she yells all night' and she told me to give her some complimentary food at night so now she has about 1oz in a bottle at 10pm as well, so she sleeps all right!...She takes up a tremendous amount of time darling even though I don't do everything for her. It's surprising.

33. Tripoli to Pisida

On 23rd January 1943 General Montgomery announced a victory message for his troops:

Today, exactly three months after we began the Battle of Egypt, the Eighth Army has captured Tripoli and has driven the enemy away to the west towards Tunisia, By skilful withdrawal tactics the enemy has eluded us, though we have taken a heavy toll of his army and air forces. The defeat of the enemy in the battle of El Alamein, the pursuit of his beaten army and the final capture of Tripoli, a distance of some 1400 miles from Alamein, has all been accomplished in 3 months. This achievement is probably without parallel in history.

After the war Montgomery looked back at the achievements of the Highland Division in its pursuit across the desert and at the Battle of the Hills and wrote:

Looking back on it all, I think my getting of the HD to Tripoli in a week was probably the best bit of soldiering I ever accomplished in my 30 odd years of soldiering. 250 miles at an average speed of 35 miles per day. One sharp little battle at Corradini and several advance guard actions...I had really accomplished quite a feat of arms.

My father was in Tripoli but a large part of his army

was still on the road when Montgomery gave his victory message. Jack and the others who had been left behind due to lack of fuel were urged to get to Tripoli in any way they could. They swarmed all over the tanks. Any trucks which still had petrol pulled one or two more behind them. Craters were filled, diversions made, vehicles and guns were pushed through the beds of wadis as the whole huge army moved slowly on towards Tripoli.

Beside the road in the area of El Nab Jack passed a group of new graves. He knew they were the graves of Seaforth Highlanders, but I don't think he knew that the men had been killed in the battle in which his own battery had fought. As he approached Castleverde the road was totally blown apart and the army moved so slowly that Jack had time to investigate an Italian lorry blown up on one of their own mines, a double Teller he thought. The lorry was completely destroyed and scattered and a pair of trousers had been blown forty yards to where it hung from a telegraph wire. Scouring the wreckage Jack found bits of uniform and a letter beginning 'Mio amato Pero'. He put it in his pocket to translate later when he would get a glimpse into the life of a faraway child he would never meet. Another child, this time on the other side, who would never know what happened to its father.

The rest of the regiment made it through to their bivouac area outside Tripoli 38 hours after my father arrived. The newcomers were tired out and fed up in spite of the victory.

The 25th January 1943 was the second anniversary of my parents' wedding. Seven months had passed since, when she was three months pregnant, my father had kissed my mother goodbye through a train window at Nottingham station. And still no mail came through to tell him about the baby. My father wrote:

Spent the anniversary of our wedding absolutely dead tired. It was the first day I had for some time without 20 or more hours work to do and consequently I was wandering about just plain half witted.

This was the nearest he got to telling my mother what he had been through since he wrote his last letter. Now they were allowed to say they were in Tripoli, but she had already heard that on the BBC.

It was 26th January 1943 and I was nearly four weeks old when Gran's telegram finally reached my father. At the time they most needed each other the war had kept my parents apart, and now things weren't going to get any easier for them either. But, for the brief moment allowed him, my father was overjoyed. My mother and I were both safe. He immediately sent off a return telegram saying "Well done Wigget. Love to you both" and, trying to come to terms with the event from a distance, he settled down to write a longer air letter:

Suppose she will be quite an established fact by the time you get this though it all seems a bit odd to me as my Wigget seems a very young Wigget herself, and as far as being a paterfamilias myself that seems even odder. How is my Wigget and did you have a bad time my poor darling? Wish I could get home for a short time to see you both as am jumping up and down with anxiety to hear the answer to a thousand questions.

What colour are its hair and its eyes? If it looks anything like me I am sorry for it but cannot think of any ready remedy. Only hope it takes after Wigget and not after me. Can think of few things more appalling than a horse faced young female James. What does Wigget think of it? Are you doing the proud young mother act to a circle of admiring relations? Feel I am not doing my share in standing off the odd thousand miles away and making sarcastic comments. However we are not sitting back and have come a bit of the way home at any rate.

That evening my father got hold of a bottle of cheap Chianti and shared it with his men, telling them all that he had a new baby daughter . He called Jack by his christian name in public for the first time since he joined the battery and Jack was absurdly gratified, he said. The battery was eating better since Jack had been appointed Battery Messing Officer. That day he found 45 cauliflowers and some peas and cabbages at a nearby farm and proudly brought them back to their bleak encampment.

My father was still desperate to get news from home:

Wonder if you can imagine how anxiously I am waiting for news of my Wigget and the little Wigget...How I wish I could go home just sometimes in stead of being on top of my job always day and night...Do let me know by the quickest means everything about the little Wigget. How I wish I could see you both.

The army had stopped moving. It was time to celebrate their victory. First there were shows in the Miramare Theatre, now sporting an HD sign above its door. Later in the war it was destroyed by bombs, but when my father reached Tripoli the magnificent Italian theatre, built to seat 1800 people, had a royal box and tiers of smaller boxes behind the raked seating. Douglas Wimberley wanted 'the Balmorals' to perform in the Miramare as soon as possible after their arrival and on 28th January they played before Montgomery and a full house. There had been a Balmorals concert party captured with the original Highland Division in 1940 at St. Valery and the tradition was continued when the Division was re-constituted. Wimberley used these shows to build up a sense of unity and 'esprit de corps' within the Highland Division. The shows always had a strong Scottish flavour: it was one of the ways in which he encouraged the Black Watch, Seaforth, Argylls, Camerons and other battalions to pull together and act as a team.

Another was to make sure the Highlanders always looked smart. Jack was not impressed:

Pep talk from the Colonel today, The degree of spit and polish this division goes in for is astonishing. All brass will be polished in spite of an A.C.I. to the contrary and now I hear that a church parade is to be provided - but no man must be less than 5'10"!

But five days later, when he was allowed in to Tripoli for the first time, he had to admit to a sneaking admiration for the result:

Troops are everywhere and some of them pretty scruffy. The HD for all its bullshit certainly looks decently turned out.

By night there were frequent enemy air attacks, especially on the harbour and waterfront. From their encampment outside the city they watched as enemy planes were brought down in flames surrounded by lights and crashes looking like fireworks. My father was told that he had been cited for the Military Cross for his fighting at the Battle of the Hills. He had caught up with his sleep at last, was relieved about the baby and delighted when his new Messing Officer collected 180 lbs. of new potatoes, an unheard-of luxury. But Jack noted that now they got monkey nuts in lieu of the biscuits they once got in lieu of bread. He was finding his place as the jester of the group. My father was, he said, 'super-genial' and now always called him Jack, and this in turn made the other officers more friendly.

Montgomery had decided to keep the troops out of Tripoli as much as possible. He wanted to keep them away from the local women. The first troops to be allowed in found the place empty and miserable; they were only allowed to stay till 5.30pm but that was long enough. "The fruits of victory look more like crab apples daily," Jack commented wryly.

Now that the Americans were fighting on our side the Allied troops were terrifically optimistic, though in reality the tide was only just beginning to turn but morale was high and even Jack had no doubt that the Allies would eventually win the war. The sudden addition of vegetables to his diet, or maybe a bug, upset my father's stomach, but he managed to throw it off quite quickly. At last, at the beginning of February, my father received a whole bundle of mail and wrote back immediately to my mother:

My love I cannot tell you how relieved I was to get a bunch of airmail letter cards from you the other day which carried the story of Wigget from Xmas to about 14th Jan. Had been waiting and waiting for just that period. Just coincided with a period of activity out here so all got hung up till they arrived in a bunch....Do wish I could be with you now my darling. Shall be itching with suppressed desire till I can get home or get you both out here. Did not think I would be as interested as all that in a little Wigget but I am, just one of those things that happen without any set explanation.

He wrote an airletter to Ga to try to get an independent assessment of the baby:

Dear Ma,

Many thanks for several letters that have appeared by many and devious routes....Am still waiting for a report from you on the offspring, have had a descriptive letter card from Peg but feel that she is being a bit optimistic. Talks about it being in some ways like me and beautiful in the same breath, which two things do not I feel quite go together. Only wish I could be with them but that cannot be just yet.

That day my mother wrote to explain that she had already had to register the baby at the Registrar's Office in Colchester:

All the walls were covered with notices about the penalties for failing to register and also for giving false information – cheery little spot!

As my father hadn't even got the letter with her suggestions about names by that time she registered me as Janet Owen, a suggestion she had never even made in her letters as far as I am aware. In any case I was always known as 'Jane' or more often, at first, as 'the inf'. And I was still giving her trouble:

Jane didn't seem to settle down very quickly and although thank heaven she gave up yelling at night she took to screaming all day which is one better but not at all what it ought to be and she seemed in pain poor little thing and got awful wind. So I don't want to inflict a screaming infant on the household because of course Mummy and Alice and everyone rushes to see what can be done and they walk up and down with her and sing and everything to calm the creature and are marvelously patient but it obviously was a tummy upset or food not agreeing or too much or not enough or something so I came to the conclusion that to get hold of a nurse who is trained and really knows was the only answer.

I was being wonderfully well looked after but my mother didn't want to impose on her family, so Nurse Prendergast was brought in. She stayed for the next six weeks, the maximum time allowed before registering with the police at a new address became compulsory. A gale blew up in England which took off a lot of tiles and left a gaping hole in the roof of my Round-Turner grandparents' house in Layer-de-la-Haye. Grandfather was home on leave. He did his best to mend it with plywood and sacking but the rain rushed through and had to be caught in zinc baths and fish kettles.

On 4th February in Tripoli the troops paraded in the Piazza Italia in front of Winston Churchill, Field Marshal Alan Brooke, and Generals Alexander, Montgomery and Leese. Churchill told the Highland Division:

"You have altered the face of the war in the most

remarkable way. The fame of the Desert Army has spread throughout the world. When a man is asked after the war what he did it will be sufficient to say 'I marched and fought with the Desert Army' ". On his return to London Churchill reported to the House of Commons:

"I have never in my life seen troops march with the style or air of the Desert Army. Talk about spit and polish, the Highland and New Zealand Divisions paraded, after their immense ordeal, as if they had just come out of Wellington Barracks."

The HD paraded in their kilts and came to be known as the 'Ladies from Hell', but Jack made an irreverent note in his dairy:

The Divisional General fell over in his carrier while saluting as the driver accelerated too suddenly.

That evening my father wrote again to my mother:

I cannot tell you how I am longing to see you and the offspring. You will have to send me one of those normally rather revolting photos of a Wigget and young taken in unnatural surroundings.

And at last my mother received my father's first cable of congratulations:

My poor sweet waiting till the 26th for the cable to arrive...

On our wedding anniversary when the 'wee girl' came in to be fed at 6 o'clock in the morning they had put into her hand a tiny little bunch of winter honeysuckle and rosemary and she was really holding it bless her! I have saved a bit of the rosemary to send to you in a letter as it means remembrance and means that I never forget my James ever, ever, ever.

I feel I have rather failed where looking after Jane is concerned – I imagined I would be able to get on and deal with her but never realised that I would feel so weak and stupid. Jane is a darling and very good tempered and placid like my J a m e s when she is feeling well but if I eat summat that she doesn't like, poor little thing, then she cries.

Darling I love you almost more than I can bear and I am longing and longing for the day you come home.

On 7th February 1943 the rain began to fall daily in torrents in North Africa. It started at 7.00 each morning and went on till 2.00 each afternoon and, as it continued in this pattern day after day, there were signs that an advance was imminent. Rommel was rumoured to have assembled 60,000 men and 200 tanks in Tunisia. Montgomery called a meeting of officers to explain his plans for the advance and on the 10th the troops received a warning that they should expect to move in 48 hours' time.

On 11th February the weather was cold, wet and windy. Jack Swaab went back to Homs with several of the senior officers to walk over the battleground of the Battle of the Hills, and to inspect the German positions at Edinburgh Castle and El Nab. Keith Douglas, who had fought there, went back too and wrote a poem about a dead German soldier. He was the very man whose bullet had pierced his own tank three weeks earlier in the battle:

> *We found the place again and found*
> *The soldier sprawling in the sun.*
> *And smiling in the gunpit spoil*
> *Is a picture of his girl*
> *Who has written 'Steffi, Vergissmeinicht'*
> *In a copybook Gothic script.*
> *But she would weep to see today*
> *How on his skin the swart flies move,*
> *The dust upon the paper eye*
> *And the burst stomach like a cave.*
> *For here the lover and the killer are mingled*
> *Who had one body and one heart;*

And Death, who had the soldier singled
Has done the lover mortal hurt.

My father never went back. He was moving on again and early that morning he set out towards the Tunisian border. As he made his way forward the road passed right by the ancient city of Sabratha but this was no time for sightseeing, the rain came down in torrents and he was soaked to the skin. All day and late into the night he struggled on and early the following morning he passed the place where the railway ended.

It was Pisida.

1998-2005   THE SEARCH III

34. The Cochrane Family

When she saw the photographs I had taken of the desert outside Pisida my mother decided she would come with me on the trip Avril organised for the following year into Tripolitania, the western end of Libya. Alec said he would come with us and we decided we would take my children, Thomas and Amy, as well. And so it was that, in May 1999, all the people closest to me came to share my particular dream; the dream that my father once really existed and that he was once a real live person who walked on this earth.

We flew out from England to Houmt Souk on the Island of Djerba in Tunisia and, the following morning as we settled into our seats in the coach, Avril introduced us to the rest of the group. Brigadier Peter Vaux, who had been in charge of the Army Garrison at Homs in the 1950s, had come with his wife Jean. Wally was an 8th Army veteran, a cockney who left his mother for the first time when he went to war. Tom, another army veteran, had been on every trip that Avril had made so far into Libya. He spent the formative years of his life there, he said, and never quite re-adjusted to living in England. Dorothy, eighty-seven, very stout and hardly able to walk, had come with a younger friend to help her find the grave of her brother, buried in Tripoli. Avril introduced the six others and finally came to us:

"And this," she said waving her arm in our direction, "is the Cochrane Family."

We were all taken by surprise. One time, long ago, my mother called herself Mrs Cochrane but that had changed when she married my stepfather when I was seven years old. Thomas and Amy have their father's surname and Alec his own Greek name. It is only I who call myself Cochrane. I went back to my maiden name after my first marriage broke up and I wanted to keep it when I later married Alec. I have no brothers, sisters, uncles, aunts, great uncles, great aunts, first cousins or even second cousins called Cochrane. Somehow that family has withered away. I was used to others thinking of me as some kind of isolated freak. But when the initial shock wore off each of us in turn realised we were delighted. It seemed we had a connecting force between us which, over the years, had been forgotten. My mother turned to me and said:

"Your father would have liked that. How he would have laughed to see us all together here!"

My mother has fifteen grandchildren and a clutch of great-grandchildren too. Thomas and Amy are two of many. As a single parent I had lived right the other side of the country from Essex where my mother still lives, so my children didn't see too much of her as they were growing up. As the bus moved forward Thomas and Amy pulled out some recent photographs of their families and children to show to my mother.

"How extraordinary that I should have spawned a whole group of fair-haired people like these," she commented. "How could I, with my black hair, have done that?"

The answer to her question was obvious yet it seemed that, over the years, she had become so fully absorbed into her black-haired step-family that she had forgotten how I and my children came to be fair-haired. She thought of us as the odd ones out. Almost as if we had done it on purpose to be difficult.

Avril sat up at the front of the bus with three

Libyans. She was in charge along with Achmed, Fatma's business partner and a huge bear-like man, and Younis the interpreter. The third Libyan was the bus-driver. He was a genuine bus-driver this time, not a secret policeman in disguise.

As soon as we arrived at the first border post I made my way to the front of the coach to discuss our stop with the leaders.

"Yes. Yes," they chorused in unison. "That's fine. Of course we must stop. This is why you have come. We all know where you want to stop. We know where the border is. No problem."

"We'll need to stop exactly two and a half kilometres on from the border," I insisted. After my failure the previous year I wanted to be sure to make a better measurement from the exact point of the border. I was glad that Achmed was so sure he knew where the precise border-line lay as I was not so certain. I looked for the milometer on the coach. It was right down low behind the driving wheel. To see the figures properly I would have to put my head down on the driver's lap and that is something that no woman, even at my age, likes to do to an Arab man. The new bus-driver only spoke Arabic, so I couldn't explain.

"Could you ask him for the mileage?" I asked Achmed.

Achmed spoke to the driver in Arabic and confirmed to me that he had taken the mileage. He didn't tell me what it was or where he thought the exact line of the border lay. We crossed the land between the two customs houses. In the Libyan shed Achmed got busy with the customs palaver. Passports were collected, papers checked. All twenty-one of us got out of the bus and queued while a border guard in a sentry-box checked our faces feature by feature. The guard looked at each passport photo then up at the right eye, at the photo then to the left eye, to the mouth, the nose, the hair.

At last we drove out through the police barrier and the pole came down across the road. It was manned by Libyan border guards holding Kalashnikovs. This was the point of no return. If the measurement from the border line to this barrier wasn't correct we could never get back through this barrier to check it.

"How is the mileage going?" I asked Achmed.

"Fine. Fine," he replied.

We drove on. We came to the point where the landscape changed and I realised we had gone too far. It seemed that Achmed hadn't been measuring the distance at all. He didn't know the distance between the border and the police barrier and now it had shut behind us. Perhaps he never knew exactly where the line of the border lay. It is simply the custom of Arab men to assume authority over a woman and I had fallen for it.

How could I have allowed this to happen? I was devastated. I had brought all these people with me and now I had let them down. High up in the large tourist coach I felt helpless. I asked Achmed to stop the bus. We did a three point turn in the road and went back to the police post where the bar came down across the road. But I had no idea of the distance between the police post and past the customs shed to the boundary with Tunisia. Everyone in the coach was watching me. They waited patiently while I tried to guess the distance back from that post to the border. They couldn't have been more charming and I felt really guilty.

"Let's try going forward two kilometres from here," I said, guessing.

I pushed my head down onto the driver's lap to read the milometer. He gesticulated wildly and shouted in

Arabic; but it was just too bad. I wrote down the numbers and told Achmed exactly the reading where I wanted to stop. We stopped. I looked again at the milometer. We had passed even my guessed number by a whole kilometre. It was the best we could do. The landscape didn't look the same. Maybe, I thought, if we walk southwards we might find the 'well used track' where my father once walked, the causeway for the railway which had never been built.

The 'Cochrane Family' got out of the coach, leaving the others sweltering inside. We walked down into the scrubby desert on a path that led southwards. This time I had my photos and the little sketch with me. But the land looked different. The tracks which crossed ours weren't as I remembered them. The camelthorn bushes didn't look the same. I was so disappointed. Here a group of people had even begun to cultivate the land. They had built themselves a thatched hut in the corner of a field and lit a little fire to cook on. Younis the interpreter began to look at my own photographs and suggest places where they might have been taken. It was surreal, and hopeless. In the end we stuck some poppy crosses into a large sand dune topped by a camelthorn bush where two tracks crossed about 200 yards to the south of the road, and Younis took a photograph of us all. It wasn't the place I had been to the previous year and I knew we had come much too far along the road. But we couldn't keep the others waiting any longer.

My poor mother looked bemused. She had expected that we would drive straight to the place where my father was buried and she had braced herself for that. She is a practical person. I think she had been wondering, if we did find the grave, how she would feel about it and what she should do. Now I had let her down. We climbed sadly back into the coach and, as it drove on towards the Roman city of Sabratha, we each found it difficult to return from the different reality of my father's world we carried in our heads. We touched our limbs as if we had had a close shave with death and I felt lucky to be alive.

The Roman city of Sabratha, when we arrived, did nothing to dispel the feeling that we were actors in a surreal film. This year the ancient theatre was full of Libyan tourists. I climbed with my mother and Amy up to some higher seats from which we looked down at the stage. We heard a roll of thunder coming from behind us, but the day looked calm, clear and still. The noise came again and louder. It wasn't thunder, but drumming and, as we watched, a troupe of dancers burst onto the stage. They were densely grouped in a swarm, like bees. Musicians danced around the fringes of the group. The main player had a type of bagpipe; he was blowing into the hollowed head of a bull whose huge curling horns stuck outwards on either side. Others played tambourines and African pot drums. The dance became wilder and faster. The dense group widened and a hole formed in its centre. Eighty-year-old Wally, one of the 8th Army veterans from our party, was swept into the newly-formed central space. He danced vigorously. Then, as we looked down, Alec was swept into the centre of the swarm and held with a pink satin sash. He danced a wild dance and a voice we could hear perfectly from way below shouted out to him in English,

"Where do you come from?"

"From London like the Queen!" he called back.

Up on the stone seating of the amphitheatre small groups of Libyans gathered around my mother, Amy and me. They all wanted Amy in their pictures with them. With her long straight fair hair she seemed different and exotic. A dark girl put her arms round my mother and drew her into the photograph too.

"What is your name?" she asked.

I was struck by the simple warmth of this girl's gesture. I couldn't remember the time when I was last able to show my mother such warmth. It wasn't just the stiff upper lip thing that lay between us, it was a separation which had happened long, long ago. Yet this girl who knew nothing of my mother could give her a hug, and I could see that she was loving it.

When our coach party arrived in the outskirts of Tripoli the vision before us was very different to that which greeted my father on 23rd January 1943. The orange groves and flower gardens of Mussolini's empire had gone. Our coach pushed its way through anarchic traffic into the centre of the city. The Piazza Italia is called Green Square now. Green is the colour of the Libyan flag. But in the paved square the only green to be seen was the fronds of palm trees, swaying high above our heads. Around the edge of the square taxis and cars were weaving and bumping. There were no traffic lights, pedestrian crossings, rules or courtesies and the signs were only in Arabic. To the west a fortress rears up above the dominating walls of the Moorish city. Gaddafi has made a magnificent museum inside it, but the exhibits, from pre-history to the present day, say nothing of World War II. The victory parades which took place at the base of its walls at the end of February 1943 have been written out of Libyan history.

The following morning we went to the Allied War Cemetery on the outskirts of Tripoli. The Italian cemetery, which had been smashed and desecrated when we walked through it the previous year, had been tidied and planted. Our guides pushed us quickly through it into the immaculate war cemetery beyond, where the military members of the tour managed a proper service around the central memorial cross. The Brigadier led the way. As we stood there in the bright sun of an African summer morning the birds chattered in the trees as he recited the familiar words.

At the going down of the sun....we will remember them.

Together we thought of another time. The Brigadier, Wally, and the two other war veterans were wearing military uniform, medals and regimental caps. They each laid sprays and wreaths. Avril laid a wreath for the Black Watch Veterans' Association. I laid a small wreath for my father. I gave my mother a kiss and as we stood for the two minute silence she held my hand. We were together in our feelings about my father's death. Long ago, when he died, we had been together too.

Dorothy found the grave of her younger brother and spent a full hour beside it. When he died the family was simply told he had been killed in an explosion. But because of wartime censorship they didn't know where he had been. They were terribly distressed. Her own mother never found out what had happened to her son or where he had died. It was thirty years after the war by the time Dorothy discovered that he had been killed in Tripoli. He had been making very large anti-personnel mines for use in Italy. Ten men were killed when one mine exploded on the assembly line. The theatre of war had moved to Italy by that time and it never occurred to Dorothy's family that her brother was still in Libya. By the time she discovered he was buried in Tripoli it was impossible to get there. When at last she found out about Avril's tour she thought she was too old and infirm to come, but a kind younger friend said she would help her. Her friend went with Dorothy wherever she went and never left her side. It was the last thing Dorothy wanted to do in life and at last it was possible. Now she found her brother's grave and those of the nine others who died with him. She left a wreath there and took a whole film of photographs to show her family on her return. After forty-five years she too was still trying to come to terms with her loss.

After the war my mother had always expected to hear that my father had been re-buried by the Commonwealth War Graves Commission but the letter never came. Now our family divided up and checked every one of the graves in the Tripoli graveyard in case we found him there. But there was nothing. The Brigadier kindly suggested that perhaps my father might be buried in one of the graves of soldiers 'known only to God'. But I knew in my heart it wasn't so.

The following day at Leptis Magna I got talking to a handsome blue-robed Libyan who had studied Archaeology in Newcastle. He had enjoyed his time in England, he said, but now he had one simple question.

"Why," he asked, "did the English allow the Americans to use their air base to bomb Libya and to kill Gaddafi's daughter?"

I cast my mind back and remembered my horror at what President Reagan had done. How could he have sent in bombers when no war had been declared? How could he justify killing that little girl? How could our government have condoned his actions? I apologised on behalf of our country. It is a pity our politicians don't seem to imagine what it will be like for the innocent civilians who live where their bombs will fall. It isn't just something which happened in the past.

At the end of our conversation the archaeologist said he would take me to see something which would amaze me, and he was as good as his word. Later that day Amy and I followed our new long-legged guide as he bounded off along the straight stone-paved street between the ruined walls of unexcavated Roman houses of Leptis Magna. The ends of his blue-dyed robes blew back towards us as we scuttled along as fast as we could behind him. He ran the whole breadth of Leptis and out beyond the city into the rolling sand dunes by the sea. We ran on, dodging between the camelthorn bushes, and as he ran our new guide stooped and caught up a porcupine quill from a prickly clump of sea-grass. He handed it to Amy who, without stopping, swept her long hair up into a knot and speared it through with the stripy quill to hold it.

The Roman baths looked so vulnerable. Only one large sand dune lay between them and the sea. The entrance lay well below the level of the beach where the sea might sweep straight in at the first storm. The little building was complete with immaculate hot baths, cold baths and steam baths. Hunting scenes were delicately painted on the underside of its tunnel vaulted roofs. In England we marvel if traces of medieval ochre painting survives on the walls of our old churches but in the Roman hunting baths outside Leptis the colours of the paintings were vivid and modern, not only ochres, greys and blacks but deep Indian reds, fresh blues and greens. The frescos show fishermen rowing their boats down the Nile. On the bank, behind the rushes and the palm trees, stands a stately colonnaded building. Although they are two thousand years old these are not ethnic but sophisticated paintings, realistic, clear and fresh. High up on the walls of the frigidarium painted hunters are stalking leopard, their evocative names are printed above their heads and our guide translated them for us as 'Swift' and 'Brilliant Lightening', which reminded me that Montgomery used to wish his men 'good hunting' as he sent them in to battle. For over a thousand years this building was buried below the sand. I learned that there are several other Roman baths and villas buried along that coast where the shoreline is continuously encroaching. As I stood with my feet on the intricately patterned Roman mosaic floors I thought again about all that lay hidden beneath the desert sand.

35. The Family in Libya

Our stop inside the boundary on our way into Libya had not been a success. We wanted to go back peacefully on our own as a family to see if we could find the place near Pisida where my father was buried. I wanted to look for Mr. Ramadam-el-Assy, the old man at the border village of Ras Ajdir, who was out when I passed by that way the previous year. I wondered if Mr. Ramadam might remember my father's grave with its little wooden cross on that land by the border.

This time, when we arrived by taxi at his house in Ras Ajdir, Mr Ramadam was at home. A daughter came to the gate and we showed her first the photograph of my mother and father on the back terrace at Hawkhurst and then the sketch of my father's grave. Mr Ramadam was lying on a simple day bed in the shady porch of his house. He struggled to his feet. Although in his nineties, lame and frail, his face was strong and memorable. He gestured us into his house. The modern sitting room was bare but for low rug-covered mattresses around the floor. We sat in a row with his daughters and grandchildren who, with infinite hospitality, gave us home-made mezedes and Arabic coffee. Younis, who had come with us, translated our questions and the two men spoke for some time in Arabic.

Mr Ramadam used to be a nomadic shepherd. Since he was a small boy he had grazed his sheep over the land around Ras Ajdir. He used to wander freely between the land which is now Libya and the land which is now Tunisia. The border was not fenced until after the war and then he and his friend, a fellow shepherd called Khalifa

Shaban, had to decide which country they wanted to live in. He decided to live in Libya where the authorities built him a house. Khalifa Shaban went to live in Tunisia.

Mr Ramadam said that in all the years he had been a shepherd on this land he had only ever seen three graves of Allied soldiers in the land between Bu Kammash in Libya and Ben Gardane in Tunisia, and these were now on the far side of the border in Tunisia. He remembered well when the Germans and Italians came through in 1943, followed by the English. There was no battle here and only three men were killed, he said. The graves lay beside two camelthorn bushes. At the time of the war the bushes were large but they had been cut back and now they were small. The two graves were near each other, one grave had had two soldiers in it and the other only one. Fifteen years earlier when the road to the border was made up and widened the authorities came and took away the bodies of the three soldiers. The local people never knew their names or where the bodies were taken. He would take us to the place, he said. We could drive there now in our car. It was after the Tunisian checkpoint and before you get to El Chucha where you see a gap in the trees on the right hand side of the road. We were thrilled with Mr. Ramadam's offer but we couldn't take it up. Achmed had our visas which were in any case only valid for a single entry and exit. So we arranged that we should pick Mr Ramadam up in our bus as we crossed back over the border on our way home in a few days time. Then, he said, he would come with us to show us the graves.

Without visas we couldn't get back to the boundary line to take a measurement from there. It had been quite a long drive to Ras Ajdir and now Younis was pressing us to drive straight back to rejoin the others. There was no time to stop again, he told us. So we got back into the taxi and drove right past the place where I had first walked towards the salt lake and planted my poppy cross.

I was confused by the new evidence that Mr. Ramadam had given us and now I began to doubt my own research. I wondered if it was possible that Gaffer had been right after all and that my father was killed and buried in Tunisia. Had the boundary moved and was that stretch of land which was once in Libya now in Tunisia? Was it possible that Mr Ramadam was right and that only three men were killed on the whole stretch of land between Bu Kammash in Libya and Ben Gardane in Tunisia? Could my father have been buried next to two others in a second grave even though only one grave was shown in Melia's sketch? It seemed unlikely. Our meeting with Mr Ramadam had posed more questions than it answered.

In 1999 we went only as far as Zliten, the last town in Tripolitania before the true desert begins and then we turned back and followed the road westwards in the same direction as my father and the 8th Army. On our way back in the coach we by-passed Homs, where my father had fought in the Battle of the Hills, and stopped for lunch at a hotel in the hilly ground beyond the town. After the meal my mother, Thomas, Amy and I wandered down to the end of the garden.

Below our feet lay a pile of cans, paper and old bottles which the hotel staff had thrown over the small boundary fence. We stood together under a eucalyptus tree looking beyond over the rough land which stretched away downwards to the north. In the distance we could see the shining surface of the sea.

The hilly ground was etched into the rough steps of ancient terracing. This was the land tilled by the Romans to provide grain and olives for export from the city of Leptis Magna. It had the surface texture of a recently ploughed field but there was no sign that anything grew there now. In a rainstorm it would quickly turn to a glutinous mass. To the east the rough-stepped land rose up into a rocky outcrop. We looked suspiciously in that direction. There was something forbidding about that hill.

I had shown Peter Vaux, the retired Brigadier in our coach party, my notes describing my father's part in the Battle of the Hills. Now, as our little family group stood together picking up eucalyptus nuts and chatting, he came up behind us,

"It could have been over this ridge that your father was looking when he got his M.C.," he said. "This is just the kind of place it might have been."

It turned out he was right. We were looking at El Nab. It looked like hellish terrain to fight over. No wonder, I thought, that Rommel decided to make his last stand before Tripoli in this place. The hotel where we had lunch was to the west of the hill. My father approached it from the east. My research had put my father's actions into the context of the desert campaign and now I could see what he was doing there and why. By the time the 8th Army reached the western edge of the desert Rommel had one very great advantage. The supplies for his army were coming in through Tripoli, his supply lines were short. But the 8th Army was supplied through Benghazi and every ounce of food, water and petrol they needed had to be brought 1000 km. across the desert. Montgomery had explained to Wimberley that unless the army reached Tripoli within 10 days from the attack on Zem Zem they ran a very real danger that, because of the difficulties with supplies, they would be forced to retreat right back to Buerat or further. Hammerforce was the frontline force detailed to break through the German defences on the main road through to Tripoli. A lot depended on the infantry hitting their targets that night and my father was aware of that. They knew they had to get through.

The Axis troops were very well prepared for the Hammerforce attack on the night of 20th January 1943. Rommel only needed to hold that position for a limited time before the whole 8th Army would be forced into retreat right back over the desert. He was severely criticised by Mussolini for not holding out longer in the Homs position.

Yet I was still having some difficulty with the part my father played in the Battle of the Hills. Did he really stand up on top of a ridge in front of the forward infantry disregarding close range machine-gun and mortar fire as his MC citation had said? I was upset to think he had knowingly put his life at such risk. He was longing to get back to see his wife and baby, so why should he stand up on top of a ridge with shells and bullets wizzing all around him? Even now that I understood the reasons it still sounded like madness to me. Was my father too brave, too selfless, or was his sense of duty too highly developed? Was it bravado? Was he brought up on too many adventure tales of fearless heroes? Was he trying to emulate his illustrious naval ancestor Thomas Cochrane? Was it something in his genes? I began to wonder, with mounting apprehension, if it was something I might have done myself if I had been in his shoes at that time. I had a sneaking sense of recognition and I didn't like that.

My father was born into a services family. He decided to become a soldier and later, when war came, he wanted to play his part on the front line where Cochranes always go. By the time of the Battle of the Hills he was up to his neck in it. After his death his unit continued up into Sicily, went home briefly before crossing to France for the Normandy landings, fought across northern France into Holland and Belgium, through the bitter cold of the Ardennes and the bloody battles of the Reichswald and the Rhine, before finally advancing into Germany. His battery was always right out at the front. It seemed to me that his death in action at some stage was almost inevitable. I sighed.

Peter Vaux, the Brigadier, could see that I was shocked by the part my father had played in that battle. He tried to reassure me that my father would not have been standing up for more than a moment or two in that forward position. My father was obviously very brave and steadfast, Peter said, but he wasn't silly. He was a professional soldier who was doing his job to the best of his ability and that job was to support the wretched Seaforth infantry who had such a horribly dangerous task ahead of them. They were being wounded and killed all the time and probably asked for his help. It was essential for him to get to a place from where he could direct their fire. The first place was no good. He might have given up but he wasn't like that, so he crept a bit further and found a good spot. It was risky, but the lives of those infantrymen depended on it. He weighed it up coolly and decided he must stay there for as long as it took. It went on for a long time and it must have been a great strain. Peter was sure my father intended to get himself and his doughty radio operator safely out of it - and so he did. That Military Cross was well and truly earned, he said.

I hoped that the Brigadier was right. On that occasion my father got back safely, but by the nature of things we only ever hear from the survivors like him. I knew that Peter Vaux too had had some pretty close calls. They make a good story after the event. Keith Douglas gives a fearsome contemporary account of the Battle of the Hills in his book 'Alamein to Zem Zem'. Douglas survived this battle and fought on till 1944 when he was killed in action in Normandy. He too left a safe staff job to go to the front. Once a war is started good men will fight and die. Again I sighed. Nobody takes into account the ongoing price to be paid by the families of the dead.

Back in Tripoli Avril had arranged a meeting for us with the British Consular Representative. I had understood there was no British presence in Libya so I was amazed when we were ushered into a spacious consular residence with quiet, well-kept gardens with watered green grass and swaying palms, only a stone's throw from our hotel. The gardens, which were completely concealed from view by a high, densely-grown hedge, led down to the corniche where we had walked by unaware. Outside there was bustle, fumes and drifting rubbish but inside was an island of peace and order with clipped green lawns and watered flower borders.

Dr. Guckian and his wife were delightful, knowledgeable and urbane. How long had they been hiding out in Tripoli where we had been told there was no British presence? With them was Mr Giuma Gider, the Libyan who dealt with the war cemeteries in Libya, Tunis and Rome, and another Englishman from the Foreign Service. They gave us bowls of strawberries and, although they could only get evaporated milk, they served us with tea in bone china cups.

Alec, my mother and I discussed the problem of my father's grave with Dr Guckian and Mr Gider. We told them about our trip to see Mr Ramadam at Ras Agdir and told him that he had said there were only three soldiers' graves between Bu Kammesh in Libya and Ben Gardane in Tunisia and that these were on the Tunisian side of the boundary. Was it possible, we asked, that the boundary might have been altered during that time?

Dr Guckian said that if the original grave had been in Tunisia this might account for the fact that my father had not been 'gathered in'. It was less likely that a temporary grave would be left in Libya, he explained, where there was a British army presence until the 1960s, than in Tunisia, which remained a French colony until it gained independence in 1956. On the other hand he was not aware of any significant alteration in the position of that boundary since WWII. He promised he would look it up for me in a reference book he had at his office and ring me at our hotel the following morning. His attitude was startlingly helpful and straightforward. It was thrilling to meet someone who was knowledgeable, friendly and keen, like us, to discover the truth.

He rang us at 8.30am the following morning and told me that the boundary between Libya and Tunisia was codified in 1911 under the Ottoman Turks. It ran inland from the headland at Ras Ajdir. There was some indication of minor adjustments in 1958 and 1959 in conjunction with the Tunisian independence. In 1988 there had been a dispute over the maritime boundary after the discovery of oil off the coast and the precise position of the sea boundary was decided in an International Court of Justice. He suggested that on my return I get in touch with the boundary specialists at the Boundary Research Unit at Durham University to investigate in detail.

When we approached the border at the end of our one-week stay we stopped, as agreed, to pick up Mr. Ramadam so he could take us to see the three graves. As soon as we got to Ras Ajdir Achmed and Younis jumped out and rushed round to Mr Ramadam's house. Alec and I ran after them but we had only gone a few steps when we met them coming back. "It's no good," Achmed said. "He's out." Mr Ramadam had promised us that he would be in that day. Had Achmed said something which had scared him? He was being very bullish and he didn't look sincere. We asked Younis to come back with us to Mr Ramdam's house. There we tried to get him to translate our questions but Younis wouldn't do it. We were defeated. We left a present we had brought for Mr Ramadam with his daughter to give to him. Now we were in Ras Ajdir we couldn't cross back though the police barrier where the border police stood with kalashnikovs to look at the land where my father was buried. Luckily I had one more idea up my sleeve. I had the name of Mr Ramadam's friend on the Tunisian side: Mr. Khalifa Shaban.

36. Graves in Tunisia

When we got through to the Tunisian side of the frontier there was a group of taxis waiting there. I told Achmed that the 'Cochrane Family' would like to leave the coach to do some more investigations; we would re-join the group in Djerba that evening. We explained our quest to our Tunisian taxi-driver, who spoke perfect French and was only too happy to translate for us. So we drove away from the border, passing through the police posts, asking the people walking beside the road if they knew Mr Khalifa Shaban. They all of them knew him and showed us the way. About 10 miles into Tunisia we stopped and walked across the sand dunes between the camelthorn bushes to a large group of hand-built rush huts where he and his large family lived. Dogs rushed out barking. But they slunk back as our taxi-driver stooped to pick up a stone. Then he put it down again, "So they trust you," he said.

Mr Khalifa Shaban wore an embroidered djellaba in cream-coloured cotton. Its neckline opened low to reveal necklaces of wrinkles on his patched brown chest. His legs were pink-scabbed below the skirts of his robe, but his features were strong and honest and he carried his ninety years with pride. His walking stick was banded with strips of beaten metal. He shook our hands then put his own hand to his mouth and kissed it. His large family collected around him as we spoke and each one shook-and-kissed in the same polite way, small bedouin women in bright-coloured hand-woven head-dresses, a son with a withered leg, and a group of children, grandchildren and great-grandchildren.

Mr. Shaban's story tallied precisely with that of Mr Ramadam. Only three British soldiers were killed in this area, from Bu Kammash as far as Ben Gardane. It happened when they came through in early 1943. At El Chucha there were two graves for three dead men: two people in one grave, one in the other. His son with the bad leg would take us to the spot, but he didn't have the right papers to pass through the police posts so he wouldn't be allowed to go along the road. He would go over the desert and meet us by the graves, he said. A battered car appeared out of nowhere. The son went into a hut to change into smarter trousers for the occasion and Amy took some photographs of the bedouin ladies with their children and gave them a bright red lipstick from her bag.

We drove back through the police checkpoints towards the border. It was forbidden, the police told us, to drive up that road if we didn't intend to cross the border. At each police post we brought out the photograph of my mother and father on the terrace at my grandparents' house in Hawkhurst. We introduced my mother and told them she was the woman in the photograph and that the man, her husband, had been killed near here. We showed them the drawing of the grave. We needed official permission to go back down this road and to stop, they repeated, but this time they would let us go. Then they waved us on. "May Allah be with you," they said.

We found the battered car and the two bedu men next to two large mounds in a gap between the trees. The son with the withered leg showed us where the two graves had been. They were to the north of the road and laid sideways, not with the head towards the mound as in the sketch. The graves lay to the east, not the west, of the mound. The whole area and the mound with its two camelthorn bushes looked quite different to Melia's sketch. A dirt track was to the north, not the south, of the mound. I looked over the graves and beyond the camelthorn mound but there was no sign of a village.

I knew immediately that this was not the place. It didn't feel right at all. We stood between the trees while I took this in and wondered what to do next. Pieces of black plastic blew around our feet and attached themselves to the stumpy camelthorns. Our taxi-driver kicked away a rusty can. My mind was straying around. I set out northwards across the desert to see if I could see the 'well used track' where my father once walked, but my mother called me back. She was thinking Khalifa Shaban's son had most likely trodden on a mine on this land and that was why he had a withered leg.

Mr. Khalifa Shaban's son and his driver wanted to go. He asked for a pen and I discovered a quite good propelling biro in my bag which pleased him. I was disappointed by the graves and I didn't know what to do next, but as I hesitated I noticed my mother bending stiffly down to pick up a stone. As she placed it at the head of the single grave Thomas, Amy and Alec began to help her. Together we built a cairn.

I fetched a poppy spray I had brought from England from the back of the taxi and some small wooden poppy crosses. I pulled the card out of its polythene cover and we all wrote our names under 'In Remembrance' written in gothic script. We stuck the poppy spray into the cairn of stones and the two little crosses into the next-door grave mound, one at each end.

Then we stood back under the trees in silence. A soft breeze pushed through the leaves above our heads. It was my mother who took the lead. Now at last we were the Cochrane Family and my mother was in her rightful place as leader of the clan. Together we paid our respects by those empty graves with a two minute silence. Whoever these three British soldiers had been, and wherever their bodies had been moved, they could stand in for my father and for all the others killed in WWII whose bodies were left by the roadside in a foreign land.

As we left I noticed the milestone by the road said Ras Ajdir 7km. I was wondering if my mother thought my father might really have been buried there in Tunisia. I didn't want to disappoint her by saying I was pretty sure that was not the case so I was relieved, after we got back into the taxi, when she said, "I feel we may not yet have got to the bottom of this mystery."

On our way back from the Libyan border in our taxi Thomas, Amy, Alec, my mother and I talked together about the war. We discussed the division of Berlin and the cold war with Russia. My mother told us about her feelings at the time of Dunkirk. Thomas was extraordinarily well informed and now Amy, who had never taken any interest in war, was fascinated too. We learned a lot from each other as the taxi rolled on towards Djerba Island.

We all had views. I have a strong rejection of war. All my life I have suffered from and witnessed the results of a death in battle. The words of Martin Luther King have lodged themselves firmly in my mind: "Non-violence," he said, "is the answer to the crucial political and moral question of our time - the need for man to overcome oppression and violence without resorting to oppression and violence." For a short time I managed to send my children to a Quaker school.

In spite of this Thomas knows all about war. It is a knowledge that boys seem to acquire, yet he would never hunt, he is strictly vegetarian and a pacifist. If there was another war he wouldn't fight, he said, pointing out that it's not that he's scared, he just wouldn't kill another human being. For him, as for me, the loss in war is always more obvious than the achievement or the glory. Young men of his generation, he said, are more sceptical of the motives of politicians than they were in his grandfather's day, and there are movies such as 'Platoon', 'Saving Private Ryan' or 'Apocalypse Now' which show war as a pointless waste. I would like to think he is right; but I am not so sure.

Thomas prefers to fight for a more ecological future, for the future of the world, he says. I would endorse that. But old-fashioned wars still go on, and once a war has begun good men like my father and Jack will do their best to win it. Ordinary young men from opposite sides, who in other circumstances might chat together as we were chatting now, are sent out to kill each other. A good soldier has to be prepared to kill or be killed; it goes with the territory.

Something happened to our family group during our week together in Libya. As the week went by I noticed my mother watching Thomas. She began to notice his independent spirit, sensitive respectful manner, quiet humour and intense loyalty. Suddenly she was gripped with a new thought about him. He was so like Jock. How odd that those genes should have come down the generations in that way, she began to say. And how odd that he should be a pacifist when he comes from generations of scrappers.

My mother has often had the thought that no war is worth the loss of even one man, but she is cynical about the effectiveness of other methods. "Well," she says "there is always bribery, I suppose." The Brigadier too was sceptical of alternatives. He was thinking back to WWII. "Imagine," he said to Thomas one evening "if you were standing on the front at Brighton looking out across the sea from which a ruthless invasion was expected daily and above you the sky was alive with bombers, behind you the smoke from burning London clearly visible, the street where you live a pile of rubble, the fate of your wife and children a mystery - would you still be a pacifist then?"

Thomas admitted that in that situation he would probably fight, but he wondered if WWII had been a special case. Since that time the British have been to war in Suez, Korea, the Falklands, the Gulf, Bosnia, Iraq and Afghanistan. Thomas felt that all these wars could, and should, have been avoided. And we should stop making and selling arms right away, he said. As I listened to their conversation I was proud that I had managed to bring up a son with these ideas; that I had broken the family chain.

Alcohol isn't allowed in Libya and although it didn't bother Alec, Thomas or me, my mother and Amy had missed it. When we got back to Houmt Souk on Djerba Island at the end of our week in Libya my mother and Amy decided to go out to get themselves a drink together before supper.

"Jock would have approved of this," my mother told Amy. "He enjoyed his drink. It was the only thing I ever thought might have been a problem in our marriage, he really did drink a lot sometimes. He loved to stay up late drinking with his friends and discussing world affairs."

As they walked along my mother asked Amy if she could look for her purse in her bag. Amy found a little tin but it was not what she was searching for. She was about to put it back when my mother said,

"You can look in that if you like."

Inside it Amy found a small army button.

"I cut it off Jock's epaulette when he went away," my mother told her. "We both kissed it and we made a love pact between us. When he left I suggested I should sew it on his uniform again, but he said I must always keep it with me, he would get the tailor to sew another button on his jacket. I used to wear it on a piece of thread around my neck and I wondered if the water would wash away our kisses when I had a bath. I discussed this with him and we decided that nothing could ever wash our kisses away and it was alright for me to wear it all the time." Now she had brought the button with her in her bag.

Over supper in Houmt Souk we talked about our week together. I had brought my family over to Libya and I hadn't even been able to show them the place I had found the previous year where I thought my father might be buried; let alone mount a more scientific search to find the precise spot, as I had intended. But nobody complained. They all said they wouldn't have missed the trip for anything. Our experiences had brought us so much closer. Now we were a tight little group.

"That was a lovely holiday," Amy said, "even though I spent nearly the whole time weeping."

Amy has always been allowed to show her emotions. I didn't bring her up as I, or as my mother, were brought up. It isn't always easy to know what my mother is feeling but she said she wasn't too upset that we hadn't found my father's grave because she felt so much closer to the rest of us. It was she who had the last word:

"It has been lovely spending time with Jock's family," she said. "Something quite unexpected to me to come out of this trip was getting to know his living family." Then she added, "I don't often see Thomas and he is a quiet fellow, but funnily enough, in so many ways, he is very like Jock. The way he moves his head and walks and the quiet way he comments on the world keep reminding me of Jock."

When my mother recognised us as 'Jock's Family' it removed a misconception which had come between us so long ago when she first married my step-father, when I was seven years old. When we got back to London after our trip I took my mother up to Thomas's top-storey flat where he had recently made a garden on the roof. On the way upstairs we met the lady from the flat below and I introduced my mother.

"I can see the similarity," she said. My mother, as usual, began to deny it.

"I can't ever see it myself. She's like her father," she said. But this time I stuck up for myself.

"There must be some similarity, I think," I replied. "I can sometimes see it too."

It may seem silly but before our trip I wouldn't have had the courage to say that to my mother. Even if I had had such a thought I wouldn't have felt able to contradict her. Dissent was not allowed in my step-family, even at this kind of level. Discussion was an unknown concept.

After our return from Libya I said to my mother, "It is sad that during your marriage to my father you were never together long enough even to quarrel over who put out the rubbish in the evening." She replied immediately and with real enthusiasm,

"Oh yes! And we would have quarrelled too!"

Yet in my step-family there was no discussion and no quarrels. I think the situation was too brittle to allow for it. Our trip to Libya brought us closer to my mother. She began to understand that we're not different to my step-family out of a desire to be tiresome. Although she may not always agree with us we have reasons for our beliefs. At last she was beginning to see and accept me and my family for the people we are, and as we accept each other. She was beginning to see us as my father might have seen us: as his family. She may even have begun to be proud of us.

When my mother first began to show me my father's letters she did it because she thought I might get to know him that way, and she was right. Now she finds that by putting my father's letters into the context of the war and of her life I have helped her too. When she read the first draft of my writing about those wartime years she recognized herself as she was then. She had thought she had moved on entirely, become a different person, but my writing helped her to join the two ends of her life and make it more whole.

My mother didn't ask me not to show my father's letters to anyone else, but I think she assumed I wouldn't. Perhaps I betrayed her trust when I did that, but so far she has been generous about it. "I find the sky hasn't fallen in," she says.

She makes small factual corrections so I can adjust the script but she seems to agree with my assessment of those times. She even said I was right about my father's girlfriend at the other end of his little sailing dingy in Kashmir, the lady who was said to have turned my father into a 'woman-hater', and she pulled out three photographs my father had taken of that lady, from his end of the boat!

37. The Dream

We hadn't yet found my father's grave but, now that I had begun to know more about him, I didn't feel the same urgency as I once felt about it. The process of writing the story of my search helped me to understand what had happened and to put it into perspective. On my return to London I went on with my writing until I came to the point when my father reached Pisida, but then I couldn't go on. I had come to know him as a live person. I was enjoying it and I didn't want to think about what came next. I stopped writing. My friends said I didn't look good. I told them there had been a death but I didn't explain. For three weeks I went into mourning.

Then one night I had a dream. For the first time in my life I dreamed about my father. It was as I turned my head that I suddenly caught sight of him. He was standing a little distance away and slightly higher than me up a grassy slope at the base of an old oak tree. He stood up tall and straight and slim under the spreading branches of the oak. Then I realised he was standing in the place above the swimming pool at my grandparents' house in Hawkhurst where as a child I used to sit to make little people with capped acorn heads, acorn bodies and pin arms and legs. He was watching me but I knew he couldn't come towards me. I had to go to him. But now I was ashamed to show my face. I should have been a little girl in my blue flowered sun-suit from America, with straight fair hair parted in the middle and looped into two blue ribbons. But in my dream I had the face I have now, the face of a middle-aged woman. I ran to the low stone wall around the swimming pool where Gaffer planted irises and, like a child who thinks it cannot be seen if its own eyes are hidden, I hid my face in my hands.

Then I realised I had to go on. My father couldn't move so it was up to me to go towards him. It was just too bad that so much time had passed that my face had grown old while his was still young, that it had taken me so long to realise that it was for me to come to him. As an adult I ran right up to him and he hugged me. It was a long close loving hug, like Amy and I give each other when we meet again after we have been apart and just as Gaffer used to hug me when he came to meet me at my boarding school.

So I had to go on. I had to pull myself together, to be brave yet again and see it through. Looking back through the History of the 51st Highland Division, published in 1953, I found again the footnote which refers to my father's death:

Just before the 5/7th Gordons crossed the frontier on 13th February they had a bit of bad luck. Major Barlow was moving up the main road when one of his men stepped on a mine. Barlow was wounded in the chest, a machine-gun officer was killed, and Lieutenant McAndrew wounded. About the same time the Commanding Officer and Major Cochrane of 127th Field Regiment were moving up when Cochrane stepped on a mine. He was killed and the C.O. wounded.

When we were talking about 'Hammerforce', the team Mongomery got together to break through Rommel's final defences in the Battle of the Hills, the Brigadier had told me it was quite usual for an artillery battery to be attached to a regiment other than its own. It came to me suddenly that my father might have been with the 5/7th Gordons when he died. I went once again to the Public Records Office and this time I looked up the 1943 War Diaries for the 5/7th Gordon Highlanders and there I found the story.

On 11th February 1943 Lt. Col. Saunders, the Commanding Officer of the 5/7th Gordon Highlanders and his Intelligence Officer set off for the border. They ploughed their way through the drenching rain and eventually came to the miserable little railway station of Pisida, the last town in Italian North Africa. On 12th February the rain continued. Again Saunders and my father went forward. The following day, 13th February 1943 in the early hours, a patrol which had been sent ahead returned to say that they had been nearly to the border and found only craters in the road and dummy guns. The Gordons' diary says that Lt. Col. Saunders moved forward from Pisida at 9.00am. My father was with him. On my old map Pisida is shown in the place where Bu Kammash is now, approximately 20km. from the border. My father and Saunders followed the infantry ('A' Company of the 5/7th Gordons) who were filling mine craters. They drove in an armoured car along a 'well used track' to the south of the road. On my 1941 map the main road is shown as asphalted as far as the border. There is no track, or proposed rail route, marked on this map to the south between the road and the Mellahet-el-Briga salt marsh to the south. The Gordons' diary tells the story:

13/2/43

At 09.00 hrs. the Commanding Officer went forward. Half way up the track on our way there the Information Officer saw a prisoner being marched back by a most bellicose looking 'jock'. The Information Officer interrogated him in his best German and found that he was fed up walking back and highly delighted to be captured. He stated there were no enemy this side of BEN GARDANE and we had no need to worry.

We carried on and this time another jock informed us that the Commanding Officer, Major Barlow, Major Cochrane,

Lieut.McAndrew the Commander of the Mx. Battalion and 3 Other Ranks had walked into an 'S' mine patch and were all out of action. Who was dead and who was wounded we did not know.

We went on till we met the Brigade Major who gave us the full story:

Major Barlow had been on the main road when one of his men stood on a mine and went up. Major Barlow got a pellet in the chest and was in rather a bad way. He was evacuated. The machine gun officer was dead, Mc.Andrew wounded.

The Commanding Officer and Major Cochrane had been moving up a much used track with 'A' Company trying to get to the frontier. Major Cochrane stood on the mine and was killed outright and the Commanding Officer who was only 5 yards away got his legs and arm peppered and collapsed on the spot. He also had to be evacuated.

It was a dismal story.

So that is what happened. It is indeed a dismal story. However one thing was clear. My father had not yet reached the frontier when he was killed and this tallied with Melia's letter and sketch. My father was killed in that narrow strip of land between the salt marsh and the frontier.

Our meetings with the shepherds did not lead us to my father's grave. Mr Ramadam-el-Assy and Mr Khalifa Shaban both told me that only three soldiers were killed between Bu Kammash and Ben Gardane as the 8th Army came through in February 1943. But they were wrong about this. Checking the contemporary records I found that at least nine British soldiers were killed along that stretch at that time, not only the three whose graves the shepherds had seen. There was my father, two men from Major Barlow's group and the six sappers who were killed soon after they crossed the frontier into Tunisia. We know that the graves of three men, probably three of the sappers, were left by the roadside in Tunisia, where our family held a special ceremony for them, until recently when the road was widened and repaired. We know that according to the Commonwealth War Graves Commission records two graves at K0204, maybe those of Major Barlow's two men, were swept away during the rainy season of 1944. My father's grave was nearby.

When I look at the map of Pisida (see the front cover) I can see that the Mellahet-el-Briga salt marsh bulges out ominously towards the sea at that point. Both K0103 and the two positions I have for the grave are nearer the centre of the bulge than K0204 and I think that the CWGC are probably right to conclude that the wooden cross on my father's grave was washed away only a year after his burial in 1944. Maybe at first the shepherds avoided walking on that mine-filled land and by the time they went there the wooden crosses had already gone. But would a flood which washed away a little wooden cross have also washed away a human body? Not necessarily, I think, and sand and salt have extraordinary preservative powers.

I was still wondering where my grandfather got the idea that his son was killed in Tunisia when I re-read a letter from Jack Swaab which is stuck in the back of my grandparents' photograph album. It was written on 2nd June 1943, nearly four months after my father's death. Here I found the story that Gaffer had told me when I was a child. It was the story he believed himself:

Dear Admiral Cochrane,

Though it might be painful to you I think you'd like to know the manner of Jock's death. Such things, wound though they do, are in my small experience better known than left to conjecture. We were crossing the border at Pisida. Jock, doing F.O.O. was right up with our infantry battalion; in fact as always he was practically running the thing singlehanded. He was first into Tunisia, cutting the wire himself. Then the infantry came through and actually advanced some distance, Jock with their Colonel and several other senior officers left his armoured car and followed them on foot. He knew there were mines about (we had quite a few casualties here because it was a mass of mines) and was scratching for them himself. The curious and tragic part was that when his party followed in the very footsteps of the infantry Jock trod on an S (anti-personel) mine booby-trapped to a Teller. There was a great flash and black smoke, and when it cleared Jock was lying there dead. The Colonel was badly wounded.

Jack could never have known that his small embellishment, his addition of the idea that my father crossed first over the border into Tunisia 'himself cutting the wire', would cause such difficulties in the future. It is true that the Gordon Highlanders, who my father was with at the time of his death, were first to cross the frontier. Jack wasn't with my father on the day he was killed and he never saw his grave. Perhaps he was never himself exactly sure where my father was killed or buried. It must have seemed an unimportant point to him at the time. If a man is dead he is dead.

I wondered what was Jack doing on the day when the news came through. Luckily he had recorded everything in his diaries. Jack set out from the base camp outside Tripoli the day after my father. He set out with his batman, Findlay, at 05.00 am on 12th February 1943. Torrents of rain were falling as he drove towards the Tunisian border. It was blowing a gale and, he recorded, 'every damn thing was soaking'. Jack and his batman were well out of Tripoli but still 85 km. from the border when his truck broke down. The big end had gone. By 7.00 pm. Jack had decided to abandon the truck and he and Findlay hitch-hiked forward along the main tarmac road which was lined by big palm trees and eucalyptus. That evening they managed to reach Zuwarah, still 60km from the Tunisian border, where they stayed overnight as guests of the 57th Horse Artillery. Jack was 40 km. behind my father on that road. The following day, 13th February 1943, Jack doesn't give the time when he first heard the news of my father's death, but it was the first thing he wrote in his diary that day:

Jock is dead. It happened soon after I caught up with the Battery near Pisida. I am absolutely stunned by the news, he was such a grand chap in all his own way. He stepped on a Teller mine and was killed outright. What makes it worse is that his wife (who I met in England) has just had a daughter. I simply can't really realise yet that he's dead. I shall miss him like hell. Oh Damn! Why is it the best people and the bravest always go?

At 13.50 Jack made another entry in his diary. By then my father's body was already buried. An anti-tank gunner, Major Reg Hamden or Maunden (if only William Melia's handwriting were clearer!) held an impromptu burial service at a spot to the south of the road. It was either in the position recorded by Lt. Col. Perry, my father's commanding officer, in his regimental war diaries or at the spot recorded by Major Melia, the second-in-command, which he said was 'approximate'. But Melia was present at the burial service and he did the drawing of my father's grave. It was twenty past two that afternoon before Lt. Col. Perry heard the news and wrote it up in the regimental diary:

14.20

News is received that Major J.O.Cochrane was killed by an 'S' mine boobied to a Teller mine at K0103. Body is buried 200 yards south of road at 200 yds east of kilo 2.

Lt.Col.Perry was well behind Jack and the rest of my father's battery. Montgomery would not have liked his style; he liked his commanders to lead from the front.

The map reference K0103 is approximately 1km to the south of either of the two given burial positions (see map p.361.) It seems possible my father was killed around K0103 and that what remained of his body was then carried up towards the road to be buried, as happened with the bodies of the Sutherland Highlanders after the Battle of the Hills. I realised now that the compass bearings I had on my first visit were probably correct for K0103, but different to either of the burial positions given in the letters, which would account for the discrepancy I noticed when I was there.

Jack's next diary entry was written at ten to two in the afternoon of 13th February, still before the time when Perry made his diary note.

They've been bringing in his personal effects, each one a reminder of incidents past. I am remembering the little jokes he used to make and how he always pulled my leg about being a reporter. The things he used to say - "That's just too bad..."

I know what Jack meant by that as I had seen a letter my father wrote to my mother from Salisbury Plain in April 1942 shortly before he left England:

A most unfortunate incident but very interesting. What happened was that upwards of 1000 stooges including your James were watching a demonstration of fighter aircraft attacking ground targets with machineguns. Suddenly one of the planes came in and strafed the spectators stand in stead of the target. One of those things listed as "Just too bad." Twenty odd have kicked the bucket and I believe the total injured including the scratches are as high as two hundred. Very good demonstration of the effectiveness of ground strafing fighters. Not nearly as lethal as I expected. Usual surprise on rising from the prone position to see the number of bodies who also got up. Then looked around for those who did not.

And now it was he who lay still on the ground and

for Gaffer and Ga, my mother and me, and for Jack too it was 'just too bad'. Jack found it impossible to believe. Everybody found it impossible to believe. Even now I find it impossible to believe. Yet I know it to be true and I have lived with it all my life. In so many ways nothing has changed since that day when Jack wrote:

It is hard to realise when somebody familiar by daily contact is dead, yet J.O.Cochrane is only a name now and that well known figure with his monocle, duffel coat and pistol strapped to his thigh is lying broken and bleeding in the sand near Pisida. And yet a part of me still expects him to turn up any moment and tell me it isn't true. But of course it is and I shall never see him again.

At 9.00p.m. that evening Jack finished writing his diary and bedded down for the night. He was still in Tripolitania, the western end of Libya, four miles from the border:

21.00 Four miles from the Tunisian frontier. The moon is bright and the stars are out. We have dug our guns in, eaten bully and veg and now, soon, we shall sleep under those bright stars. Somewhere nearby, one leg blown off, the Major is also sleeping. But he will not awaken.

It was not a pleasant thought, even now it is no better, and Jack had a terrible night. Seven months later he still vividly recalled that night:

I remember so well the reddish moon that rose that night as I lay outside 'E' Troop command post under the desert stars. The guns stood out stark against the bright sand and the plough was clear and gleaming. And how I remember the inconsolable sense of loss which swept over me, that long, lonely, sleepless night of 13 February with Jock lying in the bleak marshes where the single cratered road drove into Tunisia.

But that night Jack tried to remember the good times. He remembered my father's mannerisms, his jokes and his way of speaking:

remembering him vividly even down to that sort of snorting chuckle he used to make when he was amused at something.

Jack's teeth had been troubling him, he often had toothache and found it difficult to chew the army biscuits. He remembered how he had discussed it with my father who described his own teeth, telling Jack how 'some of the weaker brethren gave up the struggle and had to be removed'.

Another day Jack complained that he didn't have a proper job and my father replied, "Oh well, one of these days somebody will go on a course, or to hospital, or get himself killed..."

His comrades called my father callous when he made these comments and Jack referred to his laconic humour. But now exactly that had happened and Jack realised my father had cracked his last joke. He was devastated by the reality of it:

He was probably the best soldier in the Regiment. I didn't realise till he was dead how much I also thought of him as a man and as a friend. I lay there for hours staring at the Plough in the clear bright sky and feeling an overwhelming loss and sadness. And now I shall have to get used to doing without him.

As dawn broke on 14th February a gusty wind blew up the sand. It was still cold but at last the sun shone through. My father's battery went forward and crossed the border. The road was broken, dusty and littered with mines. Jack was depressed. He looked out for my father's grave; he thought he knew where it was but he never saw it. That afternoon he had a long chat with Jimmy Gegan and recorded that 'He too is bloody fed up about Jock's death'. When he was still 12 miles from Ben Gardane Jack reported six sappers killed.

I wish I felt I had something to look forward to. I find

with Jock's death I have nothing. I realise I must have been striving for his approval. I know that when he said "Stout effort!" it used to mean something.

Back home my mother knew nothing of this. On 19th February she started another densely written air-letter to my father:

I wonder how you are getting on? Whether you are in the snows and mud of Tunisia now or what you are doing, Darling I long for the day when I know where you are and what you are doing for every five minutes of the day! But my James wouldn't approve of being tied on to apron strings would he?!

Jane has begun to gurgle and burble! Only usually she makes such a funny noise that she frightens herself and makes herself start to cry! I never really heard her do a real one until yesterday and as her petticoat was going on out came an "A-goo" from the depths! She smiles a lot now and is on the verge of chuckling – really she's growing fascinating and is a 'wee rascal'. Also her hair is all falling out and the new crop that is growing is fairer still and she's got long, long eyelashes! I don't know whether I ever told you about a nevis that she's got on one side – a sort of red birthmark it is only unfortunately they grow up in a bump as a rule and this one has grown up a bit. The doctor said he could easily remove it if it grew so I shall have it done when she is vaccinated.

My father had been dead six days but for now she didn't know that. She ended her letter:

Well my darling – all my love as always and I think about you all through the day and plan things we'll do when we're together again! – Wigit.

When my mother took me back to the doctor for the vaccination he cut a slice half way round my body to remove the nevis and sewed it up with twelve huge red stitches. My mother was appalled. It looked as if I had been sliced in two. As usual the timing was just awful. It followed directly on the news of my father's death.

I only saw these letters from my mother to my father as these are the 'stragglers' which never reached him. Each one was stamped on arrival with a special stamp at the Field Post Office saying, in capital letters, "IT IS REGRETTED THAT THIS ITEM COULD NOT BE DELIVERED BECAUSE THE ADDRESSEE IS REPORTED DECEASED". They were all returned to my mother together in one bundle some months later.

38. Loose Ends

Over the years which followed our family trip to Libya I sometimes thought about the place where I went on my first trip with Avril in 1998, that derelict place with only one large old camelthorn bush with its strange long hump running to the west. Camelthorn bushes from that time do live on still, I now knew. I had such a strong strange feeling about that place and I thought that must mean something. I didn't think I would have that feeling for nothing and all the records showed the grave was somewhere there. The sun came from the right direction, the track was in the background and the place looked so strangely similar to the one which Melia drew.

My father's place of burial is less than ideal. Any day the ground could be dug for cultivation or built over, and Gaddafi's new railway is still planned along that route. I would have loved to have just one more ceremony with as many of my father's friends and relatives as I could muster. I would have liked to get in a Scottish piper to play the music he so loved. I would have liked to put him to rest in a place of our choice. But this will probably never be possible, and as time goes by fewer and fewer people who once knew him are still alive to join me.

If we face the facts of history it will not necessarily cure the pain we feel. But the alternative is worse. When he spoke to Gaffer about my father's death Jack was right when he said:

Such things, wound though they do, are in my small experience better known than left to conjecture.

My search had put many old ghosts to rest. My father was never reburied in an official cemetery but that doesn't mean that nobody cared. The army authorities appreciated his work. His men would have followed him anywhere. Those who were close to him cared, if anything, too much. This was all part of the problem. He was so full of life. And then it ended. So much too soon.

I re-read Jack's diaries.

In mid April 1943 I would have been four months old and the photo shows me with Gaffer and Ga around the time that Jack received a letter from Gaffer:

Very restrained, very like Jock. He asks me to send details of Jock's M.C. which I shall try to do. I wish Jock were still with us; he was so restful in the mess.

At the end of July he recorded that he received a letter from my mother:

Letter from Jock's wife; painfully brave.

And he immediately wrote back:

Dear Mrs Cochrane,

A few days ago your letter of 5 July reached me here on the Sicilian battlefield, and though I know it calls for no answer I want to write one. I hope this won't displease you. I've headed this letter 28/9 July because it is in fact about midnight, and I am sitting in my Command Post with its assortment of small electric lamps and hurricanes, telephones, artillery boards and what have you. It is about the only time to write letters, day time temperatures reach about 120° in the shade, but the nights, though hot and breathless, are not quite as bad as that, and one can stand in the darkness listening to the thump of the guns, and feel the night breeze cool as a caress. Out there with nobody to bother one and the stars calm and infinitely distant overhead, one has time for reflection on the sadness and insignificance of all our days and ways.

I think perhaps you'd rather I didn't speak of Jock now. If ever you write again (and please don't feel you've got to) tell me, and I shall know for future reference. But because tonight I don't know I'll take a chance and just tell you how amazing it has been the way he has not been forgotten as most of us are or will be. Men have spoken to me time and again in that casual, genuine way soldiers do, of their admiration for him and their sense of loss. My own is such that I dare not contemplate yours. Your letter made me realise how much easier is our part than that of those we leave behind, You say it is difficult not to feel bitter; I know it only too well; unfortunately I don't seem to have your courage and I do feel bitter over Jock's death and other things I have seen and heard, specially when we get the so-called Society Magazines out here.

Both at home and in the desert, Jock, with that amazing maturity of judgment for his years used to help me - and I expect many others. I miss him as much as ever. I suppose these things are the wrong ones to write to you, but I feel you are not somebody to whom the 'right' things are written.

Please forgive me if I am making things harder for you. I am glad my first letter helped a little anyway.

As a matter of fact I did know about Jane, Jock mentioned it (mentioned is exactly the word) at Tripoli. I hope I will meet her one of these days which seem so immeasurably far away.
Would you mind telling Admiral Cochrane I'll write him the odd piece of news once we've finished these people off. Things have been reasonably trying from time to time, that is why I have not been able to write for a while.

On 30th September 1943 Jack and his friends went swimming off the Sicilian coast:

Jimmy and I raced 100 yards - he won by about 5 but ended up in much better condition. The last 20 yards full out were quite a strain. However we were feeling full of beans and came back up the 400 foot of cliff in about 5 minutes. How good it is to feel healthy. It was grand on the beach. One lay in the warm sand dreaming - chiefly of going home - and hearing the repetitive surge and crash of the waves on the shingles. One stood knee-high in the foam with the sun warm on a tanned back - how Jock would have loved it all...

They cared and they missed him then. They care and they miss him still. In Tripoli my mother and I looked down from a window of our hotel to the turquoise swimming pool way below us. Suddenly a single slim figure dived neatly into the water and cut across it with a sharp crawl. For Amy a pool is for swimming. "How Jock would have enjoyed his grandchildren," my mother said. She sighed and stood quietly watching. We were thinking the same thought. What a waste. How we both wished he could have been with us all these years.

On 8th September 1943 Jack looked back again and wrote in his diary:

This is, I suppose, an historic day. Italy had capitulated on terms of unconditional surrender and is co-operating in throwing the Jerry out of Italy itself. I couldn't - don't ask me why - pluck up the correct mood to join the jubilation which is rampant tonight. For one thing I don't think the war is over by any means. I think the Germans will go on fighting for at least a year more. And secondly I am feeling very strange and distant with the large doses of Quinine we have been taking for three days against malaria. My ears are ringing and my head feels strangely detached, Instead of cheering the victory I find myself thinking of those rows of wooden crosses that line the pleasant orchards before Tripoli, and in particular of Jock's lonely grave, out on the windswept marshes of Pisida. It is so vivid I can see it now as if it were only yesterday I was there...the red house battered by shellfire on the left of the road, the wire and the concrete, and the built-up narrow road with its craters and scars and burnt out skeletons of lorries and tanks. Mines, mines and more mines. A grave - Capt. Evans D E - who was he? - I shall never know. And Jock's grave under the white moon. Jock, gone for always, and yet always present in the memory.

Other crosses, other hideous corpses. And those who fought in the desert and died in the hot sun before we ever came. All these are the price of victory.

Now my mother, who rarely reads books, read through the manuscript of my wartime chapters at one sitting. She wept as she read my father's old letters through to the very last note:

My darling one I cannot tell you how I am longing to see you and the offspring. You will have to send me one of those normally rather revolting photos of a Wigget and young taken in unnatural surroundings. Period of freedom coming to an end as I see Sunday jobs to be done looming over the horizon. Love you my sweetest always and always. May the day come soon when we can be together all the time and always. Jock.

"I would like to think," she said, "that we will meet again. If there is any such thing as a hereafter I am sure he will be waiting for me."

"He was very loyal to you," I said.

"Oh yes" she replied. "If there is such a place he will definitely be up there waiting for me."

A childhood vision flowed before my eyes. I saw my father tall and slim. He was sitting up above me and to one side of him was a long row of cats. They were all different colours but arranged in height order. Now Stouty was there as well. He had come in from a night out hunting and his ear was torn and bleeding. One day my mother may go up and sit with them too.

39. Back to Libya in 2005

From the moment we met them Alec and I got on well with Jack Swaab, his wife and two sons. But when Jack and my mother renewed their friendship I was rather nervous about it. Back then in the 1990s I still felt that my mother disapproved of me. She didn't like my left-wing political position and she didn't like me working outside the home when I was a mother. I wondered if she might persuade Jack that I was a bad lot; but the effect has been different. Over the years Jack has worked away on my behalf. He has explained my views to my mother. My views are quite middle-of-the-road, he says. His own sons' opinions are much more extreme than mine, yet he loves them dearly. Over the next five years my mother came closer to me and my family. It has been a slow but continuous process. It is only looking back on it that I realize just how far we have come. We get on well now and I have lost nearly all the anger I once felt.

I didn't really feel I needed to go back to Libya, but one day, five years after our family visit, an old friend from Architecture College rang and said he and his wife were really keen to go there. He asked if I would think of going again, and I was tempted. Now that I was able to arrange a trip myself with the knowledge and contacts I had gathered we planned a wonderful trip going right down into the desert and over to Cyrenaica to look at the old Greek cities there. I also decided to make a proper scientific check on the contemporary measurements and try once more to see if I could find the place where my father was once buried, so long ago now.

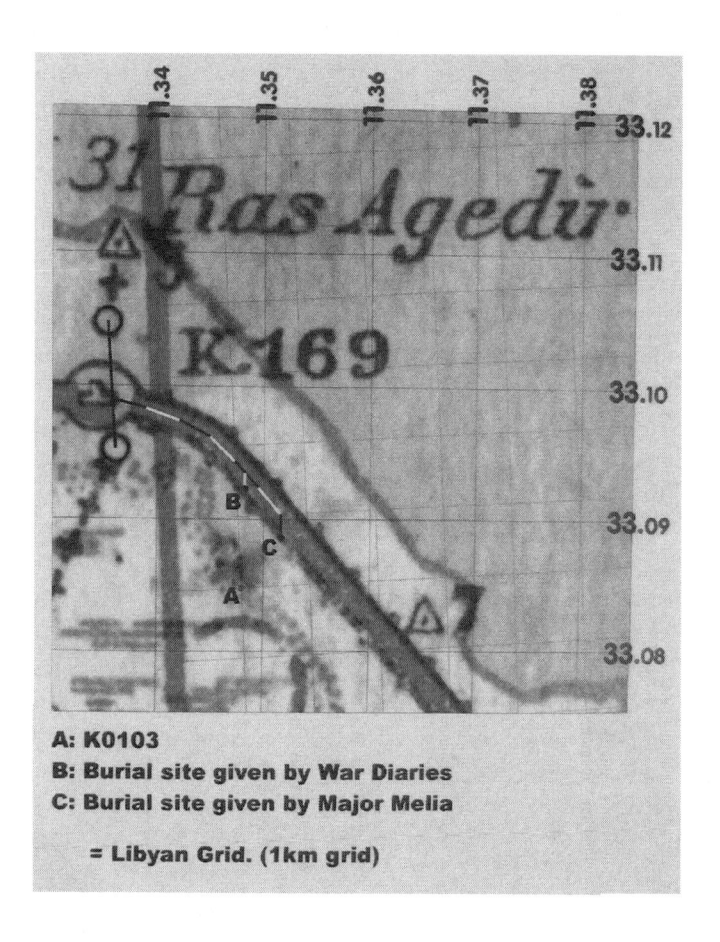

A: K0103
B: Burial site given by War Diaries
C: Burial site given by Major Melia

= Libyan Grid. (1km grid)

And so it was that in March 2005 I walked from the Tunisian frontier post and over into Libya pushing a surveyor's wheel (the thing that workmen push down the street to measure the gas or water mains below) to make a precise measurement. I was not surprised when on both sides of the border the guards were dismayed by my arrival with the wheel. On the Tunisian side, to aid my explanation, I showed them an old photograph of my mother and father together and a photocopy of the drawing of my father's grave, but unfortunately the guard spotted the edge of one of my little maps which Thomas had made for me in the same folder.

They took off the folder and left me, Alec and our two friends waiting while they consulted higher authorities. In the big bare waiting-room we chatted to an Egyptian who had been there three days. We wondered if that might be our fate too, but mercifully after 90 minutes they let us through.

Thomas had taken the old map that the 8th Army veteran had given me which turned out to be much better than anything available now. He scanned the appropriate part of the map into his computer and enlarged it to a bigger scale. Then he plotted precisely the three positions from contemporary documents. These were 'A' K0103, the official position given by my father's commanding officer in the regimental war diaries for my father's death, 'B' the position for the burial given in those same diaries, and 'C' the 'unofficial' position given in Major Melia's letter. At this larger scale it was clear that the three positions were all different to each other. K0103 was way down near the salt marsh as the compass sightings had indicated. Both the other measurements were nearer the road. Melia's position, although he said it was approximate, was on the most direct route to the road from K0103. This seemed the most likely burial position it the body had been carried directly towards the road for burial. It would then have been buried in a position where it could later be found by the burial parties for re-burial in an official war cemetery.

I had discovered that the boundary between Tunisia and Libya at Ras Ajdir has not moved in any significant way since 1943. It is now marked with a wall. I stopped by that wall to set my surveyor's wheel to zero. Thomas had also calculated the longitude and latitude of each position to three decimal points so I could pick them up on a GPS. I tried to check my GPS, a small thing like a bright yellow mobile phone, without looking suspicious. That wasn't easy, and in any case the thing turned out to be no use. I was glad I hadn't relied on modern technology and had also brought out the wheel.

My father's comrades in the Gordons were first to cross this border the day after his death and they painted their HD sign on the old shed for the benefit of the newsreel cameras. But the old shed where my father's comrades in the Gordons once crossed first into Tunisia has long gone. In its place there is now an airy steel building with swallows nesting in its roof. There we met our guide-to-be, Nuri Lamin. Nuri, who is half Libyan and half English, was brilliant. He literally, physically, had a fight to get me through that border with my wheel and I doubt if a lesser man would have done it.

Eventually I walked on, through the lorry park and out through the police post with the Kalashnikov-bearing guards, where I discovered that the wheel already registered nearly 2 km. from the border. As I walked out along the narrow sandy stretch I could see the blue Mediterranean sea to my left and the glistening salt lake coming quite close to the road to my right. Both on the map and on the ground it is clear that it would be here that those salt marshes would break through towards the sea if they were to flood. The War Graves Commission are probably right to conclude that my father's little wooden cross was washed away in a flash flood in the winter of 1944 before his remains could be 'gathered in' to an official war cemetery, but I still found myself wondering if my father's shattered body below the ground would have been washed away as well.

    I tried first for the place of burial given by Lt. Col. Perry in the War Diaries. When my wheel registered 2 km. plus 200 yds from the boundary wall I stopped and looked south. The land was cultivated here. This meant that the many mines that were scattered here in 1943 had definitely now been cleared but, on the other hand, as the land had been disturbed, my father's grave too might have been cleared away. There I checked my compass and set off to walk 200 yds. due south. After about 170 yards the field ended and the landscape turned to desert scrub with a few old camelthorn bushes, very like the landscape on the drawing. It was a peaceful place, if a little bleak. But as I reached the point and looked around, there were not one but several large old camelthorn bushes there, each one holding its own patch of earth, each one surviving in the same spot for centuries. At this point one of my friends found a bit of old washed-up wood in one of the bushes and the border policeman, who had come with us to check we weren't spies, decided we were quite mad, but not bad, and left us.

    After a picnic lunch I went back to my task and began to track the position given by Major Melia in the letter he sent with the drawing of my father's grave. I carried on down the road until I was 3 km. from the border and again headed due south across a field. Although Melia had said his measurements were approximate I could see from his drawing, his handwriting and his letter that Melia was a careful man. He was there at the time. I think he must have paced back to the road with his compass after completing the drawing and found himself near a marker-stone on the road which said it was 3 km. to the border. The old marker stones were taken away on the Libyan side but they still exist in Tunisia.

As I headed to the south the field was wider here, but again it ended about 30 yards short of my position. After that the landscape was exactly like the drawing. This time there was only one big old camelthorn bush ahead of me, all alone in the same desolate landscape shown on Melia's drawing. As my wheel clocked over 300 yards I found myself at the foot of it.

The shadows in Melia's sketch fall to the left, indicating that my father was buried with his head to the east, just as it is in the drawing. I went to the position that Melia would have been to make that drawing, and crouched as if to rest a drawing pad on my knee. There were some sandy tracks around and looking into the distance, I could see some buildings surrounded by a wall. In background of the drawing there were some buildings too:

"Do you know what those are?" I asked Nuri.

"They are some buildings used by the Libyan army," he replied.

It was perfect. It felt right. At last, I thought, I have tracked down the source of those feelings I had when I first saw that little drawing, over 20 years ago now.

A man approached us and asked what we were doing on his land. When Nuri told him that my father had been killed and buried near here, and that we were looking for his grave, he responded immediately that my father would have been killed by a mine. This land, he said, was scattered all over with mines from WWII up until the '50s when they were cleared by an Italian firm in exchange for some favour. This was reassuring news. He himself had been farming the land since the '50s, he said, but he had never come across a grave.

    I couldn't go further with the equipment that I had. I am not sure, in any case, if it would be worth it. What would be the meaning of those broken old bones, even if I were to find them here? But like the journey to Ithaka in Cavafy's famous poem I realize now that it was the journey which mattered. Over the years I have come to know my father as a man, to know about his bravery, his dry humour and his dyslexia. In some ways I am like him, it is true, but in many ways I am different. I would have loved to have grown up knowing the father I once had, for a brief few weeks of my life.

    I wound some remembrance poppies round one of the dead branches in the middle of the old bush. It seemed right. I was happy.

Acknowledgements.

First of all I would like to thank my mother for allowing me to share her memories and for her loyalty and bravery in following my journey. I am grateful for her acceptance of my version of events, which is not to say that she necessarily agrees with my views. I would like to thank the twins, Mike and Tessa, for checking my script and for their support, and to my late Godmother Ruth, my aunt Suzanne, Moll Worcester and many others for their hospitality and their conversations about times past. The views expressed and any factual errors are entirely my own.

It is an understatement, but I am endlessly grateful to my husband Alec for his love and for his unswerving support and encouragement. A big thank you to Jack Swaab for all his help, as well as for his friendship and intelligence. I would like to thank Nick Davies for his generosity, interest, help, and especially for his impromptu writing course, which set me off on a whole new learning curve. I would like to thank Peter Vaux for checking all things military and for explaining the systems and hierarchies within the British army. I am very grateful to Marsha Rowe for her sensitive and meticulous editorial work and to Jane Alexander-Orr for her final correction of punctuation and typos. Many thanks to Tabby and Fred Bourdier for their cover design, typesetting and endless patience.

A big thank you to my mother, to Alec, to Nuri Lamin, Avril Randell, Heywood and Jenny Hill, and to my children Tom and Amy Moore for coming with me on some of my journeys. I have been amazed at the number of people who have shown an interest in my trip into the dark side. For me the journey has been life-enhancing, but I never expected in my wildest dreams that others would find it so too. Thank you.

Selected Bibliography

Burrows, E.H. *Captain Owen of the African Survey*
A.A.Balkema 1979

Cochrane, Thomas. *The Autobiography of a Seaman.*
Vols. 1 & 2. Bentley 1860

Clayton, Tim & *Finest Hour. BBC TV.*
Craig Phil. *Coronet 1999*

Cordingly, D. *Cochrane the Dauntless.*
Bloomsbury 2007

Daly, Martin & Wilson, Margot.
The Truth about Cinderella.
A Darwinian View of Parental Love.
Wiedenfield & Nicholson 1998

Delaforce, P. *Monty's Highlanders.*
Donovan 1997

Douglas, K. *Alamein to Zem Zem.*
P.L. 1946

Glover, J. *Humanity. A Moral History of the 20th*
Century. 1999

Grimble, Ian. *The Sea Wolf.*
Blond & Briggs 1978

Hodgson, Vere. *Few Eggs and No Oranges.*
Persphone 1999

Hadler, S.J. & Mix, A.B. *Lost in the Victory.*
University of North Texas Press 1998

Harvey, R. *Cochrane. The Life and Exploits of a Fighting*
Captain. Constable 2000

Salmond, J.B.　　　　*The History of the 51st Highland Division 1939-45. Blackwood 1953.*

Swaab, Jack.　　　　*Field of Fire. Sutton 2005*

Timbrell, Ruth.　　　*Chavey Up, Down and Around. 1983*

Public Records Office, London.

London Gazette p.1299.

Row 10 122-124. 323/24.617 & 24.645.

WO/167/4617 127 Highland Bde. Diary 1942

WO/169/9517 127 Highland Bde. Diary 1943

WO/169/10291 2nd Btn. Seaforth Diary 1943

WO/169/　　5th Btn. Seaforth Diary 1943

WO/169/10181 7th Black Watch Diary 1943

WO/169/8963 pt.1　154 Bde. HQ Diary 1943

WO/169/8791 52nd HD HQ Diary 1943.

WO/169　　5/7th Gordons Diary 1943

J.O.Cochrane London Gazette p.1299. 18/3/1943
Microfilm M.C.Citation.